GOD'S WINEPRESS

The moving figure came nearer, and stood before him—

 See p. 29.

GOD'S WINEPRESS

A Novel

BY

ARTHUR JENKINSON

"Pity, forsooth; pity the grapes then in the winepress, for they have a sore time of it! But the wine will be good."—THEOPHILUS TRINAL.

Αἴλινον, αἴλινον εἰπέ τὸ δ' εὖ νικάτω.—AESCHYLUS.

ILLUSTRATED BY W. CUBITT-COOKE

LONDON
FREDERICK WARNE & CO.
AND NEW YORK
1896

LONDON :
PRINTED BY WOODFALL AND KINDER,
70 TO 76, LONG ACRE, W.C.

"Jesus, then, solves the problem of life . . . by teaching that all the phenomena which had given rise to a doubt of the justice of God, and even to the belief that He had abandoned this world to the power of evil, were explicable as necessary for the development of the highest good."—MASTER OF BALLIOL.

CONTENTS

BOOK I.

CHAPTER   PAGE

I   A BIRTHDAY GIFT 1

II   THE GARDEN PARTY 12

III   "ANGELS EVER BRIGHT AND FAIR" . . . 22

IV   FAREWELL 32

BOOK II.

I   THE MISSING BANK NOTES 43

II   A CRAFTY WOOER 55

III   IN ARCADY 67

IV   THE MAGIC MIRROR 78

V   A MOONLIGHT SCENE 89

VI   A WEEK OF ROMANCE 99

BOOK III.

I   THE TRAIL OF A SERPENT 112

II   ESTRANGEMENT 123

III   A DESPERATE MOVE 134

IV   A CALL IN THE DARK 145

V   AT THE SHELTER 152

VI   RESCUED 159

VII   "LIFE FOR EVERMORE" 171

BOOK IV.

CHAPTER   PAGE
I "Our Father" 182
II A Terrible Accusation 195
III A Wild Night on Somerthorpe Heath . 207
IV In the Gipsy's Van 219
V In Profundis 231

BOOK V.

I Home Again 244
II "I don't believe it" 256
III How the Curse Wrought 268
IV "In the Kiss of One Girl" 279
V God's Tools 288
Epilogue 300

GOD'S WINEPRESS.

BOOK I.

―――――

" The child is father of the man ;
And I could wish my days to be
Bound each to each by natural piety."

―――――

CHAPTER I.

A BIRTHDAY GIFT.

EDMUND STANFORD rose from the breakfast table on the morning of his eighteenth
birthday, and stepped through an open French
window into the garden. It was a lovely day in
August, full of the ripeness and wealth of summer,
and he felt that he ought to be happy, but was not,
and knew not why. He had awakened in one of
his restless moods, and had not yet been able to
shake it off.

After taking two or three turns between the flower
beds, and watching in an absent way the lights and
shadows as they danced and flickered among the
leaves of a fine old beech, he pushed open a side

B

gate, and struck down a green lane that skirted the Rectory grounds, and led to a path by the riverside.

He had not gone far along this path before he saw Evelyn Sedgewick, the Rector's daughter, seated on a low stool with her easel before her, sketching. She was so absorbed in her work that she did not notice his approach until he was almost by her side. Then a happy smile lighted up her face, and, reaching out her hand, she exclaimed :

" Oh, good morning, Edmund ; I'm so glad you've come ; for I want your opinion of this sketch. But first let me wish you every happiness to-day, and in the future."

She was about sixteen years of age, quite a girl in appearance, with deep violet eyes, and rich masses of golden hair falling over graceful shoulders.

A strange bond of sympathy existed between these two. Ten years previously Edmund Stanford's father had lost his life in rescuing her from drowning in the deep and treacherous bend of the river which she was now sketching. From that time the two children had grown up together in such familiar intercourse that they had almost come to look upon each other as brother and sister. For the last year or two they had only met during the holidays, and had begun to realize that the brother and sister theory and practice could no longer be maintained. Still, nothing had ever occurred to mar their friendship ; it continued as happy and unconstrained as it well could be.

Edmund thanked Evelyn heartily for her good wishes, and then glancing at her work, the thoughtful expression on his face deepened, and he said quietly :

"You have been sketching a spot that can never fade from either your memory or mine."

"Yes," she replied, as a tender light kindled in her eyes, "I never pass this way without feeling that I tread on holy ground. That is the chief reason why I wished to make this little sketch ; but, also, I think it a lovely bit of river scenery."

Certainly it was a beautiful view, and Evelyn had been very successful with her work.

In the foreground was a rising bit of the river's bank, fringed with reeds and bulrushes, and she had been very happy in her reproduction of their varied colours. The deep pool from which Edmund's father had rescued her at the sacrifice of his own life was suffused with light, and reflected the blue sky, and the white fleecy clouds, and the green, and gold, and purple of the banks ; while in the mid-stream a heavily laden wherry was gliding by, the sunlight smiting its big brown sail until it shone like burnished copper. Further off, on the other side, were clumps of trees, and broad fields with their golden grain. But what pleased Edmund was that Evelyn had conveyed into her picture the same solemn and beautiful thoughts which his own imagination had already woven round his father's death ; suggestions of suffering transfigured, of shuddering depths of darkness and anguish penetrated with a heavenly light.

"What I want you to notice," said Evelyn, "is the light on the sail ; do you think it could be improved ? "

"Here comes another old wherry," he replied; "the light is good, we'll watch it as it passes."

As the vessel glided by the lights were examined, and Edmund thought the picture could not be improved.

A boy was standing at the helm of the passing wherry, singing lustily, "Ye Mariners of England."

> "And sweep through the deep
> While the stormy tempests blow,"

he shouted to Edmund and Evelyn as he went by.

"Ah!" exclaimed Edmund, "he reminds me of a little poem I was reading yesterday, written by Tennyson, called 'The Sailor Boy.' Have you read it?"

"I think not."

"It is the last lines of the poem that keep haunting me:

> 'God help me! save I take my part
> Of danger on the roaring sea,
> A devil rises in my heart
> Far worse than any death to me.'

I know now what has been troubling me all this morning; it has been a vague feeling of what those words express."

"I am sure," observed Evelyn, sweetly, "that when the time comes you will take your part of danger manfully on the roaring sea of life."

"Well," he replied, "I'm glad the time has come. I'm not a bit sorry school days are over, and that next week I shall begin the real business of life."

"All the more reason why you should put away

that anxious look and enjoy the present. To-day is beautiful, and I am so glad."

"Ah! yes," he answered, looking round, "but there is thunder in the air. There will be a tempest before night."

"I do hope it will not come before our Garden Party is over. I must, however, run away now, unless you think I can improve my sketch."

"No. It is excellent; I admire it very much; it touches me deeply."

"Then will you please accept it as a little birthday gift. Whenever you look at it it will remind you of your noble father, and how he sacrificed his life for me."

With a bright look in her eyes she was gone.

Edmund sat down on the bank of the river, thinking over his life during the last ten years, and especially over the events which Evelyn's gift had brought so vividly to mind.

Well he remembered that day when his father was brought home dead. It was one lovely June afternoon, when the sun was shining brightly, and the world seemed untouched with woe.

He—Edmund—had been playing on the common, and had gathered a big bunch of wild flowers for his mother. High up in the sky a lark was singing merrily, and Jack Rickwood, the ploughman's son, showed him the lark's nest. It had five young ones in it, nearly ready to fly.

And then, little dreaming of trouble, he and Jack had a race after which he picked up his bunch of flowers and went jumping and leaping home, trying to whistle like a lark. He swung open the door of his mother's pretty sitting-room, and holding up the flowers shouted :

" Mother, mother dear, I've got——"

But the sentence was never finished ; he stood still with surprise and dread ; for he gazed on a scene that stamped itself on his memory for life.

His mother had fallen on her knees, with her arms stretched out on the table, and her face buried between them, as though she had been suddenly struck down by some crushing and awful news.

Mrs. Sedgewick was standing by her weeping.

Before he could ask a question, this lady, of whom he stood somewhat in awe, stooped down and kissed him, and he felt her hot tears fall upon his face.

He could not think what it meant, but was sure something dreadful had happened, and began to cry. She drew him closer, saying :

" Oh, Edmund dear, be good and brave, like your noble father ; your mother has only you now."

He flung his arms round his mother's neck and kissed her, and she laid her white face on his shoulder, sobbing bitterly.

" O God ! " she cried, " O God help me ! and be a Father to my poor fatherless boy."

For a time there was no sound in the room but weeping, until Mrs. Sedgewick said softly :

" Trust Him, dear Mrs. Stanford : He will hear your prayer."

Soon after, Edmund was told all about it. His father was going to the Rectory, and met Mrs. Sedge-wick with her little daughter. While they stood chatting the child slipped away unobserved to gather the flowers that grew on the river's brink. Suddenly they heard her cry out, and saw that she had fallen into the water, and was being fast carried into the mid-channel. She rose to the surface, and cast towards them a pitiful look of terror and appeal.

Mrs. Sedgewick stretched out her hands and cried :
" Oh, my child ! my child ! Can no one save you ? "

" God help me ! I'll try," replied John Stanford, tearing off his coat, although he knew the risk he ran ; for he could swim only a very little way, and never ventured beyond his depth.

But it was just possible he might succeed, and he was not the man to stand by and see Evelyn perish through fear of putting his own life in jeopardy. He sprang into the river, and struck out with fearless courage, and succeeded in grasping her as she was sinking for the third time. After a moment's pause, to gather strength for a final effort, he made for the bank. Utterly exhausted, he held up the child to her mother, and with the other hand seized a tuft of grass to save himself. But the grass gave way, and Mrs. Sedgewick had barely clutched her daughter's dress, when brave John Stanford, unable to make the least further effort, gave a short cry, and sank into the dark pool.

Nothing so sad as this had ever before taken place in Merton Magna, and the whole parish was deeply moved. For the man who had so nobly sacrificed his life was universally beloved and respected. He belonged to a family of ancient lineage, but of decayed fortunes. His father had fallen in battle early in life, and his mother, after giving him an excellent education, had placed him in a first-class land agent and surveyor's office. When about thirty years of age he had taken sole charge of Lord Merton's extensive estates, and soon after had married the orphan daughter of a clergyman—a sweet, thoughtful girl with large, dreamy grey eyes. Lord Merton and the Rector were strongly attached to him, and would have been sincerely sorry to have lost him under any circumstances; but that he should perish so suddenly, in a heroic effort to save the Rector's child, plunged them in the utmost grief. Nor was this feeling confined to the Hall and Rectory. The poor especially had learned his worth. All through that long June afternoon and evening they stood about in little groups, or sat in each other's cottages talking over the sad event.

One of these groups of villagers was gathered near John Stanford's house. In the centre of it stood a woman past middle life, whose dark olive complexion and piercing black eyes proclaimed her gipsy origin. Her name was Elizabeth Earne, and she was relating the story of how, some years before, when her son was ill of a fever, and apparently dying, Mr. Stanford had taken a doctor to see him, and had sent suitable food, and so saved his life. The kindness had made a profound impression on her mind, and had never been forgotten. She was in the midst of her tale when one of the bystanders said in a whisper,—

" Here they come ; they're bringin' him home."

As the chief servants from the Hall and Rectory passed with their burden every man uncovered, and there were few dry eyes.

" Ah ! " cried the gipsy, " loss shall bring gain ; joy shall come through pain." And then raising her hands to Heaven she prayed: "O Thou that ha' promised to be a husband to the widder, and a Father o' the fatherless, bless his poor young wife and his little son. Spread, O God, Thy everlastin' wings over 'em: yea, in the shadder o' Thy wings may they make their refuge until these calamities be overpast."

Edmund remembered being taken that evening by his heartbroken mother into the room where they had placed his dead father, and gazing upon his face for the last time. He could still distinctly recall the look of triumph which rested upon the white features, and which seemed to silently proclaim that all was well, and that death was swallowed up in life. And then he recalled how his mother stooped down and kissed the cold cheeks, and cried through her choking sobs: "My noble husband! I thank God you did your duty."

Ten years had passed away since those things happened, but they had passed quickly. Lord Merton had done everything in his power to smooth the path of the young widow, and Mr. Sedgewick had watched over Edmund like a father. Mother and son had been inseparable companions, and, living near the Rectory, a bond of peculiar tenderness had drawn the two homes together until they almost seemed one, and Edmund and Evelyn grew up like brother and sister. The Rector was delighted to see the boy becoming the very image of his father, and full of his father's spirit. And when the time came for him to choose a profession, and he deliberately expressed his wish to study law and devote himself to its practice, Lord Merton, who had great influence with one of the most important firms of solicitors in the neighbouring city of Caistor, arranged at once for his admission.

Such, then, was the past on which Edmund Stanford looked back as he sat by the river's side after Evelyn Sedgewick had left him. His eighteenth birthday had come, his school days were over, a new career was opening before him. And as a special expression of his goodwill and interest in the event Mr. Sedgewick had arranged to hold a large garden party that afternoon in the Rectory grounds. No trouble nor expense had been spared to make it a success, and everyone was looking forward to it in high expectation.

Edmund's mother had seen the day dawn with quiet thankfulness. As soon as he was awake she had entered his bedroom, and wished him every blessing, and, as the most precious gift she could offer, she had presented him with his father's watch and chain, together with a small locket enclosing some of her own and his father's hair entwined in a love knot. She gave a sigh of relief as she felt that in some respects her most anxious work was done, and that her boy must now pass very largely out of her control and training into the great school-house of life.

Through all the years of her widowhood she had never discarded the symbols of mourning. Not that she was a sorrow-stricken woman, out of whose life all joy had gone. She had seen the silver lining of the dark cloud. The sweet smile upon her face, and the soft music of her voice declared that for her sorrow had become transfigured. Still the one whom she had loved and lost remained enshrined in her inmost being, the object of an all-enduring and deathless affection. Now, however, in honour of this important occasion, she had summoned up her courage, and ordered a new gown of a soft pearly-grey colour, and intended wearing it that afternoon at the garden party.

Edmund was delighted, not merely because he loved all beautiful things, but because he adored his mother, and longed to see her as he could dimly recall her in his childhood. When, therefore, after an early lunch, she came down dressed for the party, he was immensely pleased. " Really you look quite charming, mother ! " he exclaimed, casting a keen glance over her : " why, I declare, this lovely gown makes you look decidedly youthful."

"You're a naughty boy to flatter me so," she replied, the faintest touch of colour rising to her refined and delicate face. " Where did you learn such a bad habit ? "

" It is not flattery," persisted Edmund ; " you look lovely," and he stooped down and kissed her reverently. " But you must not call me a boy any longer. Remember, I am eighteen to-day, and next week I shall begin the real battle of life."

Little did he or his mother think what tragic truth there was in those words. She looked up into his handsome face and dark brown eyes with motherly pride, and thought how tall he had lately grown, and how much he was like his lamented father.

" Yes," she replied, " you'll soon be a man now. How time does fly ! but come, let us hasten to the Rectory ; I promised Mrs. Sedgewick I would go early, so as to rest a little while before the other guests arrived."

CHAPTER II.

THE GARDEN PARTY.

MERTON MAGNA RECTORY had about it an air of great comfort and refinement. It was a handsome residence, enlarged and improved by a succession of wealthy rectors, until it looked like a fine old manor-house. One of its outward charms was the climbing plants that clothed it from base to roof in a living garment of beauty. It stood looking to the south on a piece of elevated ground, along one side of which the willow-veiled river glided. A splendid old garden—a delightful spot for a garden party—surrounded it on the south and west, and was laid out with exquisite taste. In the east there was a romantic shrubbery, which grew wilder and more secluded the farther you advanced into it, until it merged into a thick plantation of forest trees, that protected house and grounds from the keen north-east winds.

Mr. Sedgewick was just the man to make his guests happy on such an occasion. He was a clergyman whom Charles Kingsley would have hailed as a true spiritual brother—a gentleman by birth and education, of fine tastes and ripe culture, who, though possessed of considerable private wealth, gave himself up as assiduously to his duties as any poor curate could have done. He had striking and powerful features, a keen eye, a bold forehead, a winning smile, and moved about as one born to rule, not so much in virtue of office and rank, as by force and goodness of character.

Although a faithful clergyman, he was anything but a mere ecclesiastic. He used to say playfully, that everyone should be bigger than his trade. Certainly he never allowed the priest to overshadow the man. He was broad and tolerant in his views, and treated all his parishioners with equal courtesy, whether they belonged to his church or not. His life was rooted in the consciousness of God, and he endeavoured to find Him everywhere—in music and art, in science and literature, and in all common things.

Such was the man who had watched over Edmund's boyhood, deeply influenced his mind, and done all in his power to further his interests. It afforded him unmixed gratification to see him growing up a splendid young fellow, with a bright future before him. And he had not only arranged this party to take place on his birthday, that it might be a special expression of his regard, but was now throwing himself into it with the utmost enthusiasm.

He and Mrs. Sedgewick stood on the lawn receiving their guests, and had a smile and pleasant word for all. Lord Merton would have been there had he not been away in Scotland. Most of the neighbouring families were well represented, and everyone was in the best of spirits.

Among those who arrived early were Frank and Julia Ray, the latter being one of Evelyn's school-fellows, though nearly two years her senior. After a few introductions they joined a group of young people seated beneath some tall elms, where Edmund and Evelyn were arranging for various games.

"What a lovely face Miss Ray has!" remarked Mrs. Stanford when they were out of hearing. "I think I never before saw such a striking girl."

"Yes," replied Mrs. Sedgewick, "Julia is most attractive, and Evelyn is very fond of her. Still she is a very strange girl; I think no one perfectly understands her."

"Who is she?"

"She and her brother are orphans. They were brought up and educated by an aunt,—one of the dearest of old ladies, who lives in the Cathedral Close at Caistor. Frank is a medical student, and has taken his degree; but he thinks himself too young to practise, so he is going on the Continent to continue his studies there for a year or two, and Julia will accompany him. They start next month."

"It will be almost a miracle," said Mrs. Stanford, musingly, and again glancing towards Julia, "if she doesn't make more than one young fellow's heart ache some day. She has the most bewitching eyes I have ever seen."

"Ah!" replied Mrs. Sedgewick, "I hadn't thought of that; but I have no doubt I should if, like you, I had a son whose heart some girl may either gladden or break. I hope, however, Julia's eyes will do no mischief. Frank will, I am sure, try his best to look after her. But I fear she is very delicate; her mother died of consumption."

"Where are they going to reside?"

"For a time in the neighbourhood of Berlin, on account of Frank's medical studies. They will be under the care of a most judicious lady, a friend of my own, to whom I have introduced them, and then Kate Elles, the daughter of the Rector of Brentfield, is going with them, and she is a thoroughly good and clever girl. Here she comes with her father and brother."

Mrs. Stanford turned, and saw advancing towards them a tall clergyman and young lady and gentleman.

"The Rector of Brentfield," said Mrs. Sedgewick, "was a friend of my husband when he was at Oxford, and his son, Bertram, has been some time in the office which Edmund is about to enter. We have asked them to stay and dine with us this evening, so that the boys may meet."

"You are very kind. It certainly will be pleasant for Edmund to know some agreeable fellow belonging to Gresham and Walsingham's office."

The next moment the new-comers had crossed the lawn, and were engaged in cordial greetings.

Mr. Elles was a gentle, devout man, with a pale face, and mild grey eyes that seemed perpetually fixed on some object far away. He lost his wife early, and lived very much alone; for as soon as their mother died he handed over his two children to her married sisters.

Mrs. Stanford was not surprised that Kate Elles had been described as a good and clever girl. Her features suggested intellectual and moral enthusiasm. As soon as she had spoken a few words she went and joined Evelyn. With Bertram Elles Mrs. Stanford did not feel so satisfied. He was tall, and had his father's high and narrow forehead; in other respects he was unlike him. Instead of simplicity and innocence a shrewd observer might have detected a suggestion of cunning in his small ferret eyes. His mouth was disagreeable; but his voice was soft and musical, and when he spoke his features lighted up with a smile that was fascinating. And thus the impression he made on Mrs. Stanford's mind was somewhat complex. She could not make up her mind whether she liked him or not; but when the subject of Edmund's entrance into the same office in which he was engaged was referred to, and Mrs. Sedgewick expressed the hope that they would become good friends, Mrs. Stanford, with just the slightest hesitation, of which she was hardly conscious, echoed the wish.

After some general conversation, that need not be repeated here, Mr. Sedgewick left the Rector of Brentfield with the ladies, and linking his arm with that of Bertram Elles led him off in search of Edmund.

The young people had given over their games for a few minutes, and were gathered near a marquee, and refreshments were being handed round. The whole scene was one of animation and beauty. The air was filled with the hum of voices and the rippling of laughter. A row of fine old elms formed a background to the picture. In front was a raised embankment interspersed with seats and choice flowering shrubs, between which rare vases and statuettes were placed.

Here this merry party was chiefly grouped. Some were helping to hand round cool drinks and light edibles. Others were reclining on the grass, or occupying the seats. And what with the bright colours of the dresses, the graceful forms of the girls, the sound of happy voices, the general air of youthful buoyancy and gladness, it was as pleasant a picture of English country life as one could wish to see.

The merriment increased when Mr. Sedgewick approached, for he had a joke for one, and a pleasant smile for another, while he introduced Bertram to those whom he did not know, and especially to Edmund.

The three were chatting together and partaking of some light refreshment when Evelyn and Julia came up.

"Ah, Mr. Elles," exclaimed the Rector, smiling, "here are two arch-conspirators to whom I must introduce you. I can see that my daughter and Miss Ray have already devised some plot for carrying you off."

"You are an admirable guesser, papa," replied Evelyn merrily, at the same time extending her hand to Bertram. "We have come to capture Mr. Elles from you."

A look of undisguised admiration passed over the young man's face as he gazed at her. Her hat was pushed back from her forehead, displaying the rippling waves of her hair. Her face was beaming with life and intelligence, her eyes were full of happiness. She was dressed in white, relieved only by a cluster of yellow roses fastened among the lace at her throat.

Bertram might have thought her the loveliest girl in creation had not Julia at that moment given him

C

a captivating glance. The effect was to make him suspend his judgment.

Julia was a brunette, a fragile, sylph-like creature, rather below medium height, and of remarkable beauty. She wore a cream-coloured frock with some crimson roses fastened at the belt.

How long Bertram Elles might have remained entranced with this vision of loveliness it is hard to say; but he was quickly roused by Evelyn.

"We want you to join us at tennis, Mr. Elles. Will you play with me against Mr. Stanford and Miss Ray?"

"I shall be delighted to accept that honour," he replied. A smile lighted up his face, and he was suddenly lifted into a seventh heaven of happiness.

Very soon all was life and activity again. The young people broke up into various parties. Frank Ray and Kate Elles went off with some more friends for a row on the river. A large party played at croquet, while Evelyn and Bertram joined against Julia and Edmund at the nets. The Rector seemed everywhere, giving a kind word, a helping hand, a hearty laugh, as he sought to make everybody happy. Mrs. Sedgewick and Mrs. Stanford with some of the elder guests found ample enjoyment in watching the pretty scenes from the embankment, in wandering through the leafy shrubbery, or in visiting the conservatories and gardens. The whole of the place was thrown open to the guests.

The day, however, had become exceedingly oppressive; there was hardly a breath of air; and before very long Evelyn and her party were too much heated with their vigorous exercise to continue it with comfort. So the game was abandoned, and Evelyn and Bertram sauntered down the avenue of elms to the river's side, and lingered in the shade of the willows. Bertram had been brought up by an uncle, a rich banker, in London; and he found no difficulty in interesting his fair companion with stories of what he had seen in that city.

Edmund led Julia to an unoccupied seat on the farther side of the lawn, where a copper beech cast a grateful shade. "I think," he said, "this is the coolest corner of the garden to-day. Will you rest here? You look very tired. I hope the play has not been too much for you. May I fetch you something to drink?"

"Thank you," answered Julia, dropping into the chair, and letting her hat fall on the grass. She had gone beyond her strength in the game. Still she was not too exhausted to notice Edmund's solicitude as he hurried across the lawn on her behalf. And, as she watched him returning with a glass of iced lemonade, she was particularly struck with his tall, manly figure and presence.

Evelyn had often spoken with enthusiasm of her friend Edmund Stanford, whose father had saved her life; and Julia had been glad to meet him. But, bearing in mind his age, she had expected to see a boy. Edmund, however, was not merely tall and firmly built; there was also in his face a look of gravity as of one who was fast becoming a man. Although only a little older than herself, Julia felt that in maturity and strength of character he was far beyond her. Throughout the afternoon she had admired how gracefully he combined courtesy with dignity and self-respect. She was used to flattery. Young men were often enough fussing about her, and paying her small attentions; but there was something much more precious in deference, which manifestly sprang from an instinctive reverence for womanhood. When, therefore, Edmund handed her the glass, she thanked him very sweetly, and gave him a glance in which there was less of coquetry and more of real feeling than was usual with her, and which sent the blood tingling through all his veins.

He threw himself on the grass at her feet, and thought what a beautiful creature she was. Like his mother, he was struck with her eyes, and tried to make out what colour they were; but so marvellously did they change in expression that he was not sure. They seemed to have in their liquid depths a suggestion of many hues, all mysteriously blended. They were grey, or brown, or violet, according to the light and the mood. And so of her whole countenance. She seemed so sensitive to every passing change, so responsive to every touch, that, like an Æolian harp, she appeared created to voice every air that blew.

"Do you feel better now? May I get you anything more?" he asked, after a brief pause. "Or perhaps you would like to go into the Rectory and rest."

"Oh, no; this is delightful. I was only just a little over-heated and fatigued, but I am quite well again now."

As she spoke she flashed her eyes upon him, and he found it somewhat discomposing, and dropped his own; but they soon wandered back again, fascinated with the lovely vision. Not that Julia was really

more beautiful than Evelyn ; only she was more bewitching. And then she was two years older, with
feelings, passions, longings awakened to which Evelyn
was still a stranger. Moreover, he had known the
latter all his life, and that made a difference.

Very soon their conversation turned upon their
immediate future, and Edmund spoke of his hopes
and plans regarding the new life on which he was
about to enter, and Julia of the studies she proposed
to take up in Germany, and then the party was seen
to be breaking up. As Frank Ray was leaving he
invited Edmund to spend an evening with them in
Caistor before he and his sister left for the Continent,
which he promised to do. "Yes, do come and see
us," said Julia, giving him a shy glance. "My aunt
will be so pleased to make your acquaintance."

CHAPTER III.

DINNER was over, and the two Rectors retired to the study for half-an-hour to discuss some ecclesiastical business, and Edmund and Bertram went for a row down the river as far as St. Mary's Broad.

As they were leaving the house Mr. Sedgewick came to the door and said,—

"You had better not go far; I fear we shall have a thunder-storm to-night, and it may come soon."

"All right, Sir," replied Edmund, "we will not stay away long."

Within the drawing-room Mrs. Sedgewick and Mrs. Stanford sat down for a quiet chat. Opposite to them a door opened into another lofty room, where Evelyn was seated at the organ, with Kate Elles by her side. She was a skilful musician, and soon drew the Rectors from their learned retreat. They entered the drawing-room silently, and for some time Evelyn played on with more than her usual feeling and taste, until at last the piece she was rendering came to a close in a few rich and sweet chords.

After a pause Mrs. Sedgewick said,—

"Will you sing, Evelyn dear?"

" With pleasure ; what would you like ? "

" O Rest in the Lord," suggested Mrs. Stanford. " Nothing ever helped me to understand those words so well as the melody to which Mendelssohn has wedded them. It is perfect music set to noble words." And then, while Evelyn was finding the piece, she added in an undertone to Mrs. Sedgewick, " It exactly suits my mood to-night."

Evelyn sat down and sang the words with tender feeling.

When she had finished Mr. Sedgewick turned to Mrs. Stanford and said,—

" If you do not feel too tired, will you sing now? It is always a great delight to hear you."

As she rose to comply he walked across the room and drew up the blinds. Dark, threatening clouds had gathered, hiding the light.

" Shall I ring for candles ? " he asked ; " I'm afraid you can hardly see."

" Oh," replied Mrs. Stanford, " I can remember 'Angels, ever Bright and Fair,' if Evelyn can play the accompaniment from memory ; but I should be glad if you would throw open the windows ; it is unusually hot, and there does not seem a breath of air."

" Mary, dear," interposed Mrs. Sedgewick, " I think you should not exert yourself to sing to-night ; you look so very tired and pale ; but we will have the windows open, for I also feel faint."

" I will sing just this once," said Mrs. Stanford, rising, and Evelyn began to play. The girl's nature was already stirred, and the music flowed forth full of peace and sweetness.

Mrs. Stanford's whole soul seemed to go out into the song; all the yearning and pathos of a noble woman's heart,—a heart that had been pierced with a great sorrow, and yet sustained by faith and hope.

> "Angels, ever bright and fair,
> Take, O take me to your care."

And as she sang the dark clouds parted, and through the rift the descending sun shot forth a long rich beam of light. It streamed through the open window, and floated like a halo round her brow, and lighted up her pale, beautiful face with angel brightness. And still she sang,—

> "Speed to your own courts my flight,
> Clad in robes of virgin white."

And the rift in the clouds grew wider, and the light rich and glorious around her. It encompassed her whole person, and the pearly grey dress shone white as light.

The company in the drawing-room listened in silence, and Edmund and Bertram entered unobserved.

And then slowly the light declined and faded away. The heavy clouds lowered and closed in. The room grew dark. The voice of the singer sank soft and low; the passionate yearning spent itself, and she ceased.

After a pause, Mrs. Stanford, who now recognised that her son had returned, said, "Edmund, it is time we returned home."

"But you must not think of walking," exclaimed Mrs. Sedgewick. "It will be too much for you to-night. I will send round for the carriage."

"Thank you, dear, I do feel very tired now."

"Perhaps you will not mind if I walk forward, mother," said Edmund. " I shall reach home as soon as you. I shall be glad of the walk, and I would like to get a good view of this remarkable sky from the high ground on the common. I will go home that way."

He bid all good-night in the drawing-room, and was leaving the house, when his mother came into the hall.

"Don't hurry," she said, "and don't stay too long; but I daresay I shall reach home first."

She turned to re-enter the drawing-room as he moved again towards the door, and then, seized by a sudden impulse, she went up to him and kissed him, and said : " May our Heavenly Father bless you for ever and ever ! "

.   .   .   .   .   .

On a fine summer evening Merton Magna Common was a bright and pleasant spot. There the villagers would gather when the day's work was done and listen to the singing of the larks, and gaze on the gliding river as it shone like a broad ribbon of silver and gold beneath the slanting rays of the setting sun. And there the lads and lasses, unwilling to go home, would linger until long after the evening star had set her watch, and the surrounding meadows and corn-fields had fallen asleep in the arms of quiet night.

But this evening the common looked weird, gloomy, spectral, and was all but deserted. All but, I say, for though no villagers were there, on one corner of it was a small gipsy encampment, and just

outside a newly-erected tent old Elizabeth Earne
was busy preparing a supper for her son Joseph, whom
she was expecting every minute. A fire was blazing
on the heath, and its ruddy glow contrasted strangely
with the lengthening shadows and deepening gloom,
and imparted an almost sinister appearance to the
old gipsy as she bent over the flames. The fire-light
fell upon her wrinkled and swarthy features, and
sparkled in the depths of her black, penetrating
eyes, and gave a fiery glare to the red shawl tied
round her head. And yet on a nearer approach she
was by no means repulsive. She had once been a
handsome woman, and even now her features were
not lacking in dignity.

A strange, fantastic, mysterious old woman was
Elizabeth Earne, with a separateness and individuality
of character rare to find, and with a force and passion
when roused that seemed supernatural. Her son Joe
—whose life Mr. Stanford had probably saved—had
come under the influence of the Methodists, and was
now a keen, sober, industrious lad of about twenty
years of age. His mother only consented in a half-
hearted way to his slow drifting from the ancient
customs of her people; in many respects she still
kept to the old paths. Yet she liked to hear him
read the Bible, and she appreciated some aspects of
its teaching with wonderful insight, and often used
its phrases and imagery with tremendous effect.
Nevertheless she retained her faith in her own powers
—believed that she possessed a special gift, that she
saw what other people did not see, looked into the
heart of things, penetrated the soul and read its
secrets, and above all that those whom she blessed

were blessed, and those whom she cursed were cursed.

Certainly she looked witch-like enough as she bent over the fire talking in low tones to herself. But her soliloquy was soon cut short by Joe's sudden appearance. He had evidently been running, for he was out of breath.

"Mother," he said, excitedly, "your dream's true; I've just seen her."

"Alas!" replied the old gipsy, "what ha' ye seen?"

"I'll tell ye, mother. I was comin' home, and as I was late, I took the short cut by the river, and as I got near the Rectory I heard the sweetest music I ever heard in my life; so I jumped over the fence, and looked between the trees to see where it came from. And then I saw her, just as you say she looked in your dream. She was standing in one o' the rooms, and the winder was open, and she was all in shining white raiment, and she was singing like an angel."

"Ah!" said the old gipsy, pitifully, "didn't I tell ye when I saw her yesterday that I thought her time was near? and then last night I was sure o' it when I saw her in my sleep. But did ye not go up to the winder and see if it was really her? There's bin a grand party at the Rectory to day, and she was there."

"No, for while I was lookin', she ceased singing and melted away."

But his mother was not satisfied. She silently served up his supper, and then, while he was eating it, she drew on a man's rough overcoat.

" There's an awful storm comin' on, mother ; ye'd better not go far," said Joe.

" The storm 'll do me no harm," she replied, as she left the tent.

·   ·   ·   ·   ·   ·

Edmund walked up the lane towards the common, full of anxious thoughts. There had been much in the day to stir and touch him. All the vague restlessness and foreboding he had experienced in the morning had returned. His mother's look as she stood singing in the waning light still haunted him ; he seemed still to feel her parting kiss, and to hear her blessing. He wished that he had not left her, but it would seem stupid to return now.

He reached the common, and walked to the highest point, close beside a clump of oaks. There he sat down and watched the gathering tempest. All nature appeared trembling on the verge of the supernatural. Away in the west the light had become a sickly red. It streamed upwards and southwards in broad lurid beams. Masses of black clouds were drawing down, closer and nearer on every side. From beneath the clouds the light darted on the common like fiery arrows. It smote the river until it seemed to wind among the meadows like a huge fiery serpent. There was a stillness in the air that was only broken when a fitful breeze rose and swept by with a chilly shudder. The light waned. The sky grew darker. The clouds became more sullen, and the chilly shudders more frequent. Everything was weird and spectral.

He heard a movement along the road, and turned his head. Something was approaching. In the uncertain light, it seemed of giant proportions. The moving figure came nearer, and stood before him, and gazed in his face.

And then he saw that it was an old gipsy; he had noticed the encampment on the common the day before. She was tall and gaunt, her hair was in wild disorder, and she was clothed in a strange combination of garments, half a man's, half a woman's.

What light there was shone full in her face. She had come so close to him that he could feel her breath upon his cheeks. Her eyes seemed full of pity, yet he felt that she was looking into his very soul, and reading him through and through. She said quietly, almost sadly,

" It is you, Edmund Stanford! "

" Yes, how is it you know me? "

" By your likeness to your father. I knew him. He was once kind to me; he saved my boy's life."

" Ah, then you were also here when he was drowned; and when they brought him home dead you said that 'loss should bring gain, and joy come through pain.' "

" Yes."

" What did you mean? "

" I can't tell you all I meant; but you will find my words come true."

" Shall I? "

" It is as sure as death. Sorrow shall be turned into joy; knowledge shall come through suffering, victory through defeat; life through death."

" That is strange : you speak in riddles."

" Life is strange, and life is full of hard riddles;

but yet it is true that sorrow and pain and death are only tools in the hands of the Almighty, and when He has done His work there will be no more need o' them. Out o' the darkness will come . . . "

A blinding flash of lightning, and simultaneously a crash of thunder made her voice inaudible.

There was an awful silence, and Edmund looked at the old sybil in fear. She was perfectly calm, but the look of strange pity had returned to her face.

" Don't be afraid," she said, softly. " It's the Chariot o' Fire and the Horses o' Fire. The angels o' the Almighty are abroad. Where is your mother ? "

Another terrific flash, another loud report, a blow, and with a cry of pain he fell at her feet.

She helped him up again, and asked him if he was hurt.

" No," he replied, " only stunned a little ; but what knocked me down ? "

" The lightning struck one of the oak-trees, and a branch fell and it threw you down. I will help you home."

It had suddenly become quite dark, and the rain was coming down in torrents. Edmund accepted her help, and also that of Joe, who had appeared on the scene, for he felt confused, and did not know which way to go.

As they got near to his home he heard the wheels of the carriage, and several voices, among which he recognized Mr. Sedgewick's.

The next minute the Rector was by his side, and Elizabeth Earne explained what had happened.

" Are you much hurt?" he asked, in a choking voice.

" I think not; but why are you here, sir? What is the matter? Is my mother safe?"

" Yes, my poor boy, she is safe—safe for ever," answered Mr. Sedgewick.

" O God, what has happened?"

" The angels of God have taken her to their care."

It was even so. Mrs. Stanford had entered the carriage, and was smiling to her friends and bidding them good-night. Then came the first flash of lightning and the crash of thunder, just above her. The horses reared and rushed off, the Rector after them. The coachman soon succeeded in pulling them up, and Mr. Sedgewick jumped in beside her. She lay back with a smile on her refined and saintly face. He began talking to her, but there was no response. The gentle spirit had passed away without a cry or a pang.

The flash of lightning and the peal of thunder, and then the rearing and flight of the horses had proved too great a shock for her delicate frame, and the end had come in the manner—as was subsequently discovered from her diary—she believed it would come—suddenly.

CHAPTER IV.

FAREWELL.

WITH a sad heart Edmund began his career in the old city of Caistor. His mother's death had left a dreadful blank in his life. All arrangements were upset, and the whole aspect of things changed.

There was no longer any reason for keeping on the home at Merton Magna ; it was therefore broken up.

Nor was that the only change. Mrs. Sedgewick was prostrated by his mother's sudden death, and when she somewhat rallied the doctor urged a complete change of scene. He declared that her nervous system had received a shock from which it would only slowly recover, and that she must go away immediately.

Instead, therefore, of sending Evelyn back to school, the Rector made arrangements for a long absence from home, and prepared to leave for the Continent as soon as his wife could bear the journey.

Thus the bonds that united Edmund to the past were severed, and he felt himself torn from all those around whom his heart's best affections had twined. As he walked round the old place for the last time, and bid farewell to the friends of his boyhood and youth, he realized that the first great chapter of his life was coming to a melancholy close.

"How everything has suddenly changed!" he exclaimed, sadly, to himself. "A month ago my dear mother was with me, and we were happy, and surrounded by life-long friends. Everything looked bright and hopeful. But one cruel blow has changed all. In a few days I shall be left utterly alone, a stranger in a great city, to fight the battle of life as best I can."

Among those who felt the breaking up of the old order almost as much as himself was Miss Betty Thatcher. She had been his first governess, but had grown so devoted to his mother and himself that for many years she had become their constant friend and companion. She belonged to the sea-board parish of Somerthorpe, away in the north-east of the county, and there she had an old uncle, a retired veterinary surgeon, who had long wanted her to go and live with him ; but she had refused through her affection for Mrs. Stanford. Now, however, she saw it to be her duty to go to him.

"Oh, Edmund," she said, "if ever you are ill or in any trouble I hope you'll send for me. I will come to you wherever you are. We none of us know what may happen in the future ; but if ever you should want a home you'll find one at Somer-thorpe."

And Edmund thanked her, and promised that he would always keep her kind words in mind.

The next day he removed to Caistor, and began his career in the office of Messrs. Gresham and

D

Walsingham, situated in Friars' Court, a retired spot, though within three or four minutes' walk of the centre of the city.

Thirty years ago Caistor would compare with any ancient town in the kingdom for its quaint, old-world air. It could boast of a strange history, running through nearly fifteen hundred years, a history that told of the presence of Roman and Saxon, Dane and Norman, and of battle, plague, fire and flood. As you walked along its crooked streets, beneath queer overhanging houses, you could fancy yourself transported into an English or Flemish town of a bygone age.

Edmund, though he had been a weekly boarder in its ancient grammar-school, had seen little of the city; and in the intervals of business he now wandered disconsolately about its streets and lanes endeavouring to find relief from the sad thoughts that haunted him, by sketching some of the specimens of mediæval architecture which abounded—old gate-ways, and ancient ivy-grown towers, and black-timbered dwelling-houses in Elizabethan or other picturesque styles.

One Saturday in the middle of September—when the Sedgewicks departed for the Continent—came the final farewell. Soon after mid-day Edmund hurried to the railway station to see them off. He felt restless and miserable ; but, as he stood waiting, he observed a poor lame woman endeavouring to make a way through the crowd for herself and a delicate blind child whom she was leading by the hand. The woman's sorrowful face touched his heart, and he roused himself ; "After all," he thought, " how many have to bear a darker lot than mine."

Just then a voice behind him shouted, " Take care, sir! take heed there!" and he stepped aside to make way for a porter, who was hurrying along with a heavy box on his shoulder. Hard by was a big, stout fisher-woman, holding up a red-herring, and saying some-thing about it very indignantly. A corner of the box on the porter's shoulder struck her.

" Consarn you, you duzzy fule! Du you want to kill me?" she cried, giving the fellow a slap in the face with the herring. " There, bor, there's a gude sidewiper for ye ; you'll kaap clear o' me in future."

" Thank ye, owd Mother Cod-fish : it'll make a nice supper," said the porter, seizing the herring and dis-appearing in the crowd.

Roars of laughter burst from those who had wit-nessed the scene, and Edmund laughed also, saying to himself, " Fine fellow that! he knows how to profit by a nasty slap in the face."

With these reflections he did his best to smile brightly as the well-known carriage from Merton Magna drove up.

" Ah!" exclaimed the Rector, "here he is. How are you, Edmund? We were sure you would be here."

" Oh! I am well, thank you : how are you all? How is Mrs. Sedgewick?" he asked, looking towards her, and giving Evelyn a glance by the way.

" I think I am better to-day," she replied, as she lay back in the carriage, pale but calm ; " but I shall be very glad when the journey is over."

" Now," said the Rector, as they crossed the platform, "the train will not leave yet. Come into the carriage with us, Edmund. How have you been getting on?"

"Much better than I feared; Mr. Walsingham has been immensely kind."

"I was sure he would be," said Mrs. Sedgewick. "He's such a splendid man!"

"You see, Edmund," observed the Rector, "the world is neither so selfish nor so black as many paint it. There are wolves in sheep's clothing, and Satan often appears as an angel of light; but there are many noble men and women too. Don't grow hard and cynical, if you should ever get roughly handled, and never lose faith in God, and in the better side of human nature."

"I should be an ungrateful fellow if I did," he replied, his voice trembling with suppressed feeling; "I can never forget your kindness."

"Well," answered the Rector, "let me know at once should any trouble or difficulty arise, and always trust me as though I were your father."

"I will," he replied.

"How do you think you will like Bertram Elles?" asked Mrs. Sedgewick.

"He seems to wish to be friendly; but he is one of those fellows whom it requires time to understand."

"I'm afraid you will often feel lonely," said Evelyn, in a voice full of sympathy.

"I shall miss you more than I can tell," he replied, looking wistfully at her. "But I mean to fight against my worst enemy—melancholy—and work hard; and, when business is over, I shall become quite a student, and time will soon pass, and you will be back again."

" And I," said Evelyn, "intend to work hard also ; there is so much I want to do before we return."

" Oh yes," said the Rector, laughing ; " Evelyn means to become quite a blue-stocking ; I fear you will hardly know her when she returns."

" Now, papa, you are naughty : a girl doesn't need to make herself a fright, and appear all ink-stains and spectacles, because she is a student."

" It is quite beyond my imagination to picture you a fright," answered Edmund, gazing at her with renewed wistfulness.

The conversation was now interrupted by a guard, who came to examine the tickets. Edmund stepped outside the carriage. He had no sooner done so than Bertram Elles rushed up.

" Halloo, Mr. Elles, are you here ? " said Mr. Sedgewick, with a look of surprise.

" Yes ! I heard Stanford say that you were leaving by this train, and, as I had to come this way on business, I ventured to come to the station to wish you good-bye," he replied, endeavouring, at the same time, to catch sight of Evelyn, who was seated at the other end of the carriage.

" You are very kind," replied the Rector, giving him a searching glance.

" Unfortunately," said Bertram, " I have been watching on the platform for several minutes. I had no idea you were in this carriage. I thought you hadn't arrived."

" Ah," replied Mr. Sedgewick, with a curious smile, " I was having a quiet talk with Mr. Stanford."

" Take your seats, please ; take your seats," cried the guard.

" God bless you!" said the Rector, shaking Edmund warmly by the hand ; "and good-bye, Mr. Elles."

Mrs. Sedgewick came to the window and pressed Edmund's hand, while her eyes filled with tears.

The train was slowly moving. Evelyn came forward and she and Edmund clasped hands. They had been like brother and sister for years, and there was no lack of tenderness in their fare-well.

The train was going faster, and Evelyn was just reaching her hand towards Bertram, when her father, not observing the movement, drew her back ; and whispered a few final words of advice and encourage-ment to Edmund.

Then they were off.

" Well," said Bertram Elles, in disgust, " confound that parson !   I came down here on purpose to see his pretty daughter, and he neither let me speak to her, nor shake hands with her."

" It's a pity that we cannot call them back," said Edmund.

" Oh, it's of no consequence," answered Bertram, with a sneer.

As they reached the bridge beneath which the river flows that winds through the city he gave a sudden exclamation : "Why, look here," he said, " here come Frank Ray and his sister ! "

Before Edmund had time to say anything they met and were engaged in cordial greetings.

" I have just been seeing the Sedgewicks off," re-marked Edmund to Julia.

It was the first time they had met since the garden party ; and so much had happened since then, and there had been such a complete upheaval of his life, that it seemed years away.

"I should have liked to have seen them off also," she replied; "I wonder Evelyn did not let me know they were going by this train."

"I am sure she would have done so but for her mother's health. Mrs. Sedgewick has been so ill, and her nervous system is so shaken, that they wished to get away as quietly as possible."

"Ah," she said, her face lighting up with sympathy, "we were so grieved when we heard the news. It was dreadfully sad. I cannot tell you how much we sympathize with you."

"Look here," exclaimed Frank Ray, "Julia and I are just going for a row down the river. Will not both of you join us? It will be our last outing; you know we go off next week."

"Oh, do come with us," chimed in Julia, glancing first at Edmund and then at Bertram; "it will be delightful!"

"Let us go," said Bertram. "It is the very thing. I'm awfully glad we met."

It was a delicious September day. The air was soft and balmy. The sky of that delicate blue on which it rests the eye to gaze. The grand old trees along the river-side had only so far lost their summer brightness as to display a more sober green. The river was still gay with boating parties.

Under ordinary circumstances Edmund would have been delighted. Julia looked charming, and her sympathy was very sweet. But just then he was in no mood for company of any kind. He wanted to be alone. He was not sorry for the opportunity of getting rid of Bertram. "Many thanks," he replied, "I really cannot go; but do you go, Elles."

"Can you not come with us? it would be so pleasant," said Julia, with a voice and look which at any other time would have been irresistible.

"No, indeed, I cannot go to-day."

"Then shall we not see you again before we leave home?"

"May I call and see you to-morrow afternoon?" he asked.

"Oh yes, do come."

And so they shook hands and parted.

Edmund wandered on in a somewhat aimless way, until he reached the Castle Hill, where a scene presented itself not easily matched in England elsewhere, and for a time he was drawn out of himself in watching it.

It was Caistor cattle market, one of the largest gatherings of horses, cattle, sheep, and pigs to be seen anywhere. But what impressed him chiefly was the immense stir and life, and the strange characters and dresses. Shepherds and drovers in their long linen smocks, horse and cattle dealers with huge red and yellow handkerchiefs round their necks; big, red-faced butchers in blue slops, and burly farmers in top-boots and broad-brimmed hats. And then the shouting, the barking of dogs, squealing of pigs, neighing of horses, bleating of sheep, the rushing to and fro, the cries of men and women selling every variety of thing from a hot pie to a Bible. And high above all this noise and tumult the grand old Norman Castle stood solemn, silent, and majestic, its base hidden in the rich masses of foliage that flourished on the banks of its deep moat.

Suddenly he felt a hand upon his arm, and turning, was surprised beyond measure to see Elizabeth Earne, the old gipsy, by his side.

"Come with me," she said.

The command was irresistible, and he followed. With rapid steps she turned into a narrow lane, dirty and unfrequented, and then into a silent court-yard. In a far corner of this she opened a door, ascended a rickety flight of stairs, and hastened along a dark passage, at the end of which was a door which she opened with a peculiar key. Edmund followed her in, and immediately the door closed behind him. He gazed round the bare, gloomy garret, and then into the old sibyl's face.

"Ye don't need to fear," she said, quietly; "but I ha' spun the web o' your fate, and know that ye will ha' trouble, sore trouble and pain. Hows'ever ye'll win through it all in th' end. Some o' the threads are broken and tangled, and the road ye ha' to travel is dark; but ye can more than half control your doom, and when the time comes for old Lizzie to aid ye, be it early or late, week-day or Sunday, she'll come to ye."

The gipsy's strange, prophetic words surprised Edmund, but as he was about to speak she waved him loftily off.

"Away, away!" now she cried, excitedly. "If ever ye need me send here, and there are those who will bring me your message quicker than the post; but when ye least think it I shall be watching ye."

She opened the door, conducted him through

the dark passage and into the court without another
word, and then disappeared. And Edmund wandered
slowly home, wondering whether the woman was
insane, or possessed some strange insight into his
character and future.

Book II.

"In the Spring a livelier iris changes on the burnish'd dove ;
In the Spring a young man's fancy lightly turns to thoughts of love."

CHAPTER I.

THE MISSING BANK-NOTES.

ONE Monday morning, about three years after
the events recorded in the previous chapters,
Edmund Stanford was sitting at his desk in the office
of Messrs. Gresham and Walsingham. He was in
a particularly restless mood. More than once he
began to deal with the mass of papers before him,
and then threw them down again with an impatient
gesture, and allowed his mind to wander away to
some subject which evidently gave him no pleasure ;
for his face bore signs of extreme annoyance.

From these reflections, however, he was roused by
a request to attend in the partners' room.

As soon as he entered Mr. Walsingham handed
him a letter that had come from the chief bank in
the city.

"I want you, Stanford," he said, "to attend to this
letter. You know all about the case. Find the papers

Mr. Gordon wishes to see and take them to him, and ask him what he would like us to do next."

"As you are going to the bank," observed Mr. Gresham, "you may as well deposit the money. Mr. Howard will make it up for you while you are seeking out those documents."

Edmund took the letter and departed. Mr. Walsingham noticed his unsettled look, and, when he had left the room, remarked,—

"Stanford has been working hard and needs a holiday. I wish that he had been going to Switzerland instead of Bertram Elles."

"Do you?"

"Yes; he deserves a change, and, when this pressure is over we should let him go. The Sedgewicks will be glad to see him."

"As you please," replied Mr. Gresham, coldly. "Take care you don't indulge him too much. No doubt he is very clever and industrious; but I've never been quite so satisfied with him as you."

Edmund, on his part, returned to his room in somewhat better mood, and the business that had just been handed to him absorbed his whole attention.

The three years he had spent in the office in Friars' Court had confirmed him in his choice of the legal profession. From the first he had manifested a natural aptitude for his duties, and had thrown himself into them with characteristic enthusiasm.

He had set himself immediately to master the routine work of the office, and to prepare for the prescribed law examinations. Not content, however, with that, he had entered upon a further course of study with the view of making himself an efficient lawyer. He had read widely in philosophy and history, and studied with the utmost care the works of the great thinkers who had investigated the various problems of Jurisprudence.

The result was that he had rapidly grown in knowledge and mental grasp, and had brought to his work a mind trained to deal with intricate problems. Whatever he had undertaken had been well done.

Mr. Walsingham, who was really the controlling and inspiring mind of the firm, had quickly discovered his abilities, and had relieved him sooner than was usual of the semi-mechanical duties of the office, and employed him on work that required special intelligence.

For Mr. Walsingham he had formed an unbounded admiration, and had done his utmost to please him. In this way a bond of sympathy had grown up between them, which, although it was gratifying to Edmund, had not failed to excite a certain amount of ill-will.

With Mr. Gresham he had not found his path so smooth. The senior partner was devoid of imagination and sympathy. He had a haughty manner. He was a man of strong prejudices. When once his suspicions were roused they were apt to blind his judgment. Hence he made a good friend, but a bad enemy. And, as Edmund was above everything of an independent spirit, their intercourse had been sometimes strained.

Still, at the end of three years he had more than overtaken Bertram Elles in efficiency, and was becoming a recognized power in the office.

During these years he had seen nothing of the Sedgewicks, but had kept up a regular correspondence with them. For the first year they had remained in the neighbourhood of Berlin, and Evelyn, although living with her parents, had studied under the same masters with her friends Julia Ray and Kate Elles. Frank Ray, also, was prosecuting his medical studies at the Berlin University, and was, therefore, often with them.

Before the second winter had set in, Frank Ray had become engaged to Kate Elles, and soon after accepted a junior position at Guy's Hospital, and removed with Julia to London. The Sedgewicks went to the South of France, taking Kate Elles with them.

Edmund and Bertram had gone on working side by side in the office, but had never become close personal friends. For one reason, they were utterly unlike each other. There was no subject in which they found a common interest. Then there was something mysterious about Bertram. There were occasions when he would make himself exceedingly attractive, and Edmund was drawn towards him. At other times he felt that Bertram did not improve upon fuller acquaintance.

As the years passed he became more ambiguous. His life did not unfold in manly strength and freedom. His intellect was hard and sceptical ; uninspired and unfed by the nobler affections.

He had also formed an intimacy with a number of gay young men who frequented a notorious billiard saloon in the city ; often, when Edmund had gone to Bertram's lodgings in the evening, he had found that he was out, and heard afterwards that he had been playing at this saloon.

And thus many things had awakened Edmund's suspicion that Bertram was slowly slipping down hill. He was not getting on at the office, and would probably have been requested to leave it but for the way in which he had ingratiated himself into the favour of Mr. Gresham by a long course of adroit sycophancy.

Edmund, it has been said, was in much disquietude on this particular Monday morning. It may be now added that Bertram Elles was mainly the occasion of it.

Frank Ray had been struck down with fever while engaged in his medical work in London, and, although he had recovered and was moving about again, he remained so weak that he had been strongly advised to take a long holiday.

It was the height of summer, and the Sedgewicks, having heard of it, invited him and Julia to visit them. They were staying in a picturesque châlet in the Bernese Oberland, and Kate Elles was with them.

The invitation was accepted with delight ; but just as they were about to start, the venerable aunt who had brought them up was taken ill, and Julia had to hurry down to Caistor to her. She soon found that it would be impossible for her to leave her aunt, while it was also most undesirable for Frank in his weak state to journey alone.

Bertram Elles, seeing his opportunity, went to Mr. Gresham and obtained leave of absence ; so that he might accompany Frank, and also visit his sister.

Edmund had just heard of this arrangement, and he could not keep down a feeling of vexation. Often enough he had longed to visit the Sedgewicks, and a few weeks before had asked for permission to go. Mr. Walsingham had consented ; but Mr. Gresham had thrown difficulties in the way, and Edmund, too proud to press his claim, had let the matter drop. And yet the readiness with which the senior partner had consented to the request of Bertram Elles had re-awakened the sense of bitterness and injustice.

It was from these unhappy thoughts that he had been roused by Mr. Walsingham. The business entrusted to him claimed his full attention, and, before he had disposed of it, other matters unspeakably more perplexing and humiliating to himself effectually banished these troubles from his mind.

First of all he began to seek out the various papers which the banker required. He was still engaged in this work when the cashier brought him a large sum of money to deposit in the bank.

He took the money and locked it up in his desk until he was ready to go. When he had collected all the documents he again read the banker's letter, and finding in it one or two points on which he needed further information he went and consulted with Mr. Walsingham. Then he returned, took the money from the desk, and started for the bank.

He was turning over in his mind the business he had to discuss with Mr. Gordon when he caught sight of the graceful figure of Julia Ray.

She was hurrying along with an anxious look on her face, and he had almost touched her before she saw him.

"Oh, Mr. Stanford," she said, "I'm so glad I've met you ; but I'm in such a hurry. I'm going into this shop to get a prescription made up for my aunt."

"I will go in with you, if you do not object," he replied. "I can hear about your aunt and Frank while they are making it up."

"Yes, do come in," said Julia, moving towards the shop-door.

While the medicine was being prepared Edmund and Julia drew aside into a quiet corner of the shop, and engaged in conversation. They had not met for some time. He had called as soon as he had heard of her aunt's illness, but had not seen Julia. Now he watched her with absorbed interest as she spoke rapidly about her aunt and about Frank, and told of his serious illness and recovery, and of her own disappointment at being unable to go away with him.

She was dressed in some light gauzy material, suitable for the height of summer. The rich masses of her dark hair fell in rippling waves over her slight shoulders, and her eyes seemed larger and brighter than ever.

As she talked she appeared a creature of a thousand moods, sweeping the whole gamut of feeling in a moment. There was about her such a mingled air of seriousness and playfulness, simplicity and depth, such a look of innocent archness and witchery, that Edmund watched her completely enchained, and hardly knew whether she was a genuine woman or some fairy spirit of the air and woods.

They were still engaged in conversation when

E

the shopman brought the medicine. Julia opened her purse and laid down a £5 note.

"I am sorry," she said, "but I have nothing less."

The shopman went to the till, and then returned to say that he had not got the necessary change, but would send for it.

"Oh, please be quick," exclaimed Julia, suddenly conscious of the lapse of time; "but, perhaps you could give me the change, Mr. Stanford."

"No, I really cannot," he answered half mechanically. And then immediately recalling his words with a laugh, "why, yes," he said, "of course I can. I am just on my way to the bank."

And so saying he drew the bag from his pocket, and counted out five sovereigns in exchange for the note. He then bid Julia farewell, promising to call the next day to hear how her aunt was progressing.

As he entered the bank he saw the banker disengaged; so, handing the bag of money to one of the tellers, he sought an interview with him at once. Mr. Gordon led the way to his private room, and they were engaged reading and discussing the documents when the teller entered, and with a look of surprise and annoyance said,—

"Mr. Stanford, the money you just handed to me does not agree with what your cashier has put on the slip. There is £20 short; £5 in gold and £15 in notes."

Mr. Gordon paused in his reading, and glanced first at his own clerk and then at Edmund. The latter stood utterly confused and dumbfounded.

"I cannot understand it," he stammered out at last. "I certainly did a very unusual thing on my way here.

I gave change for a £5 note out of that money ; but although there would be £5 less in gold, there should be an extra note, and the sum total should be correct."

" It is most unfortunate," remarked Mr. Gordon. " I fear you dropped the notes out in giving change."

" I am confident I did not do that," answered Edmund.

" It is just possible your cashier has made a mistake," said the banker, " although I never knew him do such a thing. He is very careful."

Edmund was very much disturbed, and hurried back to the shop he had just left. The shopman who had waited on Julia was a pleasant, honest-looking fellow, and listened with real concern to Edmund's story. He was confident, however, that he had seen him put the notes carefully back into the bag. Nothing had been seen or heard of them there, and although a careful search was made they could not be found.

" Mr. Howard must have made a mistake," Edmund said to himself, as he hurried back to the office. Still it was very strange. The cashier had spent most of his life with the firm, and was absolutely trusted.

" I will go carefully over my cash," he said, in reply to Edmund, " but I am sure the money was correct when I handed it to you."

With his natural frankness Edmund went to the partners' room and told the story of what had happened. Mr. Gresham was greatly annoyed, and cast cold suspicious glances at him. Mr. Walsingham showed great distress. The cashier came to say that he had gone over his cash and found it correct, and was confident that he had made no mistake. Edmund listened in dumb agony ; never before had he felt so miserable and humiliated.

"Well," said Mr. Gresham, bitterly, "the money is gone—how I cannot tell. We must leave that for the present. Where are the papers you took to Mr. Gordon? What does he wish us to do?"

These questions brought a deeper blush of shame to Edmund's face. He had left the papers behind in his anxiety about the money, and could give no clear account of the business on which he had been sent.

"You had better go to your room, Sir!" exclaimed Mr. Gresham, in deep indignation ; "I will go and see Mr. Gordon myself."

The room Edmund was using was the centre of a group, and had three doors in it, one leading into a badly lighted passage, one into the general room, where a number of clerks were engaged, and another into a room used by Bertram Elles.

In the general room Edmund found the cashier, Bertram, and several others eagerly discussing the loss of the notes.

"Sorry for you, Stanford!" exclaimed Bertram, with an inscrutable look, "but I didn't think that you could have been so bewitched by a pair of dark eyes as to lose twenty pounds."

"I could take my oath that I never lost the notes," he replied sadly, "although what has become of them I cannot tell."

He passed into his own room and shut the door, and recalled every circumstance. "What can be the explanation of this wretched mystery?" he asked himself. "I know that I safely locked the money in my desk as soon as it was brought to me, and put the key in my pocket. No one could have touched it then. Can I have lost the money, or have been robbed of it? Has Mr. Howard made a mistake? Has the teller at the bank? Impossible. And yet what can have become of it?"

As soon as Mr. Gresham returned he was again sent for. The senior partner looked very angry.

"Are you sure," he asked sternly, "that you know nothing more of these notes than you have disclosed? Is there no light you can throw on their disappearance? We must get to the bottom of this business."

The blood mounted to Edmund's cheeks as it had never done before, and his eyes flashed fire. Now for the first time it dawned upon him that Mr. Gresham not merely suspected him of carelessly losing the notes, but, infinitely worse, of stealing them. The very thought maddened him beyond endurance.

"What do you mean, Mr. Gresham?" he asked, passionately, "by those questions? I know nothing beyond what I have stated. Of course, unless the notes are found, I will make them good, although I do not believe that I lost them."

"It is a mysterious affair," said Mr. Walsingham, looking perplexed; "but of course no one suspects you of taking them. However confident you may be I am driven to the conclusion that you lost the notes while giving change. If they should ever turn up I shall be glad; but in the meantime you had better return to your work, and while letting it become a warning to you for the future, don't let it distress you too much."

With these words, to which Mr. Gresham gave a nod of assent, Edmund was dismissed, and went back to his room with a sad heart, which was not lightened when an hour or two later he saw Bertram Elles drive off to catch the London train on his way to Switzerland.

CHAPTER II.

A CRAFTY WOOER.

" LOOK at that sheep, Mr. Elles ; I'm sure there is something the matter with it."

Two or three hundred feet up the mountain's side a sheep could be seen struggling. As Evelyn spoke she drew out her field-glass and watched it.

" Poor creature ! it is entangled among thorns."

Bertram raised his glass. He was not sorry that something had occurred to throw them still farther behind their party. He had been manœuvring every day since he arrived in Switzerland to get Evelyn alone, but now the fates were working on his side, and even she herself was unconsciously furthering his wishes.

" Yes," he said, looking through the glass, " it is caught round the shoulders, and has hurt itself in its struggles to get free ; I see stains of blood. I think I should run back to the herdsman's hut we passed a few minutes ago, and tell him about it."

" Oh, that will delay us too long. Could you not climb up and liberate it ? "

Bertram examined the spot. The face of the rock was one sheer precipice ; but by taking an oblique course he could find his way along the side of a gorge to the ledge on which the creature was held a prisoner.

" It is now or never," he thought, and then he said aloud : "Ah, I see a way up," and so saying he plunged into the gully.

All the time he had been with the Sedgewicks he had kept one object steadily in view. With the utmost adroitness and persistency he had laid siege to Evelyn's heart.

As a girl she had charmed him ; now he supposed himself seriously in love. Since he had last seen her she had grown into a beautiful woman. Julia Ray was a lovely little creature ; but there was something bewitching and elfish about her. In her society he had an uneasy feeling that he was only being played with for her amusement, and that in the end she would give him a mocking smile and elude his grasp.

But there was nothing of this in Evelyn Sedge-wick. She was the type of noble womanhood. Every line of her face was glorious in grace and beauty. Her rich wavy hair rose above her ample brow like a crown of gold. From the clear vestal depths of her eyes there shone forth the light of love, thought, courage.

She was in heart and intellect far above Bertram Elles, and he had sufficient perception of this to be somewhat afraid of her, and dubious of the result of his wooing. But he was dazzled by her beauty ; he admired her figure. He thought she could gratify his utmost desires. She was also an only child, and Mr. Sedgewick was very wealthy, and belonged to an old aristocratic family. Evelyn would be a rich woman some day, a feature of the case peculiarly attractive to him. And so Bertram felt that he would be a prouder and happier man ; that it would greatly add to his importance, both in his own eyes and in the eyes of the world, if he possessed the right to call such a glorious creature his own.

He was, however, too shrewd to make any direct advances : that would only be to court defeat. So like an essentially shallow though clever man he sought to win her by a round-about method. He put forth all his skill to wind and wreath himself into her thoughts and to awaken her interest in himself. He watched every opportunity for giving her pleasure ; yet endeavoured to create the impression that it was all done without thought.

When such a man puts forth all his skill to win a girl inexperienced in the world's ways it is a serious thing for her, and this he was doing. And not only so, he seemed to silently change in her company. Unconsciously he caught her thought and feeling and reflected them back again. He surprised himself. Desires he had not experienced for years were re-awakened. He began to think about black and ugly things in his past life, and to wish they were not there. He resolved that, in the event of his suit being successful, he would lead in future a better life, and make full restitution for all the wrongs he had done.

He would have made more progress, he thought, could he have drawn Evelyn away alone more frequently, but this he was seldom successful in doing. Most of their conversations took place where other ears beside hers were open to all he said. If he succeeded, after endless planning, in carrying her off to a quiet retreat, someone would intrude upon them before he could speak a dozen words.

A German professor of philosophy, who was also staying with the Sedgewicks, excessively annoyed him in this respect. Professor Altenstein was a young man of high ability and culture, and Mr. Sedgewick and Evelyn were frequently engaged in conversation with him. And as Bertram listened to their discussions, in which he felt no earthly interest, and noticed the friendly courtesy of the professor's relations with Evelyn and the warmth of her regard for him, he became a miserable prey to envy, jealousy and hate. Beneath his calm exterior and occasional smile there lay hidden the utmost bitterness. And thus, when the last day of his visit dawned, he was no nearer to the realization of his wish than when he came.

On this last day it had been arranged to have an excursion to the head of the wild and romantic glen in which they were residing. The party was to consist of about a dozen ladies and gentlemen from the neighbouring hotel, together with the Sedgewicks' own circle. They were to walk to the head of the glen and have lunch, and then proceed along a somewhat difficult mountain ridge until they reached another glen, where carriages would meet them and convey them home.

The day was delightful and the company in the best of spirits. When luncheon was over Mr. Sedgewick glanced round, and seeing Evelyn and Kate together, attended by Frank and Bertram, walked forward with Professor Altenstein. But Bertram soon contrived to separate Evelyn and himself from Frank and Kate—who were not at all unwilling to be left by themselves—and thus it was he found himself

with the prospect of a two hours' walk over an unfrequented mountain ridge, alone with Evelyn.

She watched him ascend the gorge to liberate the
sheep until he was lost to view among the bushes
and rocks, and then she advanced a little way along
the path and climbed a spur of the hill in the hope
of seeing Frank and Kate. She discovered them
some way on in front, but before she could make herself heard they were lost to view in the windings of
the road. Somewhat annoyed at being left alone
with Bertram, she waited impatiently for his return.
After a time, which in her mood seemed needlessly
long, she heard a shout, and looking up saw that he
had freed the sheep from its captivity, and was on
his way back.

"Oh!" he exclaimed, as he returned to her,
" I have liberated the poor creature, but I have
torn my hand. Will you please bind it up for
me ? "

It was nothing very serious, and she quickly tied
his handkerchief round it.

"Thank you, no one could have done it more
gently," he said, in his most insinuating tones.

Disconcerted by the flattery, and still more by
something in his tone, she answered coldly : " Let us
hurry on now as quickly as possible and try and
overtake our friends."

They walked in silence, and he felt ill at ease.
Then he recalled that in many ways she had behaved
very sweetly to him during his holiday, and he said
to himself, " Faint heart ne'er won fair lady." The
tumult of his feelings increased, but he held himself
well in hand ; the cool, calculating habit never left

him. He did not rush into a confession, but slowly and carefully felt his way.

"This is a most delightful excursion," he said after a few minutes. " I never in my life enjoyed anything half so much."

" I am glad," she replied, pleasantly, " especially as this is your last day with us."

" Ah ! that is the bitter drop in my cup of happiness. I must leave these glorious snow-capped mountains, these lovely flower-carpeted valleys, and go back to a dismal law-office, pore over dirty yellow parchments, and endure the presence of a pack of drivelling, dull-souled quill-drivers."

"Oh," replied Evelyn, colouring deeply, "you libel good friends. Mr. Walsingham is not dull-souled, and never drivels ; neither does Mr. Stanford, unless he has strangely altered. Indeed, I am sure *he* could never change in that way."

Bertram noticed the emphasis of this reference to Edmund, and an expression of peculiar malignancy passed over his face. But it disappeared swiftly, and he said :

" Ah ! you have no idea of the dulness and monotony of a law-office. There a man is cramped, cribbed, cabined, confined ; he scarcely feels that he is a man. But here, among these everlasting hills, beneath these fair skies, life is infinitely desirable. I would not libel good friends, but, oh! Miss Sedgewick, permit me to say that your conversations during the last three weeks have helped me more than anything else in my life. Would that such days as this could follow one another without end ! It would be Paradise regained."

" Then you would soon tire of Paradise," said Evelyn, quickening her pace.

" Oh, surely not ; this life seems to me absolutely ideal."

"I do not share your views at all," answered Evelyn, earnestly. " For the present I think I am where I should be, on account of my mother's health ; but, should she continue to improve, I hope that we shall soon be back at Merton Magna. I know my father is longing to engage in his work again, and there is so much I wish to do myself. But surely, Mr. Elles, a great change has come over the spirit of your own dream. Only yesterday you were confessing an ambition to fill a place of wide usefulness and power. I think your ideals of yesterday were far nobler than those of to-day. I have no sympathy with a life of luxurious ease and self-indulgence. But there is something stimulating and ennobling in the thought of filling a worthy place in one's day and generation, in doing useful work, and in leaving the world better than we found it."

As Evelyn spoke these words the nobility of her character shone forth, and imparted to her features a strength and dignity that startled Bertram.

Was it, therefore, the awakening in him of some nobler and truer self, or only the adroit and clever move of an unscrupulous man that led him to change the tone and manner of his appeal ? It is hard to say : most likely there was something of both in his conduct, for good and evil are strangely mixed in the lives of men, and no man is merely a monster of iniquity when you know him truly.

It is certain that the moral enthusiasm of Evelyn

struck long-neglected chords in his own life, and
made him conscious that there were still possibilities
of goodness and nobleness open to him, if he would
only turn to them.

And yet there mingled even with these thoughts
something of the cunning of the crafty plotter, who
saw that to appeal for her help and pity was the most
effectual way of awakening her interest in himself, and
so of gaining an influence over her for his own ends.

And thus Evelyn had no sooner finished speaking
than he said,

" I plead guilty, Miss Sedgewick. I am inconsistent, I am weak. Sometimes I seem to myself
as though two personalities were wrapped up in
me. I feel in me a spirit that longs to live a heroic
life, and then there is a lower self that craves for
pleasure and present gratifications. Yesterday I
thought only of climbing the steep ascent, and to-day
I have dreamt of the couch of luxurious ease. Oh,
how I wish I were like you—good, pure, strong ! Can
you not help me ? Will you not tell me what I
ought to do ? "

An expression of great concern overspread her face
as he was speaking. He saw that he had awakened
more than interest, and went on :

" Oh, Miss Sedgewick, I have come unexpectedly
to the parting of the ways. A new path opens before
me ; will you help me to tread it ? "

He extended his hand in eager appeal towards her.

" I am not good and strong," she said, " for I, also,
know of the struggle between a higher and lower self ;
but there is an Unfailing Source of help open to all
who will turn to It."

But Bertram was not satisfied with this answer, and with a sudden resolve he determined to declare himself.

" Ah," he cried, " the highest excellence is possible to you. And if I could only one day—some future day—hope that you would not deem me unworthy; if I could only indulge the hope . . . ."

Here, however, he stopped suddenly. A rock, round which the path wound, had blocked their view; and just as he was holding out his hand appealingly to Evelyn, and a confession of love was trembling on his lips, a strange figure emerged from behind the rock, and immediately confronted them.

It was an old herdsman, whose long beard flowed over his chest in snowy waves. On his head he had a fox's skin, the brush hung down behind, the legs dangled on each side among his white hair, and the head surmounted his brow. The rest of his dress was in harmony with this strange head-gear. Yet there was upon his features an expression of dignity, and his eyes were dark and keen.

Bertram was greatly disturbed by this unexpected interruption, and was eager to hurry on. Not so, however, Evelyn. She had heard enough of her companion's final appeal to be thankful for this happy deliverance. She entered immediately into conversation with the old man, asking him whether he had met their party, and inquiring about the road, to the most difficult part of which they would soon come.

The herdsman answered her questions, and then he scanned the sky and said: " Let me urge you to hasten on and overtake your friends. The wind has changed, and these mountains will soon be covered with mist."

"Oh," asked Evelyn eagerly, "is there any danger of our being delayed? My father thinks we are with our friends, or he would have turned back to seek us before now."

"The mist will come soon, and unless you know the path well you will certainly be delayed. Shall I guide you over the ridge?"

"I can assure you, Miss Sedgewick," said Bertram, who was in a fever of impatience to move on, "we do not need the help of this old fellow. I know the way; let us hurry on."

He spoke contemptuously, and waved his hand to the herdsman to depart.

His words struck painfully on Evelyn's ears, and she cried with an earnestness that stayed the old man's steps, "Oh, do not leave us; I wish you to guide me to my father."

He turned, and in so doing gave Bertram a glance which transfixed him.

"Ah, yes," he said slowly, "your path, young lady, is beset with danger; I will see you safely to your friends."

He stepped between Evelyn and Bertram and they moved on together; Bertram with a look that need not be described.

They soon came to a jagged saw-like edge of rock, bordered on the one side by a steep slope covered with snow, while on the other the mountain broke away precipitously several thousand feet into the valley below. Before them rolled a panorama of glaciers and snow-capped pinnacles shining in dazzling splendour as the sun flashed and quivered among their crystalline towers and leaping cascades.

While Evelyn was gazing on this glorious vision the herdsman said :

"Do you see yonder white cloud on which the sun is shining?"

"Yes ; is it not gorgeous?"

"But do you notice that it is sweeping towards us? And there are others behind it. In a few minutes they will be here, and we shall be enveloped in clouds."

And so it was. The cloud floated nearer, several hundred feet below them. It struck the precipitous side of the mountain with a sound like the rushing of surf upon a shingly shore ; it streamed upwards in one straight column, and then fell forwards, and the whole path was enveloped in a mist so thick and impenetrable that Evelyn could not see her own feet.

"Oh, how thankful I am you came with us!" she exclaimed.

"Yes," he replied, "you would not have known how to act. The clouds will very likely remain here all night ; but a few hundred feet below it is still clear sunshine, as you will soon see."

They had to proceed along a narrow path quite at the edge of the mountain. Without safe guidance it would have been fatal to have moved a step. After a time they began to descend, and when they had gone some distance they suddenly emerged into brilliant sunshine. Above them was the white mist enveloping the mountain, and below was the valley bathed in light.

F

Just then a shout was heard, to which their guide replied, and immediately after Mr. Sedgewick and Herr Allenstein appeared in view. Matters were speedily explained. Evelyn thanked her guide, and Mr. Sedgewick rewarded him handsomely.

During the rest of the way into the valley Evelyn clung closely to her father's side, and Bertram walked sullenly behind. His visions of a new start and a new life, with Evelyn as his good angel, melted away. The old past was still clinging to him. There was a drag on the wheel. He would not find it so easy to begin life over again as he thought. When they reached the châlet Evelyn retired to her room, and did not reappear that night. The next morning he only saw her for a few moments to say good-bye in the presence of her parents, and when he turned to go away the look of craving for something higher and nobler had given place to the sullen scowl of baffled craft.

CHAPTER III.

IN ARCADY.

ONE evening whilst Bertram Elles was away in Switzerland Edmund Stanford sat in a garden bower smoking a cigar. He felt tired, lonely, depressed. The mystery of the disappearance of the bank-notes had not been unravelled, and seemed never likely to be. For a few days after their loss he was thoroughly miserable ; but he wrote an account of the incident to Mr. Sedgewick, and then resolutely forced his thoughts from a problem for which he could discover no solution.

The Rector sent back a letter full of encouragement, and assured him of his unabated confidence. He expressed his regret that Edmund would not be able to visit them that summer ; but said that by the next spring they hoped to be back in Merton Magna, and then the old intercourse would be renewed.

This communication had done much to cheer him, and he flung himself again into his duties with all his old enthusiasm. But the strain of anxiety and overwork was beginning to tell upon him, and Mr. Walsingham arranged that he should go for a holiday as soon as Bertram Elles returned.

It was the middle of August, and Edmund was wondering where he should spend his holiday, when

F 2

a smart dog-cart was driven up to the garden gate, and the next moment a big burly farmer entered, with a comely-looking lady by his side, whom Edmund at once recognized as the oldest friend of his boyhood—Betty Thatcher—formerly his governess, and for so many years his mother's faithful and trusted companion.

Miss Thatcher's uncle was dead ; but she had had the good fortune to marry a much respected gentleman farmer—John Heaviside, of the Hall Farm, Somerthorpe.

"I can't tell you how glad I am to see you, Mrs. Heaviside," exclaimed Edmund, "and above all to see you looking so well and so happy. Why, I declare, you look years younger than when I bid you good-bye on that dark day three years ago."

"Ah ! Edmund," she replied, the tears and smiles appearing together, "I see you are growing up like all the rest of the men folk ; you know how to flatter the women, and there's nobody can do that better than my good man."

As she spoke she glanced with true wifely pride into the great honest face of her husband, out of whose grey eyes there shone a soul full of summer warmth and native shrewdness.

The farmer gave a healthy, hearty laugh at his wife's sally, and grasping Edmund's hand, said in the broad native dialect which he loved,—

"How do ye do, Mr. Stanford ? As you couldn't come to see us, Betty said we must come and see you. But we shouldn't ha' bin here to-night—right in the midst o' harvest—on'y some o' my machinery broke down, and I had to come off all in a hurry to look after some more. So Betty up and said she would come wi' me."

"Well," said Edmund, "it's an ill wind that blows good to nobody. I'm delighted to see you. I should have paid you a visit before now, but we were so busy at the office that I could not be spared."

"You look as though you were killing yourself with work and worry," remarked Mrs. Heaviside; "it's high time you came to Somerthorpe for a rest."

"I am very tired, and want a holiday," he replied; "but come indoors, and Mrs. Muriel, my landlady, will make us some tea."

"You must excuse me," said the farmer, "I ha' got to see after this machinery; it must start at midnight. I'll be back in two hours; we must not be late, as we go off at four o'clock in the morning." And so saying he turned and walked rapidly away.

Edmund admired the look of energy and decision that mingled with his genial kindness; evidently he was no country bumpkin.

"Really I must congratulate you on your husband," he said, turning to Mrs. Heaviside. "What a splendid man!"

"I was sure you would like him," she replied, with a merry twinkle in her eyes. "You see I have not gone through the wood and picked up a crooked stick."

Edmund conducted her into the house, and the two hours passed swiftly.

Punctual to the minute the farmer reappeared. "Well, when may we hope to see you at Somerthorpe?" he asked.

"I have just told Mrs. Heaviside that I shall come

in a week or ten days, and spend a fortnight with you, unless you get tired of me, and turn me out before the end of my holiday."

The farmer laughed a mighty laugh. "Tired o' ye!" he cried. "Tired o' ye! Ah! ah! I say come as soon as ye can, and stay as long as ye can. When did ye say? In a week or ten days? First-rate! Ye'll be in time for the Harvest Supper, and after that we'll ha' some partridge-shooting. Now, Betty, my dear, we must go."

Edmund walked with them to the gate, and the farmer grasped his hand and gave it a grip that sent the blood tingling to his shoulder.

"Gude night, Mr. Stanford; ye shall have the best welcome to Somerthorpe we can give ye."

And then jumping up beside his wife he drove off.

"Well," thought Edmund, as he turned into his gate, "John Heaviside is a fine specimen of the genuine John Bull.

> ' So full of summer warmth, so glad,
>   So healthy, sound, and clear and whole.'

His very laugh seems to have done me a world of good."

.   .   .   .   .   .

"And this is Hall Farm?" said Edmund, as Farmer Heaviside's man pulled up at the gate of a breezy paddock, on the further side of which could be seen a superior dwelling, which looked half farm and half manor-house.

"Yes, sir," replied the man; "and a fine owd place it is tu."

"How long has Mr. Heaviside lived here?"

" Lor', sir, Maaster wor born here, and ha' lived here all his daays, and owd Maaster, whu died laast year, wor born here tu, and his folk afore him, for I doan't know how long."

A charming old place it looked that evening as they drove across the park, in which a herd of cattle was grazing.

As they drew up both Mr. and Mrs. Heaviside appeared at the garden gate.

" How do ye do, Mr. Stanford ? " exclaimed the farmer. " I hope you ha' had a pleasant drive."

" Delightful, thank you, and I hope you are both well," he answered, as he shook them warmly by the hand. " At what a pace we have come."

" Yes," said the farmer, patting the horse's neck, " Duke is a fast trotter ; but come away indoors ; Bob'll look after your luggage."

" Really," said Edmund, when they were gathered round the well-laden supper-table, "you should not have put yourself to the inconvenience of sending your man and horse for me at this busy season. I could have come by the public coach to St. Peter's, and then walked over."

" Doan't mention it," replied the worthy farmer ; " I should ha' come for ye myself at any other time ; but I knew Bob Bacon would be careful o' himself to-day. He's a good fellow, only he sometimes puts more in his innards than he can carry. The last time he was in the old city he was found drunk in his cart on Tombland. A lot o' them boys from the grammar-school were gathered round him, and he sat on a heap o' straw a-wavin' his old hat and a-singin'

'We won't go home till mornin','

and when they took him to the Guildhall, and asked him his name, he said he was Mister Robert Pork. But he's a kind-hearted chap, and handy wi' the horses. He was a man afore he'd ever bin outside the parish. The first time he went beyond the bounds o' Somerthorpe he turned round and said, ' Farewell, Owd England.' "

" I thought he was a bit of a wag," said Edmund, laughing.

"Well," said Mr. Heaviside, rising when the supper was over, " I must leave ye to have a chat by yourselves for an hour. All's well, we finish harvest to-morrow, and the next day we ha' the Harvest Supper."

Edmund sat down with Mrs. Heaviside, who was anxious to hear his last news from Switzerland.

" Mr. Elles," he said, " came home two days ago, but in a bad humour. In fact he was so insolent to Mr. Walsingham that he is to leave the office next month. Something has not pleased him during his holiday. But he says that Mrs. Sedgewick is better, and that Evelyn has become quite a blue-stocking— whatever that may mean. He says that she spends all her time talking philosophy with a German professor, called Allenstein, to whom, he believes, she is either engaged already, or soon will be."

" I don't think that is true," said Mrs. Heaviside, emphatically.

" I am not sure but there is truth in *that*," replied Edmund, " for in several of his letters Mr. Sedgewick has referred to this gentleman as a man for whom he has a very high regard. Being a professor and a philosopher, I thought he was an old man ; but Elles says that he is a young and handsome fellow, and as he has been staying some weeks with the Sedgewicks there is no saying to what the friendship may have grown. But, of course, nothing is really settled, or I should have heard of it."

" Ah, well," said Mrs. Heaviside, still more emphatically, " I don't like the idea of it at all. I shall be disappointed if it should be true."

" The idea of Evelyn becoming engaged never occurred to me," observed Edmund, " she looked such a child when I last saw her ; but, of course, that was three years ago ; she is, however, no child now, nor blue-stocking either in appearance. I received their portraits yesterday. I have brought them to show you."

He drew from his pocket a small album. " There, what do you think of her now ? "

" I think," answered Mrs. Heaviside, after gazing in silence for a few seconds, " that it is a lovely face ; but I always believed she would grow up a beautiful woman."

Then she turned to the other portraits and lingered wistfully over the familiar faces. At the end of the album was the portrait of a girl whom she did not know—a girl with a lovely ethereal face, and large, dark eyes, full of strange light and power, which shone out from beneath a mass of hair that encompassed her head like a purple cloud. It was a face to thrill you, haunt you, bewitch you.

" Who is this ? " asked Mrs. Heaviside. " Is it the portrait of a real woman ? "

" Ah," said Edmund, " that is Julia Ray. She was one of Evelyn's school friends, and is a wonderful girl, always doing extraordinary things. Just now she is nursing a sick aunt so assiduously that the doctor warned her that she must take care, or she would break down herself. What do you think of her portrait?"

"I do not like it so much as Evelyn's. You know her?"

"Oh yes; her aunt—Miss Ray—lives in the Cathedral Close, and since she has been ill I have called frequently."

Mrs. Heaviside turned back to the portraits of the Sedgewicks and lingered over them again.

"I wish that you had been able to have seen them this summer," she said. "It seems a great pity that you could not have gone instead of that Bertram Elles."

"Yes, but it cannot be helped. I suppose that Mr. Gresham would have given me longer leave of absence and permitted me to go had it not been for the loss of those bank-notes."

"Oh yes; that reminds me of something I want to tell you. If you had been here a few days ago you would have seen a very old friend on Somerthorpe Heath, one who wishes you well for your father's sake."

"Why, who can that be?"

"The old gipsy—Elizabeth Earne: she and her son come this way twice a year. She is a marvellous old woman, and it is surprising what she can find out. She is always saying things that come true. I could not help telling her about those bank-notes, and she declared that she would find out about them the next time she was in Caistor."

"When will that be?"

"In December. Her son is going to get married

and fit up a new van about Christmas time, and while he is away she will stay in her old quarters."

" Perhaps I may look her up. When will she come this way again ? "

" Not till the spring."

The farmer now returned, and soon after Edmund retired for the night.

The next morning he rose early, and went off for a ride before breakfast. He followed a winding lane that led through beautiful woods to the sea. The sun had not yet scattered the mist which lay in delicate wreaths of snowy whiteness upon the fields, partially hiding them from view. It trembled and flitted through the woods like strange shadows, and the fine old beech-trees stood out silent and spectral. All nature seemed brooding in expectation and wonder. After a mile or two he emerged on gorse-covered hills, and the sound of the incoming tide told him that he was near the sea. The sun rose slowly and shot forth broad shafts of light. He reached a romantic spot, where a cleft in the hills disclosed a snug fishing village. After a bathe he turned homeward by a path leading over Somerthorpe Heath, on which were many hollows and open pits, over which the mist still hung. Here he caused his horse to walk slowly, and thought what a dangerous spot it would be for a stranger on a dark night.

That afternoon Edmund saw the last waggon filled with the golden sheaves and led into the stack-yard with much shouting and rejoicing.

The next evening the Harvest Supper took place. The biggest barn, its walls covered with evergreens, was filled with long tables, and round these gathered all the men who had been engaged in the harvest, together with their wives. The old men also, past work, were invited, and to those unable to come presents were sent. The tables were weighed down with good things, and great was the rejoicing of everyone.

As Edmund surveyed the scene it appeared to him typical of much that was best in East Anglian country life. Farmer Heaviside was a worthy representative of the English yeoman class. He was a reverent, God-fearing man, with nothing morbid or controversial in his nature. He did not think that religion consisted in perpetually "watchin' one's innards," or in wrangling over the mysteries of the faith. He was a plain, down-right, straightforward Englishman, with a big, broad, genial nature, endeavouring to be a good husband, master, and neighbour.

After supper there were songs and speeches. The oldest man present proposed the toasts of the evening —the health of the master and mistress, and all the company stood up and sang the ancient harvest catch. The first part had reference to the mistress :

"Now supper is over, and all things are past,
  Here's our mistress's good health in a full flowing glass ; "

After the mistress came the master :

"Here's health to our master, the lord of the feast,
  God bless his endeavours, and send him increase."

While this song was being sung the utmost enthusiasm prevailed, and cheer after cheer was raised for the master and his good lady.

Then Farmer Heaviside stood up and spoke,—

"Neighbours and friends," he said, "I thank you all heartily for drinking my health, and that o' my good wife, and I'm right glad to see you all look so happy. There are a lot o' people going about wi' all sorts o' good advice, and tellin' us what we ought to do to put the world right. But I don't see that the wisest o' them ha' anything better to tell us than what we all learnt long ago. 'My duty towards my neighbour is to love him as myself, and to do to all men as I would they should do unto me . . . . to hurt nobody by word nor deed, and to be just and true in all my dealings.' Well, my friends, I don't say I ha' lived up to that, but I ha' tried to : and now that I ha' got a good wife to help me, I hope to do better still. Now we will all join in singing, 'God save our Gracious Queen,' and then I'll bid ye all good-night."

On the following Sunday there was a Harvest Thanksgiving in the church in the morning, and another in the Methodist chapel in the fishing-village in the afternoon, to both of which Mr. Heaviside drove with his wife and Edmund.

And so the holiday passed. Edmund got several days' shooting with his host, and much of his time he spent in wandering alone over the hills, and by the sea, dreaming of his past and future.

And very, very often in those lonely rambles there flashed upon his inner eye the vision of a bewitching face, and he took out his pocket album and glanced at the last portrait in it.

So the days sped swiftly by, and it was time for him to return to Caistor.

He went back to his work braced up in body and mind, feeling that Somerthorpe would henceforth hold a warm corner in his thoughts, but never dreaming under what strange circumstances of darkness and trouble he would seek refuge there again.

CHAPTER IV.

THE MAGIC MIRROR.

JULIA RAY put on her hat and walked into the garden. Her aunt, much better though still weak, had retired for her usual siesta.

It was Sunday afternoon. The September air was delightfully warm and clear, with the faintest touch of autumn in it. High up in the sky were soft white clouds, drawn out towards the zenith like long fleecy streamers of carded wool; but nearer to the horizon gathered up into vast billowy masses, through which broad shafts of light shot a golden and rosy splendour. And beyond the clouds was arched the deep untroubled blue.

The bells had ceased ringing for the afternoon service, and in the intense Sabbath stillness the faintest echo of chanting floated through the doors of the cathedral, and trembled across the open space into the garden.

Every sight and sound was gentle, harmonious, rich. The walls of the quaint old house were covered with Virginian creepers, now in all their autumn beauty. The ancient elms of the Close had lost little of their summer brightness, and hid with their profusion of leaves all the lower portions of the stately cathedral from view. The garden was a glorious burst of colour.

On Julia's face there rested an unusually thoughtful expression. That morning she had received a letter from Frank containing unexpected news.

He had written from Switzerland to say that he had been offered and had arranged to purchase a valuable practice in the West End of London, on which it was important he should enter at once. As he had now recovered from his illness he was preparing to start immediately, and would be on his way by the time the letter reached her. He went on to say that in consequence of this turn of affairs his marriage would take place much earlier than had been contemplated; that, indeed, Kate and he had talked the matter over, and had arranged that it should be in November.

When the letter arrived Julia had only time to glance hastily through it; now she seated herself in a warm corner of the garden and perused it leisurely.

Frank had written in the highest spirits. He had made no attempt to conceal his joy over his own happy prospects. But yet there ran through his letter a tone of thoughtful consideration for his sister. He realized that his marriage would make a great difference to her. Hitherto they had been almost constantly together. He concluded, however, by saying that he hoped their aunt's condition would permit of Julia spending the next few weeks with him in London; as he would need her help in the selection and furnishing of his house, and in making all other necessary preparations for his marriage.

Julia read the letter, and then lay back in her chair musing.

So far, she had never taken life very seriously.

She was a merry, mocking little fairy, flitting about with a light, airy movement; a lovely creature of a thousand fancies and transient interests. And yet now and then she revealed a strange capacity for something nobler.

It had shown itself during Frank's recent illness. Up to that time her love for him had not appeared very deep. She had often seemed selfish and inconsiderate. But, from the moment he was declared dangerously ill, her manner changed. She watched him assiduously, regardless of infection, and by her skill and unremitting tenderness had saved his life. During those weeks of nursing a hidden fountain of self-forgetful love was disclosed that surprised all who had only witnessed her lighter moods.

But Frank was no sooner well again than she relapsed into her former self. She seemed one who would captivate you with her delicate wiles, shy glances, and ethereal beauty; and then, when she had effectually woven her silken cords round you, and made you her prisoner, would pelt you with flowers, and vanish away, to try her charms upon another victim.

Yet, with all this, there appeared to be no conscious cruelty. She did not intend any mischief. The truth is, she was never seriously thinking of love, whatever might be the thoughts of her numerous admirers and victims. She was happy in the sunshine, and flitted like a butterfly from flower to flower, content to sip the sweetness of the moment, without thought of the consequences or the future.

When Frank and Kate first became engaged she was delighted, and waltzed three times round the

"Ah Julia," she said, speaking to her own reflection in the fountain,

P. 81.

table. But this announcement of their speedy marriage was a shock to her. It awakened her to the realities of the position.

For the first time a sense of her loneliness came upon her. Father and mother had died when she was only a child. She had always been with Frank, and now he was to be married, and would need her no longer. Her dear old aunt had been very kind and very indulgent, but there was a vacant place in her heart which no aunt could ever fill.

In her excitement Julia rose and walked into the middle of the lawn, and, leaning her arm upon a marble statue of Cupid with drawn bow, watched abstractedly the gold-fish darting to and fro in a wide circular basin, into which a fountain was sending a tiny crystal shower.

The pleasant sunshine fell around her; it brought out the rich tints of her purple gown, revealed every grace of her slight figure, imparted a raven gloss to her hair, a more subtile depth to her eyes, and then repeated the whole picture in the mirror-like surface of the fountain.

Julia stood for some minutes lost in thought. Then suddenly she caught sight of her own fair image in the water, and, with that rapid change of feeling so characteristic of her, she broke into merry, rippling laughter. A happy thought had struck her.

"Ah, Julia," she said, speaking to her own reflection in the fountain, "you shall not live here all alone. You shall have a noble hero to love and cherish you, and fill your life with joy. Your Romeo will come and claim you, and you shall be happy for ever and a day."

G

The words had hardly escaped her lips when, hearing footsteps, she glanced round, and saw Edmund Stanford advancing towards her. The next second he was by her side. She could not conceal her confusion. The colour mounted to her cheeks, and her eyes fell. In so doing they again rested on the picture in the fountain. It had changed. The Julia whom she had addressed a moment before was no longer alone. A tall youth was by her side, clasping her hand, while the marble Cupid was aiming an arrow straight at him.

Speedily controlling herself, Julia exclaimed, "How glad I am to see you, Mr. Stanford! It is good of you to come so soon. I heard you were expected back yesterday. I do hope you have enjoyed your holiday."

"Yes, thank you, immensely," answered Edmund, looking admiringly at her. And, judging that her embarrassment was occasioned by his abrupt appearance, he added, " I must apologise for coming upon you so unexpectedly ; but, just as your servant was about to announce me, your aunt's bell rang, and I said I would come and announce myself. I saw you absorbed in thought for some moments, and, pardon me when I confess that I thought you, together with this marble statue, and dancing fountain, and with that background of noble elms, made a picture which I should like to paint. I could not disturb you until I heard your happy laugh. Evidently you have been occupied with pleasant thoughts, which I almost envy, for mine have been sombre all the morning."

" Oh dear," replied Julia, feeling more embarrassed than ever, " I hope you have had no bad news."

They were the first words that came to her lips, but she hardly knew what she said.

" No ; only I feel more dull and lonely than ever after my little holiday at Somerthorpe. But I want you to tell me all about yourself, and your aunt, and what news you have from Switzerland. Shall we go and sit down in yon pleasant corner ? "

They walked across the lawn, and Julia sat down in the chair she had lately left. Edmund drew another close beside her and seated himself. Frank's letter had fallen to the ground. Julia picked it up, and handing it to him, said :

" You were asking about Frank ; here is a letter I received from him this morning. It is full of unexpected news."

Edmund read the letter, and expressed his pleasure at Frank's happy prospects.

" But," he added, " although this is all very delight-ful for him, it can hardly bring the same unmixed joy to you. His gain will be your loss. You have been so much together. That thought is evidently troubling him."

" Oh," replied Julia, " I am glad for Frank's sake. He has always been good to me, and deserves to be happy. And Kate is worthy of him. I knew her long before he did, and always found her faithful and true. What do you think of her brother ? "

" Bertram ? " said Edmund, with some hesitation. " Well, we have not much in common, and although we have been a good deal together during the last three years, he is still somewhat of a mystery to me. But he can make himself very attractive when he likes."

" That is my feeling," she said. " He's not like Kate ; but I've not seen much of him until lately. He has been here almost every day since his return from Switzerland, and sometimes he has been quite charming."

" Ah," replied Edmund, glad to think that Bertram would soon be out of the way. " You are aware that he leaves our office next week ? Do you know what he intends doing in London ? "

" Oh, has he not told you ? He will enter the bank, with his uncle, Mr. Bruce, and as soon as he has received some instruction in banking he is going out as one of the firm's representatives in Canada."

" Indeed," answered Edmund, thinking that the sooner he was on the other side of the Atlantic the better he would be pleased. Then he added : " I don't think he particularly enjoyed himself with the Sedgewicks."

" He told me that he had been awfully happy ; that he and Evelyn had walks together every day, and that he had found her delightful."

" I imagined from the way he spoke to me that he had thought her quite a 'blue stocking,' absorbed in conversations on philosophy with a German professor. But she will be home next spring, and we can judge for ourselves."

" I am sure you will be glad to see them back, and especially Evelyn—you were so much together."

" Yes," he replied, " but we may not be able to start again on quite the old footing. Three years will have made a great difference. Still, I shall be delighted to see them back. On the whole, these years have been very dark and lonely to me—without

father, mother, brother, or sister, alone in this great
city, with all the friends of my boyhood and youth
suddenly swept away."

"Ah," said Julia, "our fates are somewhat alike.
You have no brothers or sisters, and I have only one,
and he needs me no longer. We are both fatherless
and motherless—almost alone in the world."

"That is so," remarked Edmund, looking into her
eyes, where the tears visibly trembled; "you lost your
father and mother early, did you not?"

"Yes. My father, as you probably know, was an
officer in India, and both Frank and I were born
there. I was only five when my father fell in a
struggle on the North-East border. The most vivid
recollection I have is the look of agony in my
mother's eyes when the news came that he had been
killed. Mother returned home with us, and died
soon after. Aunt Ray brought Frank and me up,
and we have hardly ever been separated until now."

"I suppose you remember nothing of India?"

"Nothing definite, just vague floating pictures.
Often I think I should like to go back. Sometimes I
dream of marble palaces and lovely gardens, and
fancy I am there. By the way, I was reading the
other day a curious old book on dreams. Do you
believe in them?"

"I can scarcely answer you yes or no. I don't
believe in dreams in any vulgar sense. Most of them
are, no doubt, quite trivial, due to some slight dis-
turbance in our sleep. But many dreams are, I
think, significant. They may not reveal the future,
but they certainly tell us something about ourselves
—the mysteries of our being, the secrets of our inner

life, and so, indirectly, the dangers and possibilities that lie before us."

" How can that be ? "

"By indicating the direction our thoughts incline to travel when they are not directly under control. In that way they reveal us to ourselves."

" I understand."

" But if the dreams of the night are significant, how much more are the dreams of the day ! Have you ever heard the saying, 'Our wishes are a forefeeling of our capabilities'? Those who have achieved the noblest careers have often had in their early years some mysterious foreshadowing of life. 'The Child is father of the Man,' as Wordsworth says, and not seldom in the child's thoughts and wishes there must be a prophecy of the future."

"Our wishes are a forefeeling of our *capabilities*," mused Julia ; " but what about our *achievements*, Mr. Stanford ? "

" Ah, there you touch upon a vital distinction," he replied. "We may fall short of our destiny. How many are capable of a life they never live ! We may miss our providential way, and hide our talent in a napkin. There are a hundred ways in which we may fail to rise to the height of our calling."

It was Julia's nature to respond like a harp to every touch. She unconsciously yielded to the strong emotions of another. Hence she caught the glow of Edmund's moral enthusiasm. She sat twining the long stalk of a picotee round her fingers, more lovely in her seriousness than Edmund had ever seen her in her lighter moods. As he gazed upon her he was more than ever struck by her remarkable character and beauty, and became doubly conscious of a tender emotion which had so often lately sent the blood tingling through all his veins. A new tenderness was in his voice as he said,—

"I am afraid I have disturbed you, Miss Ray, by my moralisings. I ought to have been more considerate of your feelings to-day. Pray forgive me."

"Oh, don't say that!" replied Julia. "Your words have done me good, and I cannot thank you enough for them."

As she spoke she lifted her eyes to him, and there shone in them a light he had never seen before.

There was a pause for a few seconds, and then Julia said,—

"I was reading, one day last week, Tennyson's 'Lady of Shalott.' Sometimes I think that, like Elaine, I possess a magic mirror in which I see fair pictures that I should like to weave into the web of my life. And then the visions fade away, and I do not attain my ideal. But I am sure your words to-day will help me."

"It is very good of you to say that," replied Edmund eagerly; "and if I could be permitted to help you more and more it would be a great joy to me. In one respect, however, I do not altogether like your reference to the 'Lady of Shalott.' For when she looked into her crystal mirror, and saw Sir Lancelot ride by, and followed after him, the curse fell on her. Should you ever see such a vision in your magic mirror, and follow also, I hope that it may be with happier result to both lady and knight."

But no sooner had he spoken than he turned towards the house, having heard approaching footsteps, and so did not notice the look of surprise and confusion on Julia's countenance. The servant had come to announce that tea was ready.

"You will stay and have tea with us, will you not?" said Julia, only partially recovered; for his words brought vividly to mind what she had seen that afternoon in the clear crystal depths of the fountain.

"I shall be delighted to do so," he replied.

CHAPTER V.

A MOONLIGHT SCENE.

JULIA led the way to the drawing-room, and, leaving Edmund with her aunt, ran off to her own room, and endeavoured while making a slight change in her toilet to control her emotions.

When she returned her aunt accepted the help of Edmund's arm, and they descended to tea.

She was an intimate friend of Mr. Sedgewick, and his regard for Edmund had prepared her to receive him cordially from the first. Of all Julia's numerous admirers he was the only one to whom she gave the least encouragement.

She was looking out of her window and saw him join Julia in the garden, and was not at all displeased when, an hour later, she perceived that he was still engaged in eager conversation with her. She had even hurried forward the tea in the hope that he would remain.

Not that she had any of the instincts of the ordinary match-maker. But she was one of those charming old ladies, unspoiled by time, who remain for ever young in heart, and who find a perennial delight in promoting the welfare of others.

She had been beautiful when young, and not unlike Julia both in features and character. And in those days she had had her own romance, which, ending badly, had nearly wrecked her life. But she recovered, and gained in the course of years that sweetness and tranquillity which are sometimes found in those who have suffered most.

Very dearly she loved her niece, and her own early mistake made her the more watchful over her. She knew that Julia had the capabilities of a noble womanhood, but she was not blind to her faults. She saw weaknesses in her which, in conjunction with her captivating beauty, might, under possible circumstances, involve her in some unfortunate escapade, and blight her life.

It therefore gave Miss Ray pleasure to see a young man of Edmund's stability and attractiveness frequenting her house. She was too shrewd to suppose that it was wholly on her account that he had made his almost daily calls during her illness. And now, as they sat at tea, she was well pleased to observe the courteous attentions he paid to Julia, as well as to herself, and the sly glances of responsive sympathy which Julia returned.

Even her niece's absent-mindedness as she presided at the tea-tray only evoked a smile of gentle raillery.

" You are day-dreaming, my dear," Miss Ray said, pleasantly.

" Day-dreaming ! " replied Julia. "Oh, auntie, you should have heard what Mr. Stanford was saying in the garden about day-dreams. He thinks they are ever so much more important than the dreams of the night ; and I was glad to hear that, for my waking dreams are always pleasant."

" Were you having one of your pleasant day-dreams when Mr. Stanford called this afternoon ? I happened to be at my window, and I saw you gazing very absently into the fountain. Even when Mr. Stanford arrived he seemed unwilling to disturb you."

Julia's spoon slipped from her fingers and fell down. She stooped to pick it up, and certainly it took her a very long time.

" I can bear witness," said Edmund, smiling, " that I heard a most merry laugh ring out. I quite envied the happy thoughts which must have occasioned it ; but it would not be right to ask what they were about. I should not like to confess some of my day-dreams."

And then he added, speaking more particularly to Miss Ray,

" We were talking about other things besides day-dreams. I was glad to hear the good news about Frank. I must apologise for not mentioning it before. I'm sure you will be glad."

" Yes ; both at his professional and domestic prospects. We have known Kate Elles for many years, and she is all that I could desire in a wife for Frank. I am very thankful ; for, as one of my favourite authors says, ' There is no earthly relationship which has so much power to ennoble and exalt as marriage, and on the other hand none which has so much power to wreck and ruin the soul.' "

" My mother often made a similar remark," observed Edmund. " I notice," he added, addressing Julia, " that Frank wants you in London to help him to prepare his new home. I hope you will not have to leave just yet."

"What do you say, auntie dear?" asked Julia.

"We must settle that to-morrow; but if you are going to church this evening, it is time you were getting ready. What do you intend doing, Mr. Stanford?"

"You know," he said, turning to Julia, "that the Dean has arranged for a series of short, popular evening services in the nave of the Cathedral? They begin to-night."

"Oh yes," replied Julia, "I had heard, but had forgotten about it. I should very much like to go."

"I shall be delighted to accompany you," he said, "if your aunt will permit me. I could then see you safe home again."

"I shall be quite satisfied when I know that Julia is with you," answered Miss Ray, with unaffected sincerity.

Julia, feeling very happy and excited, ran off to get ready.

They said little to one another as they walked round to the great west door of the Cathedral. It was a beautiful evening. A gentle breeze whispered among the broad elms of the Close, and here and there a dry leaf fell pattering to the ground. The bells had a far-a-way sweetness of tone. The stately Cathedral rose up solemn and vast against the pale blue sky. Possibly the beauty of the quiet twilight hour, with its brooding mystery, its lengthening shadows, its soft silvery light, cast a spell upon their spirits, and helped them to collect their thoughts. Or it may be that already something of that awe had fallen upon them which touches the soul as it approaches a crisis in its history.

Edmund and Julia did their best to enter heartily into the service. Still the thought of being so near to each other was never absent from their minds, and was very sweet. A close observer might have noticed that their eyes met more frequently than was really necessary; and that when they stood up to sing out of the same hymn-book, and their hands touched, a richer colour mantled Julia's cheeks, and a softer light passed into Edmund's eyes.

The sermon, at any rate, received their whole attention; for the preacher had many things to say that seemed directly intended for them. His text was: "For none of us liveth to himself, and no man dieth to himself"; and he besought his hearers to remember that men and women may make this world and the next brighter or darker not only for themselves, but for those whom their lives touch. He had much to say about the power of a noble love to lift life to a higher level, and to turn the morbid, listless youth into a man of enthusiasm and energy, and the giddy, thoughtless girl into a wise and unselfish woman.

To all this they listened with attention, and when they left the Cathedral Edmund drew closer than before to his companion, and felt that the hour had come when he must speak.

And it is likely he would have done so as they slowly loitered home in the beautiful moonlight but that they were not alone. The path was filled with those who like themselves were returning from the service.

When, however, the garden gate had closed upon them, and they were alone, Edmund said:

" Do you need to go indoors just yet ? Shall we go to yon quiet retreat, where we had our pleasant talk this afternoon, and sit down for a little while ? "

As he spoke he clasped her hand.

Julia glanced up shyly for one moment, then her eyes fell, but she did not withdraw her hand as he led her gently to the bower.

The night was glorious. The moon, at its full, shed down a flood of silver light that filled the garden with a soft, mystic splendour, save where the trees and shrubs cast their deep shadows. The quaint old house, standing far back amid a profusion of climbing plants, looked a haunt of ancient peace. A breath of wind went whispering by like a youth murmuring a love story in a maiden's ear. The flowers exhaled a thousand sweet odours. The fountain poured forth a crystal stream, which rose up like a tall, transparent flower-bell, and then curving over collapsed into a shower of sparkling diamonds ; while the marble statue of Cupid, whiter than ever in the moonlight, gleamed out from amid the dark evergreens as though he were the presiding spirit of the hour.

For a few moments they sat silent, gazing on the lovely scene, and happy in an unspoken love.

Edmund felt the blood leaping and throbbing through his veins, and the confession of love was trembling on his lips, when in the perfect silence they heard the garden gate give a peculiar click, as though someone was endeavouring to enter noiselessly.

Julia experienced a nameless and inexplicable dread, and a sudden shiver passed through her fragile frame.

" What is it ? " she whispered.

" It can only have been the wind," he answered. " I hear no footsteps."

She drew perceptibly closer to his side.

" Nothing shall ever harm you, if I can prevent it," he said tenderly. " Oh, Julia, will you not trust yourself altogether to me ? I love you with all my heart."

She knew that he loved her, and had half fashioned in her mind the pretty hesitating reply she would make when he spoke to her—half yes, half no, which would call forth a fuller confession from him. But now, as she heard the tender words, and felt the clasp of his hand, and saw the beseeching look in his great honest eyes, she was wholly conquered.

" Am I worthy of you ? " she whispered.

But even as she spoke he clasped her in his arms and kissed her.

" My darling," he said, passionately, " for ever mine, don't speak of unworthiness. If what we have heard to-night be true, love will make us more and more worthy of one another. I am only sorry that I have so little to offer you at present, beyond love ; but henceforth I shall have a new energy, and a new motive for making the best of life."

" Oh," cried Julia, " you are true and noble already, and I will try and be worthy of your love."

As she spoke she lifted up to him a tear-stained face, which he reverently kissed again. And then, with that strange capacity for rapid change of feeling so characteristic of her, she said with an arch smile, which had yet a good deal of seriousness in it,

" I want to ask you a question."

" What is it ? "

" Were you ever in love with anyone before ? "

" No, my darling ; why do you ask that question ? "

" Because, until lately, I had thought that there was someone else whom you must love, and whom you would be sure to marry."

" Whom ? "

" Evelyn Sedgewick."

Edmund started. " Why ?   What could make you think so ? "

Julia hesitated, and then said slowly :

" You grew up together, and were so fond of each other, and Evelyn is so good, and beautiful, and rich."

" I never thought of her in any other light than as a very dear friend ; just as I would think of a sister."

" Strange ! "

" Do you think so ?   Well, for one thing her wealth would have created a difficulty."

" Indeed ; and yet you ask me !   I inherit all my mother's fortune."

Edmund again started : " I did not know that," he said.

" No," replied Julia, smiling at Edmund's exclamation.   " It is not generally known.   I was not aware what it really meant myself until a week or two ago, when I came of age.   Are you sorry I am an heiress ? " she asked, archly.

" Yes ; I wish you were not better off than I am myself ; and yet, dear Julia, I could not now recall my words."

" But suppose I were to send you away for what you have said ?   I have a host of admirers who will not object to my fortune," she replied.   And then the desire to tease was gone.   Again she nestled close to his side, and her eyes beamed with happiness.

"Dear Edmund," she said sweetly, "forgive me. I shall not send you away. You have made me very happy to-night. If the money is a difficulty I can easily get rid of it; for I hold it absolutely in my own right. But how pale and cold you look. Let us go into the house, and tell dear auntie."

Edmund rose to his feet. He had not yet recovered from his surprise. As they moved to leave the bower there was a rustling of leaves immediately behind where they had been sitting. A branch broke, and footsteps were heard on the gravel path.

Edmund sprang round the trees, only to see a man leap the garden wall and disappear.

Julia would have fallen to the ground had not her lover returned just in time to save her.

"Do not be alarmed, dear. Your aunt was telling me before tea that your neighbour's fruit-trees were robbed a night or two ago. No doubt it was someone prowling about for the same purpose again."

But Julia was not satisfied. "I think we are being watched. Who can it be?" she said, trembling: "let us hasten indoors."

They walked into a broad path, and entered the house, as soon as Julia had recovered from her agitation.

Few words were needed to enlighten Miss Ray. She saw what had happened as they entered the drawing-room hand-in-hand, and after kissing them both she solemnly blessed them.

That night Edmund lay awake for several hours thinking of Julia, and when at last he did fall asleep he dreamt of her.

She appeared like a beautiful vision in the sky;

H

her eyes shone like stars, and her hair floated around her like purple clouds. But she was seated upon a massive gold throne, and it was so high that he could not reach her.

Then he dreamt that he was painting her portrait; but somehow he could not get the features right, for her expression changed continually.

Finally, when they were perfectly happy together, a strange horrid creature with black wings swooped down and snatched her from him, and disappeared, leaping over a wall.

He awoke in great excitement, and it was some time before he slept again ; but then his sleep was undisturbed, and when he awakened in the morning the sunshine filled his room, and the new love that filled his heart made it sing with joy.

CHAPTER VI.

A WEEK OF ROMANCE.

EDMUND was not more than half dressed when he unlocked a little case and took out his mother's jewels. He had never touched them since he put them away with a sad heart after her death. There were not many—three or four rings, a few bracelets, a necklace; but all rare and of fine quality, and he lifted them up and looked at them tenderly.

"Would that she were still living," he thought; "but I'm glad they once met."

The most valuable thing in the collection was a small antique ring. It had been in his mother's family for generations. The stones were of great beauty, and exquisitely set in chased gold. It was the most precious thing he owned, and he was glad that he could offer Julia so choice a gift.

After breakfast he wrote to Mr. Sedgewick, and informed him, in a letter overflowing with happiness and hope, of his engagement.

As he walked to business the whole world brightened and beamed around him with a new gladness. The flowers had a sweeter fragrance, the grass a fresher green; the clouds were touched with a purer radiance, the trees with a richer splendour. Never before had the blood run so warmly through

H 2

his veins ; never had the river of his life flowed so sweetly or so full. All through the day love made divine music in his soul, and lightened every duty. Even towards Bertram Elles he somewhat relaxed, and readily did several things to oblige him, especially as he was suffering from a sprained ankle, incurred, he said, whilst playing cricket on Saturday.

So also with Julia. She was transfigured. Hitherto her heart had been like a garden in early spring ; but now summer had come, and all the secret loveliness burst into blossom. Her nature showed itself richer, fuller of beauty and fragrance. And united with these higher qualities, previously almost hidden, the lighter traits of her character only imparted an added charm—like the dew upon the flower, the bloom upon the fruit. She moved about the house and garden radiant as a beam of light, and waited upon her invalid aunt like a ministering angel.

She attired herself for dinner with special care, and when she gave a final glance into the mirror was glad for Edmund's sake to find herself so fair.

The drawing-room was empty when he entered ; but soon he heard her footsteps, and his heart bounded for joy. Half unconsciously he murmured the lines :

> " She is coming, my own, my sweet :
>   Were it ever so airy a tread,
>   My heart would hear her and beat,
>   Were it earth in an earthy bed."

It was their first meeting as acknowledged lovers, and it would be hard to say which was the more deeply stirred. A rich colour mantled Julia's face as she came towards him with a coy bashfulness that was irresistibly charming, while Edmund's profounder feelings were akin to religious awe.

Never before had he seen her look so beautiful. She had selected a silvery-coloured gown of gossamer lightness that shimmered and scintillated with every movement, as the sea when gently stirred on a summer's night, and the moon is full. A scarlet sash relieved its severe beauty, as did also the clusters of scarlet geraniums twined among the fine old lace at her throat and among the rich masses of her dark hair.

He drew her to himself with reverence, and whispered, " My love, my life, my fate."

But Julia had recovered herself. She gave him one of her most bewitching glances, and, with a touch of her old coquetry, asked :

" Are you sure? Were you not sorry last night when you found that I was an heiress?"

She laid her hand in his, and her eyes baffled him with their mingled seriousness and merriment. " Are you quite sure?" she asked again.

" Of course I am quite sure, you little fairy," he replied, looking at her with admiration ; " and I will bind you closer still with this golden link." He slipped the ring on her finger.

Julia's mood changed immediately. Every suggestion of light gaiety faded away. As she examined the ring a look of tenderness overspread her face.

" Thank you so much, dear Edmund," she said. " It is a lovely ring, and it belonged to your mother. She had it on the day I saw her, and I shall prize it above all my jewels for your sake and hers."

Edmund was delighted, and briefly told her something of the ring's history.

At dinner the conversation was chiefly about Frank and Kate, and their approaching marriage. Frank had sent a telegram to say he had arrived in London, and wanted to know when he might expect his sister.

" I think, my dear," said Miss Ray, " that you should not delay longer than the end of this week. I am well now, and can spare you ; but I might have another attack of my old complaint, and then it would be difficult for you to get away. Will you go on Saturday ? "

Julia looked wistfully out of the window. Under other circumstances she would have been pleased at the prospect, and been ready to hurry off at the earliest opportunity ; but it was different now. She glanced at Edmund.

" Don't you think the beginning of next week would do ? " he asked. " Saturday will be a holiday at the office."

He was realizing now, more fully than he had ever done, how dull and lonely his life had been since his mother died. He had been cast into a great city among strangers, and had made few friends, and so the years had passed in almost unbroken toil. He had given himself up to his profession with enthusiasm, and had studied in his lodgings with immense ardour, and had thus increased in knowledge and efficiency far beyond that of ordinary men of his age ; but each year his heart had craved with a deeper longing for sympathy and love.

And now that the winter of his life seemed gone he rejoiced in the sunshine, and wanted to prolong his new-found happiness. Julia would, of course,

be back in November; but that was a long way
off.

And so it was arranged as they desired.

After dinner Miss Ray settled herself in a cosy
corner of the drawing-room, and soon fell off into a
doze. Edmund and Julia drew to the window, and
while the grey twilight slid down, softer than sleep,
on the old Cathedral Close, they let out their life-
secrets to one another in sweet confidences.

Very wonderful and beautiful is this unveiling of
hearts, when two young lovers, who have lived chaste
and dutiful lives, begin to discover themselves to each
other, and tell of their inmost hopes, ambitions, desires.
Each brings to the other a new world of thought,
feeling, imagination, and their growth in mutual
knowledge becomes a series of delightful surprises.

So, at least, it seemed to Edmund and Julia that
evening. As they talked on Julia became conscious
of regions of thought and feeling in Edmund on
which she had never previously entered. She was
like a dweller in a flat country who wakes up to find
himself, for the first time, in a land of mountains,
with all their mystery of light and shade and purple
splendour. And Edmund discovered that beneath
Julia's fairy lightness of movement and sparkling
effervescence, there were unexpected and unexplored
depths.

They talked on while the light faded slowly, and
a pale radiance streaming up from behind the elms
showed that the moon was rising.

Julia knew that Edmund was an excellent pianist,
and so, taking advantage of a pause in the conversation, she asked him to play.

He rose at once, and went to the piano. For a moment or two his fingers hesitated among the keys, and then glided into the " Moonlight Sonata." Never had he put more soul into his touch, and the soft, silvery notes of the *adagio* gave perfect musical expression to the melting sweetness and brooding mystery of the scene outside as the lights of day merged and blended into the mellow radiance that was rising. Presently the moon glided in serene splendour from behind the trees, and sailed into the clear, unclouded heavens, and at once the bright, sparkling, brilliant notes of the *allegretto* expressed the radiancy of glory that filled the sky.

The beauty of that particular evening was unbroken by cloud or storm ; but Edmund played on through the *presto agitato* telling of the struggle between light and darkness, good and evil, with the ever-recurring hope of final peace and joy, when all evil and darkness shall be overcome, and the light shall shine full and clear. On and on he played until the music rushed to its conclusion in one glorious burst of triumph.

"Oh, thank you," cried Julia. " I never before heard the ' Moonlight Sonata' played like that ; I understand it now."

" It suggests Life," remarked Miss Ray, who had awakened at the first notes, and had been listening attentively. " Life with its cloud and sunshine, storm and calm, and over all Eternal and Almighty Love."

"Yes," observed Edmund, "it is a remarkable thing, but almost every great work of art deals, in some form or other, with the one great problem—the everlasting conflict between Light and Darkness, Good and Evil."

On another evening Edmund took with him a piece of manuscript music which he had set to some words from Tennyson. He offered to sing them if Julia would play the accompaniment. She sat down gladly and began to play. The first chords were soft and sweet, but quickly passed into a passionate movement. They were set to that song of unutterable longing which Maud's lover sings :

> " O let the solid ground
> Not fail beneath my feet."

Edmund had a baritone voice of unusual sweetness and compass, and sang with a wild self-abandonment and pathos that brought the tears into Julia's eyes.

There was silence for a moment, then she looked up and asked him, shyly,—

" Are you quite, quite sure now, dear ? "

"Yes," he replied, and slipping his arm round her slender figure he led her to the sofa by the window.

" I will tell you," he said, sitting down beside her, " how I came to write that music. It was one afternoon whilst I was at Somerthorpe. I had walked several miles, and at last sat down in a lonely spot among the hills overlooking the sea. Everything was beautiful around me. The wide expanse of waters was a deep blue in the distance, an emerald green near the shore. It spread out until sea and sky united and melted into each other. Here and there I could discern a white sail. The hills, covered with purple heather and golden bracken, were gorgeous in the sunshine. Nature was lovely, but my heart was sad. The silence and loneliness oppressed me. As I sat musing, my life rose up and passed before me. One by one the most sacred ties had been severed. I was alone in the world. Yet I longed with a great longing for love. I craved for another heart which would beat in responsive sympathy to my own. Then the words I have just sung came to my mind, and with them the music. The words made the music. As I walked home singing them to myself I thought of you. Your face haunted me ; all through the night I saw you in my dreams. I felt that I loved you, and I made up my mind that I would try to win you. And now that you are mine all indifference about life has vanished. I am no longer ' vext with waste dreams.' Life now opens out like a glorious sea, full of infinite possibilities."

So the evenings of that first week of their betrothal passed.

For the Saturday, some of Julia's friends arranged a picnic party to St. Olave's Broad, and invited the young lovers to join them.

Luncheon was tastefully laid out in the fine old garden that slopes down to the margin of the beautiful Broad, and as soon as it was over the party scattered in various directions.

Edmund and Julia went off in a boat by themselves.

The Broad looked, that afternoon, its loveliest : a sparkling gem of silvery water set in green and gold ; a fairy region of happy dreams and unbroken peace, hidden far away from the common world in a deep seclusion of ancient woods and gently sloping hills.

Edmund rowed to the extreme end of the Broad. Julia leaned back among the cushions at the stern, with half-closed eyelids, wrapt in a fairy dream of delight. She looked as though some subtle essence of loveliness, distilled from all the harmonious sights and sounds around her, had silently slid into her soul, and diffused itself through her whole being, until

> " Beauty born of murmuring sound
> Had passed into her face."

The sky overhead was without a cloud. The lake was a deep blue, save where the sun's direct ray made it sparkle and flash like molten gold and silver.

They floated past quiet bays, fringed with beds of swaying reeds and stately bulrushes, rich in tints of brown and yellow, beyond which sloped upwards noble woods, just beginning to flush into autumn splendour, while the more open spaces were covered with golden bracken and purple heather.

After rowing some three miles they entered a sequestered bay in the most lonely part of the Broad. Had they been on some coral island far out in the Pacific Ocean they could hardly have found a fairer spot, or been more entirely by themselves.

" Here in this fairy solitude," exclaimed Julia, " you must rest before we return."

" Yes," replied Edmund, " it will be delightful."

And he proceeded to moor the boat to the roots of a tree whose wide-spreading branches offered a pleasant shade. He sat down beside Julia. A few whispered words, sacred to lovers, passed between them, and then, too happy for speech, they relapsed into golden silence.

They remained so still, each lost in sweet dreams, that the winged creatures around them regained their confidence, and came near. A kingfisher, in gorgeous plumage of red, blue and green, dashed past, and hanging on a swaying reed watched for his prey. A goldfinch settled upon a thistle, and searched for the downy seeds. The coots passed in and out of the beds of rushes. The twittering swallows glided swiftly overhead. Bees droned among the aromatic plants. A brown butterfly flitted from flower to flower. From the woods came the cooing of the ring-doves, and high in the fair sky several larks were singing rapturously.

"Oh, Edmund!" exclaimed Julia, "is not this delightful? What mystic harmony of lights and shadows! What beauty of form and colour! Surely we have floated into some fairy world of joy and loveliness, far away from the busy world! Does it not seem like a dream too beautiful to be real? Would that we could dwell for ever and ever in such an enchanted world."

"I am glad you are enjoying it so thoroughly," he replied; "I was never so happy before."

"I was just wondering," said Julia, in a low sweet voice, and with rising colour, "why we should not always live in such a world of beauty as this—say in a lovely villa, like those two we passed with gardens sloping to the water's edge. Why should you toil for years and years in the city when this delightful life is already within our reach?"

Edmund visibly started, but he soon controlled himself, and said quietly :

" A most fascinating day-dream! I have entertained it a thousand times ; for beauty appeals to me in all its forms. I am often weary of the world, with its eager mammon-worship, and eternal problems for which there seems no solution. A thousand times I have wished that I could withdraw from it to some sheltered retreat like this, and live in unbroken communion with Nature : listening to her eternal music, watching the ever-changing expression of her beauteous face. If you have read Tennyson's 'Palace of Art' you will understand the feeling, except that I never desired to live alone in my beautiful retreat. But I have wished to follow Art for Art's sake alone, and dedicate my life to the worship of the Beautiful. And now you say that that lovely dream might be realized. I understand ; and yet forgive me when I reply that it is a temptation that must be resisted ; it is all a mistake, and I am sure that they who live for selfish enjoyment will find life ending in hollow mockery."

" But Wordsworth lived a noble life, and yet he deliberately forsook the world, and retired to the lonely hills."

" Yes, because he understood himself, and knew that he could serve mankind better by so doing. But where Wordsworth succeeded a thousand ordinary men would fail ; and I am sure that my place is among men, and my life-work to help them. And I feel certain, dearest, that such a life would not suit you at all. To-day you feel all this beauty, and think you would never grow weary ; but you would soon be disappointed. And now, my sweetheart, have I too roughly dissipated your pleasant dream? Forgive my thoughtlessness. Perhaps I should not have spoken so eagerly, but that the temptation appeals so strongly to me."

"You must not consider my words too seriously, Edmund dear. Hitherto I have been a thoughtless girl, thinking how I could best enjoy myself."

"My darling!" exclaimed Edmund, drawing her closer to himself, and kissing her, "you are all I could desire, and I wish I were more deserving of the rich gift of your love; but our love for each other will strengthen and elevate us both, and make us more and more worthy of one another, and give us nobler ideals of life and duty."

"You have made me happier than I ever hoped to be," said Julia, for it was her nature to respond at once to the strong feeling of another; "and I am sure your ideas about life are higher than any I have ever had." As she spoke her eyes shone with an almost unearthly gladness.

"And I," said Edmund, "feel through every nerve and vein and fibre of my being the touch of a new life."

Very soon after this they returned to their friends, and then, having had tea in the gardens, they all went back to the city. The picnic had been an immense success.

Sunday was another happy day for the two lovers, and on the Monday morning Julia left for London.

So passed the first days of Edmund's betrothal to Julia Ray. It was just one week of romance, and always in his thoughts stood apart as a brief period

of ideal beauty and rapturous delight.   And although
in after years he had to look back upon it through
an intervening period of darkness and agony in which
all that makes life worth living seemed lost, yet he
never failed to cherish it as a sweet memory.

BOOK III.

"'Glory to God—to God!' he saith,
'Knowledge by suffering entereth,
And Life is perfected by Death.'"

CHAPTER I.

THE TRAIL OF A SERPENT.

IT was a bright morning in November when Frank Ray and Kate Elles were married. The little church at Brentfield was crowded in every part, and when, an hour or two later, the happy pair drove off for their brief honeymoon, all the wedding guests and the household followed them to the entry gates, and sent them on their way with a volley of hearty cheers and old slippers.

Edmund lingered behind with Julia at the gates until the merry party had returned to the Rectory, and then, linking his arm with hers, drew her unobserved into the conservatory.

He was anxious to be alone with her. An inexplicable suggestion of dissatisfaction had shown itself in one or two of her recent letters. It was too indefinite and intangible to refer to, but it had made him uneasy.

When, however, they met that morning just before the marriage ceremony, her greeting was so glad and affectionate that it scattered all his fears. He concluded that what had troubled him was nothing but a morbid fancy of his own, and endeavoured to put it away as a feeling unworthy to be entertained.

"I never saw you look so lovely as you do to-day," he exclaimed. "My eyes have worshipped you all the morning."

"Naughty boy," replied Julia, her face beaming with gladness. "You ought to have been looking at Kate, not at me : to-day she should be the centre of interest."

"Yes, for Frank and the rest, but not for me," he answered, as he bent down and touched her brow reverently with his lips. "I can't tell you," he added, "how much I've been longing to see you during the last week or two. Time seems to have been moving with leaden feet. I don't believe I could have waited much longer. I should have grown desperate and come up to London to see you again, even though I had only ᵗᵒ clasp you once in my arms, and hear you ᴄ ɪat you still were mine."

"O doubt ᵃᵣt," she murmured, slightly dropping her eyes, "why did you want to hear that?"

And then, without giving him time to reply, she went on in serio-comic tones, but with an eager look in her eyes : "I think I ought to distrust such strong statements, sir. Love, I am told, doesn't fill a man's whole life as it does a woman's. You have your work and your studies to occupy most of your thoughts. Confess, now, that you could do quite well without me."

I

" Ah ! " he answered, " how I should have felt had I never seen you I can't say ; but we have met and loved, and now without you life would have no meaning for me."

The strange, wistful look left her eyes, and they became luminous with joy and love. He took her in his arms and kissed her, and for a moment she felt a blissful content.

" Now," she said, after a few minutes, " you must let me run away. I must go and help to send off the bride's cake."

Edmund moved uneasily and hesitated : something was troubling him.

" Could you not," he asked, gently, " be excused, and go for a walk with me ? I did not like to tell you before, for I knew that it would vex you, but I'm sorry to say that I must leave this afternoon."

" Leave this afternoon ! " cried Julia, starting, and the colour fading from her face. The news struck her like a blow.

" Yes," he answered, regretfully, "I knew you would be cruelly disappointed, and so am I, but it really cannot be helped. I have to go to London to-morrow morning by the first train, in order to see some solicitors before the opening of the Law Courts, and it is imperative that I should have an interview with Mr. Walsingham to-night."

" It is too, too bad," exclaimed Julia, unable to conceal her vexation. " I never for one moment thought but that you would arrange to remain for the party to-night. We have been separated all this long time, and yet you can't spare me one night from business. It is very, very inconsiderate of you."

Her happiness was all gone in a moment.

"You grieve me to hear you say that," he replied, again drawing her close to himself. "You know I am not inconsiderate. If I could do otherwise I would; but I must see Mr. Walsingham to-night, and get some papers and my final instructions from him. This is the most important business he has ever entrusted to me, and he is most anxious that it should be successfully carried through."

"I hate Mr. Walsingham," cried Julia, giving her foot an angry stamp. "The idea of your engaging to see him to-night! Surely some other arrangement could have been made. I am bitterly disappointed. It is just what I have been fearing; business stands in your thoughts before everything."

Edmund was distressed, but held himself firmly in hand.

"My own dear girl," he said, with the utmost gentleness, "your words hurt me very much; but I cannot think you really mean them. It is strange how you misjudge me. Who can have put such thoughts into your head? Business, or, as I should say, Duty, does, I hope, stand high in my regard; still I would not permit any earthly thing to come before you. But I cannot fully explain matters here; we shall be interrupted. Do go and change your dress, and let us go off into the woods; they are still beautiful. I long to have you all to myself for an hour. I would not for the world leave you with this misunderstanding."

Julia's eyes dropped, and a tear trembled on her cheek. She was conscious that one word more would compel her to yield. Neither she nor Edmund, however, realized how much depended on its being spoken. But just as the word which would have altered their whole future hung upon his lips, voices and footsteps near at hand caused them both to start. Julia slipped from his arms.

"I am sorry I spoke so hastily," she said, "but if you have duties so have I."

She touched his cheek coldly with her lips, and hurried away to her room and locked herself in.

Two hours later there came a tap at the door. Too unhappy to wish to see any one, she asked who was there. A servant replied that she had brought her a note. Julia opened the door and eagerly grasped it.

"I am very, very sorry, miss," said the maid, "I should have given it to you an hour ago ; but I was busy and laid it down, and forgot all about it."

Julia tore it open. It was from Edmund.

"I want to see you so much before I leave," the note ran, "but I have received a telegram from the office, and must go immediately."

Julia glanced into the mirror. Her face was stained with tears and her eyes red, but there was no time to bathe them. She ran downstairs. As she did so she heard the clatter of a horse's hoofs along the drive. She sprang across the hall and flung open the door, but only to see Edmund disappear through the Rectory gates, his horse at a full gallop.

"I hev a kind o' notion, miss," said the old groom, who was passing round the house to the stables, "that Mr. Stanford ha' bin waitin' to see ye for a long time, but that he couldn't wait any longer. He ordered his horse an hour ago."

Julia returned to her room, bitterly disappointed.

As to Edmund he rode rapidly towards Caistor with a heavy heart, trying in vain to understand Julia's conduct, sure that there must be something behind it that he ought to know ; but what it was he could not imagine.

Since their engagement everything had moved on happily until within the last week or two. Julia was in London helping Frank to get his new home in order, and Edmund was settling down to work with the enthusiasm of a man who had definite aims, and meant to achieve them.

Had anything been needed to confirm their betrothal it came in the form of letters from Switzerland. Mr. Sedgewick read Edmund's letter announcing his engagement with some feeling of regret.

" And yet," he said to himself, " it is nothing more than what I might have expected. Still it is strange to think how life seems to hang on a series of accidents. How easily it might have been quite different."

And so musing he passed into the next room, where Mrs. Sedgewick was looking out on the glorious panorama of the mighty Jungfrau chain, and Evelyn, seated near her, was reading.

" I have news that will surprise you," he said ; " Edmund and Julia are engaged. Here is a letter I have received from him ; I will read it to you."

When he had finished Mrs. Sedgewick said : " I am surprised. They are very young. I wish Edmund had waited two or three years longer ; but oh, those bewitching eyes ! " As she spoke she recalled in her own mind Mrs. Stanford's remark.

"I am not sure that Julia is quite the sort of girl for him," said the Rector; "but I must write and send him our good wishes, and give him some sound advice."

"And when you write," said Evelyn, looking paler than usual, "give him my every good wish. I do hope that Julia will make him very, very happy."

"And mine also," added her mother. "I wish we were back again at Merton Magna."

That night Mr. Sedgewick wrote to Edmund a letter full of encouragement and good sense, and Evelyn wrote to Julia congratulating her that she was loved by so noble a man, and wishing her every blessing that life could impart.

When Julia had been about a month away Edmund went up to town and spent a few days with her and her brother. Never were two young lovers happier together. Edmund showed Julia Mr. Sedge-wick's letter, and Julia gave him Evelyn's to read, and they vowed that nothing should ever come between them or mar their confidence in each other.

Kate Elles was in London just then, spending a week or two with her uncle, Mr. Bruce, the banker, and this circumstance naturally took Julia there very often, and of course, while Edmund was in town, he went with her.

But he instinctively disliked the banker from the moment of his first introduction.

"Bertram Elles over again," he thought, "only older, cleverer, and more unscrupulous."

The lower part of his face was heavy and gross, his forehead high and narrow, his eyes small, restless, and furtive. He was effusively attentive to

Julia, whereas his manner towards Edmund was particularly cold.

The latter was not at all pleased that Julia should be thrown into the society of this man and his nephew, between whom there seemed to exist an excellent understanding. With the exception of Kate Elles, who was a brave and high-minded girl, every member of the family repelled Edmund. The whole household reeked of the two things he most abominated, worldly scheming and sanctimoniousness, mammon-worship and cant.

Still, considering the relationship, he did not see that he could say anything. It would only make Julia feel very awkward and uncomfortable. So he congratulated himself that it would only be for a short time, and remained silent.

One evening after Edmund had returned to Caistor, Bertram found his uncle in the smoking-room rather later than usual.

" I had a good long talk this evening with Julia Ray," the banker casually remarked. " She's really a very attractive girl, and a rather rich heiress, is she not ? "

" That's a fact, uncle," answered Bertram. " I learned it first accidentally, through overhearing a conversation one night, and then I made private inquiries, and she's far richer than this fellow Stanford has any idea of."

" Well," said Mr. Bruce, sympathetically, " I felt quite sorry for her to-night. She's getting worried out of her life about this house-furnishing. Her brother is too busy with his new practice to look after anything, and she has no experience. We really ought to do more to help her. I will spare you from the bank at any time if you can give her any assistance; in fact I told her so, and she seemed very glad."

And so Bertram went to Julia's aid. He ran after work-people and trades-people; he wrote orders, answered letters, checked accounts, kept the cash-book, made out the inventory, and helped her in a hundred little ways that filled her with gratitude, and raised himself immensely in her esteem. Mr. Bruce also stepped in with advice, and suddenly showed a surprising desire to save her from anxiety and give her pleasure. When he could not go himself—and he was often engaged—Bertram went on his behalf. And thus the latter was very much in her company.

And then, when Edmund was referred to, as of course he would be, Bertram put forth all his skill to depreciate him with faint praise. He was such an excellent lawyer, such a thorough student, such a conscientious worker, who would allow nothing to come before business; he could always be relied on for steady, plodding work. But it was scandalous how Mr. Walsingham, who was only a canting hypocrite, imposed upon him. He really made him quite a drudge; but he just got over Edmund by flattery.

All this, not so much said as vaguely hinted at, worked like a secret poison in Julia's mind. Edmund usually wrote every day; but if, by any means, he missed a post, or his letter was shorter than usual, or slightly less ardent in tone, it was misinterpreted. Julia was unhappy; she began to fear that Edmund had only given her a little bit of his heart; that she would only fill a small place in his life ; and that he would turn out one of those men who are so engaged with the world's affairs that their homes become little more than places to eat and sleep in. And thus the vague suggestion of discontent found its way into her own letters, and awakened the fear in Edmund's mind that all was not quite right.

Such was the state of things up to the morning of Frank and Kate's marriage. Edmund rode over from Caistor, and arrived just before the wedding ceremony. And when Julia entered the library, where he was waiting to greet her, and he saw her exquisitely arrayed for the wedding, and looking like an embodied dream of loveliness, he gave an exclamation of delight, and forgot all his fears.

And Julia, as was her nature, responded at once to his eager embrace, and all her trouble vanished.

But then came the shock when he told hei that business would compel him to leave again that afternoon. It was so sudden, so unexpected, so much like the very thing she had been dreading—the repeated reference to Mr. Walsingham emphasizing the feeling—that she lost all control of herself. All her jealousy of his work, all the suspicions that had been so adroitly awakened in her mind, came back with ten-fold power. The poison did its work effectually, and in utter vexation, and anger and grief, she refused to listen patiently to him ; but with a passionless kiss sent him away sick at heart and bewildered.

As to herself, when Edmund had gone beyond recall, she went back to her room and wept bitterly. At one moment she thought she would follow him, at once, to Caistor and tell him how it was that she had not seen him again. And then she resolved that she would do nothing of the kind.

"Why did he go away? Why did he not tell Mr. Walsingham that he could not undertake the business? If he had loved her as he ought he would not have left her. But if he did not care, why should she?"

So she thought; but she did care very much indeed. For beneath all her vexation and petulance there was a genuine love of Edmund. And could he have returned just then, and spoken one gentle word, she would have rushed into his arms and told him all that was in her mind, and he would have learned what was behind her conduct, doing all the mischief.

But he was gone, and Julia sat alone in her room, desolate and angry. Then she suffered from a violent headache, and had to lie down for some time.

When she rose again the frivolous elements of her character had got full possession of her. Her old love of coquetry and petty conquest asserted itself. She dressed herself with the utmost care, and went down like a dream of beauty. She dazzled and captivated everyone, and so thoroughly did she weave her silken cords round Bertram Elles that he fell wholly under her power, and was more madly in love with her than he had ever been with Evelyn Sedgewick.

CHAPTER II.

ESTRANGEMENT.

WHEN Edmund and Julia met again they both felt restrained and awkward. A jarring note had been struck, and its vibration was not stilled. The sweet harmony of their first love was broken. The scene in the conservatory at Brentfield was like a stone thrown into a tree full of singing birds : there was silence and consternation.

Both were affected by it, but each in a different way. Edmund's nature was of so fine a grain and texture that the least blow upon it left a scar for long afterwards. But Julia's bitter words were worse than blows ; they had struck him like stiletto stabs, and he bled inwardly. His sense of justice had been outraged. He was, however, proud and reserved ; he asked for no explanation, and did his best to hide his misery, but did not succeed very well.

On Julia the interview had acted like a chilling and biting wind sweeping over a summer garden. The flowers, which had so lately burst into bloom, closed their petals, and her old nature re-appeared in ampler vigour. She hid her unhappiness more successfully than Edmund, and seemed indifferent to what had occurred. Only the light of newly-awakened love faded from her eyes ; they remained brilliant, but cold.

The new depth of feeling, as of a creature breathing thoughtful breath ; the new earnestness, as of one eager to realize loftier ideals of life and duty ; the blissful repose, as of a heart at rest, was gone. She had become again just her old self—a phantom of delight, dazzling every one with her delicate wiles, her sparkling effervescence, her fairy loveliness, but cold and fickle.

So nearly a month passed, and she and Edmund were drifting wider and wider apart. He sought relief from his unhappiness in intenser study and devotion to business, and so confirmed all her false impressions, and she gave herself up to all manner of trivial occupations.

December came in with day after day of heavy rain. The rivers overflowed, and the meadows were flooded. Then followed an interval of hard, black frost, and the skaters had a glorious time. They were out all day long and far into the night. The ring of steel on the ice seldom ceased.

Edmund got away from the office more often than he felt quite justified in doing, though not sufficiently often to satisfy Julia. But Bertram Elles hurried down from London, professedly to enjoy the sport, and he was at her command at all times. The relationship which now existed, through the recent marriage, made possible a greater degree of intimacy than before, and he was not slow to take advantage of it. Edmund did not hide his dislike to the intercourse, and Miss Ray threw out sundry gentle warnings ; but Julia took no heed, and went her own way.

Things were fast coming to a crisis. Misunderstanding, jealousy, and unfounded suspicion were driving apart two who really loved one another, and at any moment there might come a complete rupture. What the effect would be on Edmund, were it to occur, it would be impossible to say. His life might be spoiled, as many others have been, in the same way. But Julia would be almost certain to fling herself into Bertram's arms, and, as he was only an unscrupulous and faithless schemer, her life would be wrecked.

This, however, was not to happen. Providence has strange methods of working, and of saving the soul, even by anguish and loss, from the error of its ways.

Shortly before Christmas Edmund received an invitation to spend a day with Lord Merton. His lordship had not seen him for some time, but had been so gratified with the reports he had received from Mr. Walsingham that he wished to have a good talk with Edmund about his future, and invited him over to Merton Magna. He was to stay to dinner, and return to Caistor the next morning.

Lord Merton fixed Edmund's visit to take place on a day when a grand carnival was to be held on Brookside Meadows, a wide expanse of marsh land situated some two or three miles from the city, and just then covered with ice.

The invitation had been received and accepted before either Edmund or Julia knew anything of the carnival ; but no sooner did Julia hear of it than she urged Edmund to write and put off his engagement with Lord Merton, so that he might take her to Brookside Meadows. And when he said that it would be impossible for him to do such a thing, and, further, expressed the opinion that the carnival was not an entertainment for her to patronize, she was displeased, and hinted that he cared more to go and dine with Lord Merton than to please her. Edmund repudiated the accusation with considerable heat, and saw that their estrangement was entering on an acute stage.

The day for the visit arrived, and Edmund had barely started when Bertram called on Julia and proposed that they should go to the carnival. At first she hesitated, conscious that if she went she would widen the breach between herself and Edmund. She mentioned his objections to the carnival, but Bertram swept them loftily aside. And so in the end she consented to go.

"After all," she mused, " am I not free? It will be time enough for Edmund to control me when I am his wife. It is a hard thing if he is to prohibit me from associating with one who may almost be called a relative, and who has been so exceedingly kind to me. If I submit to this dictation now, where will it end? Besides, of course I shall tell him that I have been, when we next meet, and if it should awaken a little jealousy he will be more considerate for the future."

And so she went, and Bertram was glad, and did all in his power to make the morning enjoyable. He had a double reason for keeping away from the crowd and shielding Julia from the objectionable aspects of the carnival. So he hired a dainty sledge, to which he yoked himself, and swept away over the polished ice, until, far from the crowd, he drew up breathless. The day was bright and cloudless, though the wind was keen ; but Julia was well wrapped up with furs, and he was glowing with excitement. And there all alone they loitered, and Bertram spoke honeyed words, until he feared to say more lest his purpose should become too plain.

Then they dashed back again and joined a somewhat reckless party of Bertram's friends, bent only on amusing themselves in the liveliest way. Julia revelled in the excitement. It was what she wanted ; for it enabled her to forget herself. The misgivings that had haunted her were swept aside with an impatient gesture, and she wholly abandoned herself to a whirl of delightful sensations.

When it was time to leave for lunch, and one of Bertram's friends asked if they were not intending to return in the evening when the meadows would be lighted with coloured lamps, and the skaters would bear torches, Julia was foremost in supporting the proposal.

" Oh yes, do let us return," she cried ; " I have never skated by torchlight in my life, and when all these festoons of tinted lanterns are shedding down their many-coloured lights the effect must be very picturesque."

" Yes," replied one young fellow, " but you must not forget that at night the parties here are not very select. A rough element may be present, and there will probably be a good deal of drinking and feasting in these booths."

" What matter ? " cried Bertram, impatiently. " Let's come and see the fun. We can keep well together, and need take no harm. On these miles of ice there is room for all sorts without crowding."

" I shall enjoy the excitement," said Julia. " I

feel restless ; life is too tame. I could welcome an adventure."

" Bravo, Julia ! " exclaimed Bertram, and his fervent hope was that she would remain in this mood.

And so about a dozen of the party arranged that they would return at night together.

On their way home Julia invited Bertram to luncheon ; but he excused himself on the plea that he was expecting letters that would require answering immediately, really because he was reluctant to meet her aunt. He arranged, however, to call for her soon after dinner, and then, with a tender look and a significant lingering clasp of the hand, he left her and walked on to his lodgings in great exuberance of spirits.

Julia seemed visibly within his reach. A touch, he believed, would sever her connection with Edmund. That morning she had gone directly against his wishes, but had shown no regret or misgiving. On the contrary, her enjoyment was unmistakable. Never before had he seen her in such high spirits ; never before had she smiled so sweetly on him ; never had he felt so supremely happy. Certainly she was all but his. He might say he was sure of her.

As he thought of the meeting again in the evening he grew quite excited. Then he checked himself, and recalled the fact that after all he could not positively call her his yet, although no doubt she was within his grasp.

" And as that is the case, why do I delay ? " he asked himself. " Why wait till she herself has snapt the slight bond that holds her to another ? Why not declare my love to-night, and win her? She is in just the right mood; I will strike while the iron is hot."

The more he thought of it the more convinced he was that the time had come.

If there was any secret hesitation behind his resolve it was finally banished when he reached his lodgings.

" Old Abraham Jacobs has been here again to see you," said his landlady, " and has left a note."

Bertram sprang upstairs to his room, and snatching up the note with an oath, tore it open and read :

" I have called to see you about business. I need go into no details ; but I warn you that I will not any longer trust your assurances of a speedy marriage with a rich young lady. Unless you pay up I will apply to those who will give me my money, but the disclosures I shall make will ruin you."

There was no name, nor date, nor address ; but Bertram knew the handwriting only too well. In his fierce bitterness, and anger and dread, he sat staring into the fire, mechanically crumpling up the note in his pocket, while his brain was busy in trying to find a way out of the difficulty.

" There is only one way," he mused. " That old blood-sucker will stamp and rage and threaten if I do not produce the money ; but, after all, if I can prove to him that I am really engaged to Julia Ray, he will wait. Better still, if the old rascal should hear that she has eloped with me he will keep quiet, knowing that it will be all right."

When his landlady came to clear away the luncheon

K

things she found that he had touched nothing, and when she was about to expostulate he impatiently ordered her to carry the food away.

And so he sat on, gazing into the empty grate long after the fire had gone out.

While he sat thus making his plans Julia entered her aunt's drawing-room shortly before dinner, looking unusually excited and restless. Miss Ray noticed that she had on a warm outdoor costume.

"I was not aware," she remarked, "that you were going out this evening, Julia dear."

"I am going," answered Julia, with a defiant toss of her head, "to Brookside Meadows. There is to be a grand skating-match to-night by torchlight."

"Surely, Julia, you will not be so rash," said Miss Ray, earnestly. "Your cold is already worse through going out this morning, and to-night a bitter north-east wind is blowing. You run great risk of laying yourself up for the winter. I cannot think why you are so reckless just now."

Julia gave a rather mirthless laugh, and said, "Oh, I shall take no harm."

"Well, my dear, I think you are making a serious mistake. You are not strong enough for so much exposure and fatigue. I am exceedingly surprised that Edmund should have given his consent to such a mad freak; it is not like him at all."

"He has not given his consent; he knows nothing about it. You forget that he is dining to-night with Lord Merton," replied Julia, somewhat bitterly. "I am going with Bertram and a party of his friends."

Poor Miss Ray sank back in her chair as if struck by a sudden blow. An expression of great sorrow passed over her venerable face. She had noticed the growing coldness between Edmund and Julia, and knew that Bertram's presence had not helped matters. She was grieved that Julia had been willing to accept his attentions to the extent she had, and yet they had been offered with such an air of innocence that beyond a mild protest she had not known how to interfere. But he was clearly going too far now.

"Julia dear," she said, in faltering accents, "be warned by one who loves you as a mother, and who, but for such a mistake as I fear you are in danger of making, would have been, long before you were born, the wife of one of the best of men." The thought of that long past brought tears to her eyes, and she paused to regain her composure. Then she proceeded : "You are not acting rightly towards Edmund, and I am sure he is unhappy. You love him, do you not ? "

"Of course I do," replied Julia, curtly, not venturing to look up.

"But you are not happy together. How has it come about, dear? Tell me ; I may be able to help you."

Julia, however, had never clearly traced the origin of the misunderstanding. She had put herself in the wrong, and then found it much easier to imagine herself the victim of neglect and indifference than to find the root of the trouble in those suspicions which Bertram had awakened in her mind. So she merely answered :

"Things have never been the same since Frank's wedding-day. Edmund returned to business as soon as the ceremony was over, and I was angry and disappointed, and that is how it began."

" Has not Bertram a good deal to do with it ? " asked Miss Ray. " He tried to depreciate Edmund to me ; but I silenced him. I doubt whether his aims are honourable. I promised Edmund several days ago that I would put you on your guard, and I regret now that I have delayed. I fear that he is trying to supplant Edmund in your affections, and really you have given him encouragement."

" I hope Edmund has not been trying to set you against Bertram," answered Julia hotly. " Bertram has been kind to me ; but he knows that I am engaged. and is much too honourable to do what you fear."

" Well, Julia dear, do be careful. I have a strange foreboding of trouble. I was sorry when I saw you go off again with Bertram this morning ; and I am sure this engagement for to-night is a terrible mistake. I believe you love Edmund, and I am sure he is wholly devoted to you ; but you must remember that a man of his character will not be trifled with."

All during dinner Julia sat occupied with her own reflections, and as soon as it was over she retired to her room. It was not the first time such thoughts as her aunt had given expression to had come to her. Through the afternoon a change had been passing in her own mind. Her better self had begun to assert its influence, and she could not shake off the feeling that she was not doing right. She was not acting in a way that was true to Edmund, and was fast compromising herself with Bertram. Things could not go on in this way much longer ; there would be a crisis of some sort.

And now, as she thought over what her aunt had said, her conscience told her that it was only too true. In the light of those remarks Bertram did not appear the hero she had begun to think him. She was sorry that she had promised to go with him. But what should she do now? In a quarter of an hour he would be calling for her. She must decide quickly. For a few minutes she stood irresolute, the voice of her better self urging her to give up the project, and all manner of minor considerations pressing her to keep to her engagement. Bertram would be displeased and disappointed ; he would say she was changeable and fickle. So, in a sudden outburst of defiance, she resolved that she would go, only she would be more careful for the future, and would make Bertram see that she intended to be true to Edmund.

CHAPTER III.

A DESPERATE MOVE.

BERTRAM was not slow to perceive that Julia had passed into another mood since he left her at mid-day. She sat by his side in the coach that was conveying the whole party to the carnival, listening in a pre-occupied manner to the talk of the others, and taking little part in it, and it required all his skill to draw her into conversation.

The excitement and self-abandonment of the morning were gone, and he was perplexed to know how to bring them back. He wondered what could have wrought the change, but shrewdly guessed that Julia's aunt had been talking to her. There had probably been an unpleasant scene, and she had not yet recovered from it. Yet even this, he thought, might be construed in his favour; for it showed that his was the stronger influence over her. Had that not been the case her aunt, no doubt, would have been able to have persuaded her not to come.

The more he considered the matter the more he was satisfied that this conjecture was correct, and it only showed him the danger that beset all his plans and hopes so long as Julia came under her aunt's influence. In fact he could never be sure that he had really won her until he had got her away from her present environment, and that he must endeavour to accomplish at once. The great thing was to prevail on her to take an irrevocable step. That was the conclusion he had reached before leaving his lodgings, and, indeed, he had made certain arrangements in the hope that such would be the development of affairs.

It would be an achievement, no doubt, to prevail on her to break with Edmund, and to accept of his attentions ; but that would leave things very insecure. Julia's moods were not to be relied on, that was clear. And then he would have, he was quite sure, her aunt, and brother, and the Sedgewicks all against him. Would she be able to hold out, even for a short time, against such a combination ? He was not certain. No ; he must endeavour to push his conquest further than that ; and get her to take a step from which she could not draw back.

Thus his previous decision was confirmed, and with that end in view he began to recall all that was most exciting in the morning's adventure, in the hope of restoring the former frame of mind.

He was engaged in this effort when a young fellow, seated at the further corner of the coach, called out :

" Elles, have you heard that an old gipsy has pitched her tent on the ice, and has been doing a roaring business in fortune-telling all the afternoon ? "

This was interesting news, and the general conversation in the coach ceased at once.

" I saw nothing of her in the morning," replied Bertram.

" They say that she put up her tent about mid-day, and, by Jove ! there seems to be something uncanny about her. George Holmes left her tent quite excited, and declared that she must be in league with his Satanic Majesty. And my sister Polly went in. She was sure she would be able to find out the old sibyl's tricks; but she returned as white as a ghost."

" I wonder whether she will be there to-night?" said Bertram.

" I don't know ; but I should think very likely. She must be making a lot of money."

" Shall we all go and have our fortunes told, Miss Ray?" cried another of Bertram's friends. " You said in the morning that you would welcome an adventure."

" I would rather go in the daylight," replied Julia ; " and I should like to know something more about the old gipsy."

"Oh, she's a wonder," exclaimed the first speaker, "there's no doubt about that. She can read you like a book. But she's mighty particular ; she won't see everyone."

" I should not like to consult her," said one young lady, with a shudder.

" Nor I," remarked another. " Just think of an old witch poking into all the dark corners of one's heart to see what she can turn out."

" A needful work sometimes," said Julia, " and difficult to do for one's self."

" Better, then, to see a father confessor instead of an old gipsy," answered the previous speaker.

" One is about as good as the other," laughed the youth at the further end of the coach. Bertram sat silent and full of thought.

When they reached Brookside Meadows a brilliant and fantastic scene burst upon them. The night was dark but clear. Overhead the sky was bright with innumerable stars. From a row of booths a flood of light streamed out upon an eager moving throng. Many-tinted lanterns were festooned from tree to tree. The air was filled with multitudinous sounds— the rushing and grinding of steel on the ice ; the hum of hundreds of voices ; the clanging of a noisy band ; and, rising above all, peals of laughter from merry groups. The skaters carried torches, and as they swept past singly or in parties, now in straight lines, and now in graceful circles, illuminating the black ice, the bare trees, the clumps of withered reeds, and each other's faces, the air seemed filled with fiery flying serpents and falling stars.

The whole scene was very stimulating and exciting, and as Julia and Bertram stood watching it the latter remarked :

" It does look a novel scene, does it not ? It would have been a pity to have missed it."

" It certainly looks very picturesque," replied Julia, giving, however, a shiver as the keen wind swept by.

" You are cold," said Bertram, " let me take you for a spin," and before she could say yea or nay he had clasped her hands and they were off.

Right into the midst of the maddest, merriest part of the crowd he shot with her—in and out, round and round, straight onward and in sweeping curves, circling past the clanging band, up between the booths, with their flaring lamps, and along the line of festooned poplars, from which there fell a flood of golden and rosy light.

And there he paused, and felt his heart beat quickly as he gazed on the lovely creature by his side, radiant in the glow of unearthly light, her eyes dilated with the excitement of rapid motion, and the whirl of life around her.

His spirits rose high. He clasped her hand with a warmer touch, and off again they sped, in wider and wider circles, further and further from the crowd, and then on and away into the liquid luminous darkness, and they were alone again, the rush of life behind, the silent stars above, the wide vast marshes before.

"Ah," he cried, "this is divine; this is worth coming for! What sense of freedom is here! It is beautiful, glorious! it is life, not stagnant, stupid, sordid existence, which is only another name for death, but life such as you and I long to live, full, free, rich, rushing on for ever!"

As he spoke he clasped her hand more tightly, and drew her closer.

"You said truly, in the morning, that life is too tame," he went on. "That is just it. Most people don't know what life is. They are devoted to conventionalities and small proprieties. They are bound down by rule and custom, and the fear of Mrs. Grundy. Their blood is no thicker than water. The grand passions are regulated and starved. Life with them means endless grinding at the mill. Love with them is just the cooing and billing of doves in a cage. But you and I, Julia, must have freedom, ecstasy, rapture! We must have life's wine cup full to the brim ; we must drink the nectar of the gods!"

Now if Bertram had given vent to all this rodo-montade in the morning it would have intoxicated Julia. She would have been completely carried away with it. But her mood had changed. Now it fell flat and insipid. It produced quite the opposite effect to what Bertram intended. Instead of stirring her blood, and bringing back the excitement of the morning, it awakened questioning and doubt.

"What does all this mean?" she asked herself. "What is it to lead up to?"

She did not respond to his firmer grasp when he drew her closer, but immediately withdrew again; and at last said:

"We must turn back; our friends will wonder where we are."

"Oh no," he replied. "They are all enjoying themselves, and let us do the same. Is it not divine to glide on together in this way? I would that it might last for ever."

"But I must go back," cried Julia, beginning to cough. "The wind here is too strong for me."

They turned back at once, and for a few moments sped on in silence. But Bertram's affairs were in too desperate a condition for him to let his opportunity slip:

"I was speaking about life," he said. "Don't you see, my dear Julia, that what keeps the world from true life is fear—fear of nature? Men and women are afraid to trust their own noblest passions. Half of what we call civilization is nothing but an arbitrary system for regulating and restraining what should be free. The first thing to do is to claim our birthright, the right to choose our own path, and live our own life."

But Julia's mind was on the alert now, and she replied incisively:

"Yes, freedom is divine; that is freedom within the bounds of law, all else is license."

"Quite true," answered Bertram, shifting his position, and speaking in his softest and most insinuating tones. "And yet, Julia, how much our lives are hampered and entangled by mere custom, habit, and dread of the British Philistine. A great happiness, for example, is placed within our reach. It would make our lives full, rich, strong. Why do we not grasp it? Because we should be doing something unusual. We should set a few silly tongues wagging ; a few foolish people would hold up their hands in horror. This dread of what people will say has too long haunted us. What is needed is a band of daring spirits not afraid to set the world's stupid prejudices at defiance. I am sure you agree with me, Julia : do you not ? "

He looked down into her face ; but was disappointed and startled. There was no sign of acquiescence, no indication that she was ready for some mad escapade ; but there was something which showed unmistakably that the conversation was distasteful to her. Presently she said :

" I think that what has more often stood in the way of our happiness has been too strong an inclination to do as we like, ' to follow too much the devices and desires of our own hearts.' But here we are back again ; look, there are our friends." And disengaging her hand, she darted after them.

" Glad to see you back again, Miss Ray," said one of the young men as she glided up. " We had better keep well together ; there's some queer folk about, and they are evidently watching us. I just now ran against somebody standing under the shadow of those trees, whether man or woman I can't say, but one of the strangest and wildest creatures I ever saw in my life."

" Perhaps the old gipsy's husband," said Julia, " or possibly the old gipsy herself. Go and see, Bertram, if she's still there."

" All right," he replied, " you keep all together ; I will go and look after the old witch."

He struck across the ice until he reached a dark and solitary spot, and then stopped. He was at his wits' end. Time was passing, and nothing was being accomplished. He had left his lodgings confident of success ; but Julia seemed further off now than she had been for days past. Most bitterly he upbraided himself for not pressing his suit in the morning. Why did he let that opportunity slip ? But it was no use wasting time, every moment of which was precious, in idle regrets. Things were desperate ; he was standing on the very verge of ruin. And yet if he could only win this girl, who appeared a few hours before within his grasp, all would be well. Surely that was not going to prove an impossible feat !

To and fro in the darkness he slowly moved, his brain busy with the problem. Even when a boy he was constantly plotting for some private end, and since he had become a man he had seldom been without some questionable business or intrigue. And yet he had achieved nothing. There was not an enterprise on which he could look back with satisfaction, and there was much on which he dared not look back at all. For the most part he had been engaged in devising schemes to save himself from the dangers and difficulties into which his crafty disposition had brought him. Often enough he was weary of the struggle, and wished that he could begin life again as an honest man. And over and over again he had resolved that if he could only free himself from the meshes of old sins, he would lead a new life. But the time never came. It seemed a cruel and hard fate that one who was willing to make a new start should be kept back by the consequences of past wrong; but so it was. And yet surely there must be some way out of this difficulty? He must seek some further aid. He must bring some new influence to bear on Julia. But what?

Then he remembered the old gipsy. Why not go and consult her? No, that was not quite it. He would go and *bribe* her, and then take Julia to see her. Yes, by Jove! he had hit on the right plan at last; for Julia was evidently inclined to visit the old witch.

Without a moment's delay he sped across the ice, and drew up to the door of the gipsy's tent.

"Come in; I'm expecting ye," said a harsh, decided voice, and Bertram entered, not, however, without vague, superstitious fears, which he vainly tried to hide

A curtain dropped over the door, and the gipsy motioned him to a stool. Then she took up her pipe and smoked on in silence.

In the centre of the tent was a low fire, on which was placed a simmering cauldron. A strange odour rose from it that began at once to affect his senses.

The gipsy had on a long, red cloak; her hair was dishevelled, and hung about her shoulders in snaky coils, whilst black, piercing eyes shone out from beneath shaggy brows. Her hand was long and skinny, and on one finger there sparkled a ring of a peculiar eastern pattern. The lamp was placed

"Come in; I'm expecting ye."

P. 142.

behind her, and threw her face into deep shadow, but the light fell full on Bertram, and he felt that the Sibyl's eyes were fixed on him as though she would read his very soul.

"Well," she said, presently. "You've come at last?"

" Not to have my fortune told," he replied, trying to put on a bold face. " I've no faith in that ; but if you'll help me I'll make it worth your while."

" Help you to win a dark-eyed lady?" said the gipsy, with a cunning smile.

"Yes, by Jove! that's just it. How did you know?"

" By my art, which you say you don't believe."

"Well, I want you, old mother, to help me to win her."

" But she loves another."

" No ; she only thinks that she is bound in honour to him."

" And you want her ? "

" Yes ; will you help me ? "

" What would you like me to do ? "

" Tell her that you can read her heart : that there is only one that can make her happy, and then describe me to her."

" Describe you ! inside or outside ? "

" Both, confound it, if you like ; only you'll get nothing unless you persuade her that I'm the one she must marry."

" You'll have to bring her here."

" Of course."

" And what will you give me ? "

" I will give you £5," he replied, conscious of a strange feeling coming over him.

The gipsy gave a contemptuous laugh.

"That's not enough," she cried. "Would you buy a pretty lady with a big fortune for £5?"

"Well," said Bertram, "I will give you £10."

"Let me see the money."

Bertram pulled out his purse. As he did so a bit of crumpled paper fell upon the floor and rolled under the stool. The old gipsy observed it, although he did not.

"There," he said, counting out ten sovereigns. "I will give you them as soon as she says that she will be mine."

"Very well," replied the gipsy, with a sinister smile. "Now go and fetch the young lady."

The curtain that had covered the door rolled up, and she motioned him to depart.

Then the gipsy dropped the curtain again and picked up the bit of crumpled paper. When she had read it she crooned with satisfaction, and put it away inside the covers of a little black book. She then went outside her tent to a corner where the meadows were open to her view. There she stood in the darkness, watching and listening, her quick brain and her quick eyes and ears taking in everything.

Presently there came across the ice a low cry, distant, but unmistakable.

"Julia, Julia!"

The old gipsy started.

"'Tis he," she murmured to herself. "He's come just in time."

She went back to her tent, threw off her red cloak, and put on a long coat, and a man's soft hat, turned out her lamp, and disappeared in the darkness.

CHAPTER IV.

A CALL IN THE DARK.

EDMUND rode over to Merton Magna, pleased
with the prospect of visiting his noble friend
and old home, and his joy would have been undisturbed by a single dark thought but for the misunderstanding that had arisen between him and
Julia.

It was, therefore, a considerable disappointment to
him to learn when he arrived at the Hall that
Lord Merton had taken a sudden chill, and was
confined to bed, and that he could only see him for
a few minutes.

The interview was, however, very pleasant. His
Lordship expressed his unabated interest in our
hero's welfare, and then said that he must make himself as comfortable as he could in the library, and
come back another day.

Edmund said that under the circumstances he
would prefer to go and visit a few of his old friends,
and then return to the city the same evening.

The result was that about the time that Bertram
and Julia were starting for Brookside Meadows
Edmund was mounting his horse to return to Caistor.
It had been his intention to leave earlier; but he had
seen very little of Merton Magna for more than three

L

years, and everyone wanted to have a word with him, and to learn how he had been getting on, and what news he had of the Rector and his family; and so the time had passed only too quickly, and for a few hours he had enjoyed a respite from the thoughts that now almost continually haunted him. No sooner, however, had he got clear of the parish, and heard the regular beat of his horse's hoofs on the hard, frost-bound road than the old trouble returned; and he began to brood over what was nearest his heart.

Bit by bit he lived over again the last few months. His thoughts flew back to the afternoon at Somer-thorpe, when he became fully conscious of his love for Julia, and prayed in his loneliness that the sweet heavens might endure until he was quite, quite sure that she loved him.

He recalled how he found her the following Sunday in the garden, dreaming, as she afterwards confessed, of him. He lived over again those blissful evenings during the week of their plighted love, when—

> "The moonshine, stealing o'er the scene,
> Had blended with the lights of eve,"

and they opened out their hearts to each other in whispered confidences.

Above all, he thought of that lovely day on St. Olave's lake, when their happiness was too deep for utterance, and Julia wished that the blissful moments could go on for ever and ever.

Yes! Julia had loved him, he was confident of that. They had been happy, and enjoyed one deep draught of the rich wine of life. But it was over now. His golden vision of happiness had vanished.

He had learned how frail and fickle a woman could be.

The process of disillusionment had begun in the conservatory at Brentfield, and every day since it had been going on, until the conclusion could no longer be avoided—Julia had ceased to love him.

But why? He could not tell; he could only conjecture, and the supposition was a very horrible one. She must have transferred her affections to Bertram Elles. However that might be, the one thing of which he was certain was the wretched fact that she had ceased to care for him. It must be so, or she would not be so dazzlingly cold, so superbly indifferent, so splendidly passionless.

And yet his mind, having reached that conclusion, dashed itself against it, as a young wild creature of the woods beats itself against the bars of a cage. For he loved her so passionately, and found it so hard to give her up.

And he resolved that he would not give her up until he had heard the fatal words from her lips. But he could not endure the uncertainty any longer. For her sake, as well as his own, they must come to an understanding with one another. There must be some explanation. All intercourse with Bertram Elles would have to be absolutely broken off, or they must part. A crisis, he felt, was at hand, and the sooner it came the better. Were it not so late he would have gone to her that very night, and asked her what it all meant; but to-morrow he would know the truth. He would look and search into the depths of those wonderful eyes, and read it there. Nay; she should tell him with her own lips. And then, when the engagement was dissolved, as he was sure it would be, what would he do? Would he be able to put her out of his thoughts, and out of his heart? What would happen to her? Would she be happy? He could not believe it.

From these reflections, however, he was roughly roused by his horse giving an awkward stumble, and immediately knocking up lame. He sprang from the saddle, and found that it had cast a shoe. It would be impossible to go on without having it replaced. What should he do? He glanced round to see where he was. The night was dark, but clear, and he saw that he was about three miles from the city. Away yonder were Brookside Meadows, and there were the lights of the carnival.

He grasped the bridle, and walked on by the side of his horse until he came to a small inn. Often enough he had passed it in his school days, and knew the landlord and his wife well. He stopped and called, and immediately both appeared at the door and recognized him.

"Ah! Maaster Stanford," exclaimed the landlord, "I saw ye pass this mornin', and I sed to the gude wife that I'd warrant you were goin' on a wisit to Lord Merton. How is his Lordship?"

Edmund answered the landlord's inquiries, and put a few questions of a friendly character, and then mentioned the difficulty he was in about his horse.

"Well, Maaster Stanford," said the landlord, "du you come in and warm yerself aside the fire, and I'll go and get yer hoss shued. But you'll ha' to wait a bit, for th' smithy 'll be closed."

And, so saying, he took the bridle and went off

Edmund followed the landlady into her kitchen, and stood before the fire chatting with her about her family. Then he remarked:

"You are very quiet here to-night; but there will be plenty of noise and life across the meadows at the carnival."

"You are right enough there," replied the landlady; "but we are out of the way of it, and I'm not sorry."

Edmund pulled out his watch.

"I think," he said, "that, as I am here, I'll walk across your fields and have a look at the skating. I'll be back in half-an-hour; my horse will not be ready before that."

"Then you'd better let me get you a lantern," said the landlady. "The moon is not up yet, and you must take care, you know. The ice isn't very good on this side o' the midders: we're so sheltered with trees from the frost."

"I'll take care," answered Edmund, who was already at the door. "Never mind the lantern; I can see."

He turned into a side lane, leaped a field gate, and was soon on to the ice. Guided by the lights, which he could see in the distance, he crossed over a lonely and deserted portion of the meadows, and more than once heard the ice crack ominously beneath his feet. But he was soon over, and reached a temporary shelter put up for the convenience of skaters who wanted to rest at that extreme corner of the skating course.

It was nothing more than a ragged piece of tarpaulin stretched over poles to break the force of the wind, and in front of it a plank, supported on two casks, did duty for a seat. By the side of it a low fire still smouldered in a portable grate.

The shelter was situated some distance from the parts where the principal skating was going on, and was quite deserted. But it afforded a full view of the whole scene, and Edmund, not caring to go farther, sat down and watched the moving picture before him.

Skaters with flaming torches went flashing past; the clanging band struck up a lively tune; shouts of laughter rang across the ice from the booths; and beyond, in the distance, the festoons of tinted lanterns produced a pretty effect.

After watching the scene for a few minutes he rose to go; but something about a group of skaters, that swept nearer than the others, held his steps. He was still pausing, looking after them as they sped forwards, when a tall man, whom he at once recognized as Bertram Elles, went flying in their wake. At the sight of him a feeling of great anger and bitterness arose in Edmund's heart, and he vowed to himself that if his engagement with Julia was broken off, Bertram should not escape severe punishment. Again he was turning impatiently away, when his eye caught the group a second time, and he paused and sat down again.

This time, as they passed, he noticed that Bertram was still hanging behind, but that he was no longer alone. A lady was with him, and he seemed to be trying to get her separated from her companions; for he stopped, and pointed with his torch to a distant part of the ice; but she turned away and endeavoured to reach her friends. He saw Bertram skate after her, and hold her with something like compulsion,

Edmund's face burned with indignation, and he resolved that if Bertram persisted in his conduct he would go the lady's assistance. Her face was turned from him, so that he could see nothing but the general movements—the effort of the lady to escape, and of Bertram to detain her. Then suddenly she turned, and the light of Bertram's torch fell full upon her face and figure, and Edmund started. The blood rushed to his head, and he grasped his riding-whip more firmly.

Yes, there could be no doubt about it : it was Julia. And Bertram, the scoundrel, was trying to get her away alone, and she would not go. For a second or two he watched their movements with wild, dilated eyes, and then he started to his feet.

" Julia ! Julia ! " he cried, and sprang round the shelter in the direction she was going. But in his excitement his feet slipped from under him, he fell backwards behind the shelter, his head crashing violently against one of its supports.

CHAPTER V.

AT THE SHELTER.

HOW long Edmund lay unconscious he could not tell; but while he was still dazed, and quite unable to rise, he heard Julia speaking eagerly. He opened his eyes, and through a rent in the tarpaulin saw her standing near the fire, and Bertram by her side. The latter's torch burnt brightly, and revealed her face looking frightened and ghostlike.

"I am certain I heard him call me," she said, excitedly. "Oh, where can he be?"

Edmund tried to rouse himself and say, "Here I am"; but, instead, he again relapsed into unconsciousness.

"Impossible!" replied Bertram, unable to hide his irritation, "Stanford cannot even know that you are here; but you are dreadfully pale; do come and sit down."

"I suppose I must," she murmured, sinking dwon on the plank. Bertram stood facing her with the look of vexation still upon his face.

Julia had never been really happy during these weeks of estrangement from Edmund, although she had done her best to appear so. Many times she had wished that the misunderstanding could be cleared up. She had longed for reconciliation, only she wanted him to seek it. And so she had drifted on, inwardly caring for him, yet treating him coldly, and giving Bertram Elles an unwise encouragement.

Conduct so inconsistent could not but bring many rebukes of conscience, and much disquiet of heart, however happy she might appear to be ; and her occasional outbreaks of recklessness were really efforts to forget herself, and were immediately followed, as we have seen, by greater misgiving and regret.

Had she followed the impulses of her better nature that evening she would have withdrawn from her engagement with Bertram. But it is one of the penalties of wrong-doing that each false step makes another one nearly inevitable. And thus she had so far trifled with Bertram that he had gained an influence over her, and she could not bring herself at once to do a thing which would displease him, and lower her in his estimation. And so she had gone with him, though reluctantly.

This inward struggle had, however, put her upon the alert. It had awakened the suspicion that his intentions were not so honourable as she had hitherto been willing to believe. It had made her quick to perceive the drift of his conversation, and anxious to put an end to it. And as soon as she had got rid of him, by asking him to see if the old gipsy was near, she had joined the rest of the party, resolved on no account to leave it with him alone.

While he was absent she had skated hand-in-hand with a friend whom she had not met since the picnic at St. Olave's Broad. A reference to that happy day brought a great lump into her throat. " Oh," she thought, " if Edmund were only here I would go to him and tell him how sorry I am for all the misunderstanding, and assure him that it shall never occur again."

It was while these thoughts were filling her mind that Bertram rejoined the party. And how it happened she could not tell, so adroitly did he accomplish it. But she had hardly noticed his return before she found herself again alone with him, and heard him pressing her to go with him on a visit to the gipsy's tent. This she positively refused to do, and hastened to get away from him to her friends.

It was just then there came that strange, unaccountable cry out of the darkness, which well-nigh made her heart stand still, though no one else appeared to have noticed it.

What could it mean? She felt sure that it was Edmund's voice; but if so, where was he? Could she have been mistaken? Was it only her own unquiet heart appealing to her like a voice without? Was it some warning voice from heaven, like that which arrested Saul of Tarsus? Could it be Edmund in trouble, and calling for help?

She could not tell; it was a mystery. As she sat in the shelter wondering what it could mean the deathly pallor remained upon her face, and she still trembled.

All she knew was that out of the darkness there had reached her a strange pathetic cry, like the voice of Edmund, calling her by name, as if he wanted her, and had come to claim her, and that now the thought of him so completely filled her whole mind that it seemed as though Edmund himself must be present, felt though unseen, impressing his whole soul upon her, and appealing to her to be true to him.

Whatever it was, it had re-awakened her deeper self into acute consciousness, and she was ashamed to think how cruel she had been to him who was after all her true and only love.

These thoughts, of course, only occupied a few seconds, during which Bertram paused, expecting to see her regain her composure. As she did not do so he grew desperate, and, abandoning his customary caution, began :

" It is a pity that you should worry yourself about Edmund Stanford. He is not here. He preferred to go and dine with Lord Merton. Even if he knew you were here I don't suppose that he would take the trouble to come and look after you. Why did you ever listen to him ? He will never make you happy. He does not love you as I do."

Edmund, who had come partly round, listened to these words with a throbbing brain. He tried to rise and confront his slanderer, but fell back again, barely conscious.

Julia, however, had leaped to her feet with a sharp exclamation. The torch which Bertram held lighted up her face, her eyes were dilated with anger, and seemed to emit visible fire.

" How dare you say that ? " she cried. " I never thought you could be so base."

For a moment Bertram quailed before her, and then he recovered himself, and in measured tones, that very successfully hid his rage and disappointment, said :

" Come, Julia, I have a right to be heard. You ask me how I dare say these things. I might reply that you have given me encouragement ; for unless you have been trifling with me—and I cannot believe you would be so unkind—you must care for me. But, besides that, I dare speak because I love you ; love you as Stanford never can or will."

As he spoke he could not withhold his admiration. Never before had he thought her so well worth winning for her own sake. She stood before him with face white as marble, but proud, queenly. As he looked at her his rage melted, he forgot his desperate circumstances, his voice sank, and, as far as was possible to him, it was love that spoke now :

" Oh, Julia," he cried in pleading accents, " listen one moment longer to me. You have won my heart, and if you send me away with a refusal you will break it. I shall go away without hope, my life will be spoiled. I have been waiting for you to snap the bond that holds you to Stanford ; but I can wait no longer. I lay myself at your feet. No one else cares for you as I do. Join your life with mine, and leave this wretched old city, and it shall be my one endeavour to make you happy."

Again Edmund longed for strength to spring up and take him by the throat ; but surely, even if he had it, he ought first to hear what Julia would say to these proposals, and how she would meet Bertram's charge that she had given him encouragement to make them. He must listen, he felt he had a right to, and he did so with a strained eagerness that almost made his heart stand still.

" Bertram," she replied, in words that seemed wrung from her heart, and sounded like a succession of sobs, " I have wronged you, wronged Edmund, wronged myself ; may God forgive me ! I have been foolish and cruel. But I never supposed you thought of me in this light. You knew I was engaged to Edmund. You have been very, very kind ; but I do not love you, and never shall ; I love Edmund Stanford."

"You only think so," he pleaded, passionately. "You are not yourself to-night ; you are not well. I noticed it when I called for you. Something has unsettled you. Why, you even imagined just now that you heard Stanford calling you. But this mood will pass away ; to-morrow you will see everything in the true light. Let us go home now, and at least give me leave to speak to you again."

"Never, never," cried Julia, with tears in her eyes. "I am the victim of no illusions now ; I have walked amid false lights and shadows too long. To-night I am my true self, and I know that I love Edmund, and shall never love another. I have been cold and cruel to him ; but he will forgive me, for he is generous and noble, and I know that he loves me, and I am sure that he called me just now. He may be miles and miles away, although he seems to me strangely near, and in some trouble ; but in any case I will go to him, and I will tell him all."

"Then you have deceived me," cried Bertram, passionately, advancing towards her.

"No, I have not," replied Julia with gleaming eyes. " In any case, you have done the greater wrong, for you have slandered Edmund, and tried to supplant him. I see it all now. It is you that have come between us all along. You awakened the first suspicions and doubts, and it is you that have tried to keep them alive. And now I see that you have

been working for your own ends. But I will go to
Edmund, and ask him to forgive me ; for I love
him, and shall love him to the last hour of my life.
And now leave me! Do not dare to touch me! I
will go home alone."

And so saying, she swept away into the darkness.

Edmund staggered to his feet and followed.
Bertram also dashed forwards ; but the next moment
he was struck by an unseen hand, and found himself
sprawling on the refuse heap by the fireside.

Julia avoided the skaters, for most of them were
Bertram's friends, and made for the road across the
unfrequented meadows over which her lover had so
lately passed. Edmund followed, his heart singing
for joy, although he was in great pain from his fall.
Julia was flying along quickly, for she had on her
skates, and hearing someone following, she thought
it was Bertram Elles. The moon was rising, and
Edmund could see her before him. She was,
however, rushing towards the spot where the ice was
not safe ; already he felt it cracking beneath him.

" Julia ! Julia !" he cried. " Stop."

She heard him, and swept round.

" Oh, Edmund, is it you ? "

" Yes."

" I am coming to you."

But even as she spoke the ice gave way ; he heard
a crash, a shriek, and saw her sink into the bitter
water.

CHAPTER VI.

RESCUED.

THE events of the last few minutes had thrown Edmund into tremendous excitement. Wave after wave of feeling—love, joy, hatred, grief—went surging through his soul; yet he never lost his presence of mind, save for the few seconds when he lay dazed by his fall. Now every sense was doubly alive. Thought was stirred to its utmost activity. He grasped the situation in a moment.

Another step forward and the ice would give way beneath him and so delay his rescue of Julia. Quick as thought he sprang aside, and reached a spot where it was stronger, and then moving lightly round, came up to the place where she was immersed to the waist.

" Oh! take care," she cried, her teeth chattering so that she could scarcely speak, " the ice is quite rotten, and the water is bitterly cold."

" It is stronger here," he answered, dropping on his left knee and placing his right foot as far from it as possible, so as to distribute his weight. Then he reached forward.

" Now," he said, " lean this way." As she did so he slipped his arms round her waist, drew her nearer, and then rising quickly, lifted her out of the water and clasped her to his bosom. He sprang with her across the ice, and safely reached the lane a few hundred yards from the inn he had so lately left. Then for one brief moment the flood-gates of his soul gave way, and he held her in a loving embrace and kissed her passionately, and called her his own by every sweet and endearing name. And Julia, with a choking sob, flung her arms round his neck. Where he had come from, and what had happened to so completely break down the barrier between them she could not tell. She only felt a thrill of exquisite joy through her whole being, and that they were one again.

But he knew that not a moment must be lost.

" Let me," he said, " unfasten your skates. There is an inn at the corner of this lane ; you must remove these wet clothes immediately. Will you walk, or shall I carry you ? "

" I will try to walk," replied Julia, grasping his arm ; " it will help to restore warmth."

She was shivering with cold. Her wet clothes clung heavily about her, and she was drenched to the skin. They had not proceeded fifty yards before she broke down, her head sank against his shoulder, and her limbs, overcome with numbness, refused to move. A sob fell from her lips, everything seemed to fail and fade and vanish from her, and she would have fallen to the ground but for his support.

He took her in his arms and hurried forward. As he did so the light of the rising moon fell upon her face. Her eyes were closed, her lips and cheeks were livid, and she lay so motionless and helpless that an agonizing cry broke from him. He feared that she had ceased to breathe. But no, the exclamation had roused her, and for a moment she opened her eyes, and tightened her arms about his neck, and then again relapsed into unconsciousness.

" Thank God! " he thought, " she is still living." But even then the big beads of perspiration stood on his brow, less from his exertion than from fear of the result of so much exposure to her. There came to him a giant's strength, and he ran on, but with a wild storm of feelings raging within him.

" What will be the effect of this on her delicate frame ? " he asked himself. " Will she be able to stand it ? She who has always been so careful against cold and exposure ? Who ought not to have been out on such a night at all ? What if it should prove fatal ? What if he was to learn that she loved him, and was faithful to him, only to see her die ? "

He could not think it, could not believe it ; but in the agony of his heart he cried, " O God, save her ! save her ! have pity on us," and ran on as fast as he could, and when he drew near to the inn he gave a shout that brought the landlady to the door.

. . . . . .

Whilst Edmund was thus engaged in the rescue of Julia a very different scene was being enacted not far from the shelter.

Bertram Elles quickly gathered himself up from off the ash-heap, and stared around, feeling very stupid and confused. " Where was Julia ? " he asked himself. Who was that who sprang up and darted after her, as she went off ? Above all, who knocked him down ? He felt sore and dazed, and could not

M

put things together very well ; but he was satisfied now that Edmund Stanford was on the ice, and that it was he who followed Julia. And it must have been some confederate of his that had struck him to the ground. He was still standing, swearing vengeance on Edmund, when he heard a crash and a cry. What was that? Was it not Julia's voice? Had the ice given way and she gone through? Should he go and help her? No ; hang it ! let Stanford save her, or let her drown. She was nothing to him now. The game was up, and he had better get away as quickly as possible. There was still time for him to catch the night mail. He would write to old Abraham Jacobs, and tell him he should have his money in a month, and he would go and make the best terms he could with his uncle, and then depart to Canada, and never set foot in this hateful old city again.

So he turned on the ice and glided away. He heard some of his friends calling him ; but he avoided them, for they would have awkward questions to ask about Julia. He resolved that he would get back to the city alone and unseen, and be off to London before any of them had time to look him up.

But he had not gone far before a tall figure strode across the ice and confronted him, and a voice, which he recognized as the gipsy's, asked scoffingly :

" Where is the young lady ? Why did you not bring her to me ? "

" Curse the young lady, and you too ! " exclaimed Bertram, turning away with an oath.

" Oh, fie ! " said the gipsy, following him and speaking still more jeeringly, " to curse the bonnie dark-eyed lady because she loves a better man than you will ever be. Curses, like chickens, come home to roost. I know you; I read men's hearts like a book. You have chosen to walk in the dark; *but God will find you in the dark.*"

She gave a hoarse laugh, that sounded in his ears like the croak of a raven. He flashed round white with rage and fear.

"Leave me, you black old hag," he cried, striking at her, "or, by God, I'll knock you down!"

"You knock me down!" she answered, warding off his blow, and seizing him by the throat, and shaking him as a dog would a rat. "I could shake your wicked soul out of your body if I chose, you liar, slanderer, and thief; but you shall live, and bear an old woman's curse."

She stretched her long, skinny arms over him, and then, raising her black, piercing eyes to the sky, she cried, in a hoarse whisper, that made his blood run cold:

"God in Heaven! let Thy wrath rest on this man! may the Avenger of Blood follow him over the seas; let him be tormented with Furies by day and night; when he lies down to sleep may evil dreams haunt him; and for him may there never be any peace, until Thy Angel of Justice is satisfied!"

She flung him from her into the darkness, and went her way, and he crept off the ice like an accursed thing.

.   .   .   .   .   .

When Julia again opened her eyes she found herself lying before a blazing fire. A motherly-looking woman was bending over her, and a girl was kneeling

M 2

at her feet, unlacing her boots. Edmund was standing by, holding a steaming glass in his hand. For a
moment she glanced round bewildered, unable to
think what it meant; then everything came back to
her, and as her eyes rested on Edmund they filled
with tears. He gave an exclamation of thankfulness
when he saw that she had recovered consciousness.

"Oh, don't cry," said the landlady cheerfully; "you
will soon be better."

"Drink this," said Edmund, holding the glass of
hot spirits-and-water to her lips. She touched it, and
then shook her head.

"You must drink it," he said gently, but firmly.
"Take it quickly, and then I will go and hunt up a
cab, and arrange about my horse, and in the meantime you will get your things changed."

Julia drank it down with a wry face, and Edmund
hurried away to arrange about their getting home.
Very soon he was back with a cab, and found her
with her strength partially recovered, but with a perceptible increase in her cough. She had exchanged
her dripping clothing for some the landlady had
supplied—thick woollen stockings and a warm frock,
whose imperfect fit was hidden by the rich masses
of her hair, which had fallen to her waist.

"Ah," she cried, giving him a bobbing curtsey, and
endeavouring to control her tears in the presence of
the landlady by a facetious remark, "I hope you
consider my appearance very becoming."

"Charming," he replied, smiling. "You must let
me sketch you in it some day."

"The young lady would look well in anything,"
said the landlady; "but now you must let me throw

this thick woollen shawl right over your head and
shoulders, and then you must get home and to bed as
quickly as ever you can, and to-morrow you'll be
quite well."

They thanked the landlady for her kindness, and
then drove off.

"Are you still cold?" he asked, tenderly; for he
felt her give an unconscious shiver. As he spoke he
drew her closer towards himself, and folded his arms
round her.

"No," she replied, with a faltering voice. Then a
sob broke from her lips, followed by such a storm of
weeping as he had never seen before.

"What is it, my darling?" he asked, holding her
close to his heart. "What is troubling you? Do
not weep, I know all, and I love you more than
ever."

"Oh, Edmund!" she sobbed at last, "I am
ashamed to think how cold and cruel I have been
since Frank's marriage. Can you ever forgive me?"

"My own dear love," he replied, "I have nothing
to forgive. I have been very unhappy, for I thought
you had ceased to love me. I had come to the
conclusion that you had transferred your affections to
Bertram Elles; but I understand it all now."

And then he told her everything—how one or two
of her last letters from London had troubled him,
how he had been perplexed and hurt by the scene in the
conservatory at Brentfield, how he had been distressed
as the estrangement widened week after week. He
told her of the thoughts that had tortured him on his
way back from Merton Magna, and how he had
resolved to ask her whether she really cared for him

or for another. And then how his horse had cast its shoe, and he had come accidentally, or, as he would say, providentially, on the ice, not knowing that she and Bertram were there, and how, through his own fall, he had become unintentionally a witness of the scene at the shelter. Above all, he told her of his great joy when he learned in this unexpected way that all the trouble had come about through a slanderous tongue, and that she was really true to him.

" And now," he said, " this unhappiness is all over. I shall never doubt your love again, and you will never doubt mine, will you ? "

" Never, never," she answered ; " but I did trifle with Bertram, though I cared for you all the time, and now I feel that I do not deserve to be so nobly loved."

"We have both been in the wrong," he said. " You least, for you have been cruelly deceived by a lying tongue ; but the suspicion and misunderstanding are all over, and we shall never, never again give place to them."

And thus there came to these two young things one of those divine moments into which more of real life is crowded than into years of common experience ; a moment of reconciliation, forgiveness, and joy which wiped out the memory of all the bitterness, and their spirits rushed together, and they felt the perfect love which casteth out fear.

Very soon they drew up at Miss Ray's gate. Edmund persuaded Julia to go straight to her bedroom, both because it would be better for herself, and also would save her aunt from the sudden shock of seeing her so oddly dressed.

He went to the drawing-room and briefly related what had occurred. Miss Ray, realizing the gravity of the accident, hastened to Julia, and almost immediately after sent a message to Edmund, begging him not to wait, but to call on his way home and ask the doctor to attend.

Julia's cough was worse than when she went out, and her aunt knew that after such a shock the most serious consequences might ensue. A fire was lighted in her bedroom, and a hot, nourishing drink got ready.

By the time these things were done the doctor had arrived. He was an old friend of the family, and thoroughly understood Julia's constitution. Edmund had seen him and informed him of what had happened, and although he spoke cheerfully he inwardly feared the result.

" And so my little lady has been having a cold bath in the open air this frosty night ? " he said, advancing to the bedside and laying his hand on Julia's wrist, at the same time watching her closely. " Rather unfortunate, that."

Julia was about to attempt a humorous reply, when her cough checked her. He noticed the cough, and took her temperature.

" Well," he said pleasantly, " you must try to get a good sleep to-night, and to-morrow morning I must examine your chest. In the meantime you must be kept quiet and warm."

After a few further directions with regard to the administration of some remedies which he said he would send down immediately, he withdrew.

" What do you think of her ? " asked Miss Ray, anxiously, as soon as they reached the dining-room.

" Her pulse is rapid, her temperature high, and she is unnaturally excited," he replied ; "and it is most unfortunate that she has this nasty cough. It is impossible to say, at present, how she will stand the shock. She must remain in bed, and the temperature of the room must be kept warm and even. We shall soon learn how she is likely to bear it, and in the meantime we must hope for the best."

When the medicine arrived, and her aunt went to administer a dose, Julia noticed that she had made preparations for sitting up all night.

" Oh, auntie dear," she said, " pray don't sit up, I'm sure it's not necessary."

" My dear, the fire must be attended to, and you must have your medicine regularly ; I should not like to trust the maids."

" I'm so sorry to give you so much trouble," replied Julia. " Had I only taken your advice it would not have happened."

" Never mind, dear, perhaps it is all for the best," remarked Miss Ray, thankful that Bertram Elles had been found out, and that Edmund and Julia were reconciled.

" I feel sure it is." Another fit of coughing hindered Julia from saying more for a few seconds ; then she added quietly and sadly, almost as though she were talking to herself, " Yes, a shock was needed. All my life I have been a giddy, thoughtless girl. But to-night I have passed through a crisis ; something has fallen from me. The old life, I trust, is dead, and a new life begun."

As she spoke her aunt bent over her and kissed her, and Julia flung her arms round the dear old lady's neck and wept afresh, tears of penitence and love.

"Oh, auntie dear," she cried, "you have always borne patiently with me, and to-night Edmund has been most noble and generous ; I am sure that God sent him to me. I do not deserve such love ; but, dear auntie, pray for me, so that, should my life be spared, I may for the future live it more worthily."

And her aunt bent down and kissed her again, and said : " May our Heavenly Father bless you, dear child, and help you to live the higher life to which He has called you."

It was some time before Julia could fall asleep, but when she did drop off what she had gone through that night—the incidents on the ice, and the moral crisis that followed—combined into a dream so realistic and vivid that it had the spiritual effects of revelation.

Again she was out on the ice, fleeing from some nameless evil. Night had come on, and there was no light of moon or stars. At every step she slipped and stumbled. Suddenly she heard a crash, and felt the ice give way, and herself sink into the bitter water. She struggled to save herself, grasping at the withered reeds and broken ice, but all in vain ; she was sinking deeper and deeper, and the cold icy water was rising higher and higher.

Then she heard her name called, and supposed that it was Edmund ; but was too much exhausted and blinded with the freezing water to see who it was. Someone clasped her in his arms, and bore her away in safety. As he placed her on the ground he said in a voice that seemed the soul of sweetness and music :

" Julia, I have loved thee with an everlasting love. To find thee I have passed through the horror of great darkness, and the chill night air, and the swollen stream of death ; and now that I have saved thee wilt thou not love and follow me ? "

And as He spoke she fell at His feet as dead ; for she knew that it was not Edmund, but the Lord Jesus Christ. And with her head bowed very low she said :

" Lord, I am not worthy of Thy love ; I am only a giddy and sinful girl."

But He took her by the hand and raised her up, and said : " Thy sins are forgiven thee."

Not until then had she dared to gaze into His face. It was the most divinely human countenance she had ever seen. On His head was a crown of thorns, His hands and feet were pierced, but His garments were kingly, and a light shone from His person before which the night vanished.

And she said : " Lord, I would follow Thee, but my garments are wet and soiled."

And He answered : " Thou shalt be arrayed in fine linen, clean and white ; for the fine linen is the righteousness of saints."

So vivid was this dream that she could not shake off the impression of it when she awakened. She seemed to have passed through a gracious experience, and her heart rose up in silent prayer and praise.

CHAPTER VII.

"LIFE FOR EVERMORE."

THE doctor's voice was as cheery as ever, and his face wore its usual look of imperturbable serenity, when he entered Julia's room the next morning. He drew a chair beside her, and seated himself as though he was only a friend who had called in to hear how she had passed the night. And yet, in truth, he was very anxious about her, and began noting, with a quiet, comprehensive glance, every symptom, however slight, so suggestive to his practised eye.

He was not merely a life-long friend of Miss Ray, but also a frequent visitor at her house, and for some time he had seen that things were not going well with Julia. He had looked into her eyes and read the sure signs of disquiet, and had reached shrewd conclusions as to the cause. He had known her since she was a child, and was very fond of her, and had watched over her with an almost fatherly interest.

As he sat by her side, holding her hand gently in his, and making a few pleasant remarks, he was observing everything. He noticed a light in her eyes he had not seen for some weeks.

"Ah," he said to himself, "there is a change there. Her poor little heart is at ease. I wonder whether last night's accident has had anything to do with it?"

And this impression deepened as he proceeded to examine her more carefully, and saw that she was developing symptoms of serious illness—a high temperature, a bad cough, and greater difficulty in breathing. Yet for all these alarming signs—the significance of which, she, having lived so much with Frank, understood, she manifested a beautiful patience and sweetness that quite surprised and charmed the old physician.

"Strange girl," he thought, "and something wonderfully attractive about her too. If she only lives we shall see more of it as she gets older; but I don't like the look of things. She will have enough to do to pull through."

"You don't think her quite so well this morning," said Miss Ray, anxiously, when they had left the room.

"She is almost better than I hoped to find her after what had taken place," the doctor replied. "One thing is greatly in her favour : she is wonderfully patient, and she looks more happy and at rest than she has done lately."

"I do believe the dear child has passed through a crisis," replied Miss Ray. "Something has gone from her. Hitherto her best life seems to have been kept back by an alien element ; but now it has broken through. I thought you would notice the change."

"Yes. I never saw her more sweet and winsome. I must go now ; but I shall come back in the afternoon, and in the meantime I shall send off for a trained nurse."

A graver expression than usual passed over the doctor's face. He seldom betrayed his thoughts so fully. Miss Ray noticed it, and asked with a trembling voice,—

"Oh, doctor, do you think——"

She could say no more. He understood, and replied,—

"We must do everything for her that can be done; she has youth, and for the rest we must commend her to Him who alone knows what is best."

But Julia did not improve as the day wore on. To the experienced eyes of the physician it was evident that she was seriously ill, and that it would only be with a very great struggle, if at all, that she would recover.

Edmund called several times during the day to hear how she was, and in the evening Miss Ray took him up to her for a few minutes. When he entered the room she was sitting propped up in bed with pillows, and he was distressed to see how ill she looked; yet he entertained no thought but that she would recover. The light kindled afresh in her eyes when she saw him, and she put her arms round his neck and kissed him.

"Dear Edmund," she said, "I hope you took no harm last night. Are your head and shoulders much bruised?"

"My darling," he replied, "I'm all right—a little stiff and sore from my fall, nothing more; but I am grieved to see how ill you look."

"The doctor says that I'm quite as well as he expected to find me." And then she drew him closer, and said softly, "Dear Edmund, I'm so glad the

dreadful misunderstanding is all gone.   I know what
true love is now."

"My darling," he whispered, "this is only the dawn,
the spring ; the golden summer of our love has yet
to come."

She gave him a wistful, longing look, and said with
an exquisite smile,—

"I hope so, dear Edmund, if it be our Heavenly
Father's will.   I have been longing to see you, and
to tell you what a sweet peace I feel.   Your love
has led me to the very fount of love."   And then she
proceeded to tell him of her remarkable dream, and
the impression it had made on her mind ; and
Edmund, deeply touched, said that for the future they
must help each other to live a nobler and more pur-
poseful life.

By the next day, however, she was decidedly worse,
and her cough was so bad that Edmund only spent
a few minutes with her, as he slipped softly into her
room with some fresh flowers.

On the Sunday the bishop called to see her.   Miss
Ray was one of his old and deeply respected friends,
and Julia, so slight and winsome, had, when a mere
child, secured a warm corner in his heart.   He saw
that beneath all her lighter moods there was something genuine and noble, which would eventually
burst into flower.   He hastened round, as soon as he
heard that she was seriously ill.

Julia was very thankful, for during the previous
night she had been in great distress, and had
begun to fear that she might not get better.   And as
the dark shadow slowly loomed up before her, which
crosses sooner or later every path, it would have been

strange had her faith not been sorely tried with
many doubts and misgivings. She was young, and
had never thought of that last mystery as having
anything but a most vague and unimaginably
remote significance for her. And yet now it seemed
to be drawing painfully near—oh, so near—just
when her life was breaking into richer promise,
and the world was growing more beautiful, and
love was making all things a thousandfold more
desirable than before. How could she resign it all,
and relinquish Edmund and all her earthly hopes
and friends, and face that dark and lonely region
which mortals have ever feared? What new and
strange life was hidden in that mysterious realm?
And what if her faith should fail in the hour of her
utmost need?

Such were the thoughts that troubled her. No
wonder that when she turned her eyes on the venerable bishop he saw in them a lingering look of terror,
and a pathetic wistfulness that claimed not merely
his tenderest sympathy, but wisest and surest con-
solation.

"Yes, my dear child," he said; "I am sure that
behind all the shows and accidents of life, Love,
Eternal and Almighty Love, is the one all-enduring
reality, Love that holds us in safe keeping, and will
not suffer that shadow to touch any true interest of
our lives."

"Thank you," she whispered; "and now," she
asked with touching pathos, "will you pray for
me? Ask our Heavenly Father that I may
recover, if it be His will: for, oh! I should so
much like to live; but if He has ordered otherwise,

pray that my faith may not fail as I tread the dark valley."

And then in low and tender tones the bishop prayed as Julia desired, and asked that the Good Shepherd would gather her, as one of the lambs of His flock, safe in His own arms, and carry her in His bosom, then would all be well with her, now and for ever, whatever might betide.

But Julia's days were numbered ; she grew rapidly worse. The cold that was troubling her before the night's exposure had made it impossible for her, with a hereditary weakness of the chest, to throw off the effects of the shock. A severe attack of double pneumonia developed, and speedily ran its fatal course. The highest professional skill was called in, but proved powerless to arrest the disease. Frank and Kate were summoned from London, but only to await the inevitable end.

Inexpressibly strange was it to see how calmly Julia resigned herself to this sudden termination of all her dreams of earthly bliss. Instead of needing the support of her friends to meet a hard and cruel fate, it was she who cheered and supported them. Like a plant that only flowers before it dies, but then flowers gloriously, all the hidden beauty and sweet- ness of her nature rushed into bloom during those last days, and in her case death seemed literally swallowed up in life. But is not that frequently the case with the young? It would sometimes seem as though a special grace were vouchsafed to those who in dying have most to resign. The old, and over- worn, and wretched are often found clinging to the last miserable remnants of life with a feverish and tenacious grasp, while the young, beautiful, and gifted will let it go at the first touch of the icy fingers. It was not one who was old and sad, but a maiden on whose fair brow the last year's floral crown had hardly faded, who asked :

> " And what is life, that we should moan ?
> Why make we such ado ? "

It would be impossible, however, to describe the distress of Edmund during those brief, dark, winter days. He gave up going to business, and hovered about the house, unable to render much assistance, and so, for the most part, keeping out of the way in the library ; but always within call, and listening in dumb agony to the reports which hour by hour grew more hopeless.

From time to time he was permitted to see Julia for a few moments : she often asked for him, and as soon as he appeared she was glad, and gave him a sweet smile and a tender word ; but he saw that she was swiftly slipping away from him. As the inflammation increased she suffered a good deal : there was more difficulty in breathing, and her mind often wandered. But as soon as full consciousness returned she manifested the most perfect patience, and a sweet peace filled her mind.

In one of these intervals of clear consciousness, when she knew that she was dying, she asked to be left alone with Edmund. He was in the library, and was at once sent for.

When he entered the room she was partially sitting up, supported by pillows. A glint of afternoon sunshine fell around her, and though her face was deathly

N

pale, with deep dark circles round the eyes, it was lighted up with a wistful smile.

Edmund saw only too clearly that his beloved was passing away, and as he bent over and gently kissed her a sob broke from his heart.

" Oh, don't grieve, dear Edmund," she whispered with difficulty and frequent pauses. " All is well . . . God is Love . . . Had it been His will . . . I should have liked so much to have lived . . . and been your wife . . . but now I know that that is not to be . . . I am going to be with Jesus . . . I am going to meet my dear father and mother . . . and your father and mother . . . I am sure they will know me . . . and love me."

" My darling, my saint, my angel," cried Edmund, " may God bless you and guide you safe home, and may He help me; for life will be dar and lonely without you."

" He will be with you. . . . You must not grieve when I am gone . . . but live a brave and noble life . . . I thank our Heavenly Father for your love. . . . I shall not cease to love you . . . and you will not cease to love me . . . as all pure spirits love one another in God. . . . Perhaps this pain is sent to fit me for the work of a ministering spirit . . . and I shall serve Him there . . . and you here. . . . By-and-by God will send you joy and love again . . . and you must accept them . . . and not make your life sad when He would not have it so . . . I know you will not forget me . . . and I shall never forget you . . . And now kiss me, dear, again . . . for I feel so tired."

Edmund bent over the beautiful form and kissed her gently, and almost immediately she fell into a short sleep. When her aunt and the nurse returned she was still sleeping, clasping Edmund's hand tightly, as though she did not want him to go.

When she awakened again her mind was wandering, and she did not seem to know what she was saying ; but it was easy to see on what her thoughts were working.

" The everlasting love of God," she murmured, " that's where I rest. . . . For ever and for ever . . . all in a blessed home."

That same evening Frank and Kate arrived, and she embraced them affectionately, and said to them much the same as she had done to Edmund, telling them not to weep for her ; for that all was well, and as it should be.

After that she dozed frequently, and on the whole had a better night, and, the next day, so far rallied that there was a glimmer of hope that she might yet struggle through. She beckoned Kate and Frank to her side, and, clasping their hands, told them that whatever happened they must never distrust one another, and never allow anyone to come between them. She made no reference to Bertram ; but seemed anxious to indicate, by her own gentleness to Kate, that her brother's conduct must not cause trouble between her and Frank. Her dear old aunt she embraced again and again, and thanked her for all her loving care, and asked her forgiveness for whatever sorrow or anxiety she had ever given her.

" I was often giddy and wayward," she whispered, slowly, as if she were summing up her life. " Yet I always wished to be good. Edmund's love came like a sweet summer to me ; but I was like some

N 2

fruits that will not ripen until they feel the touch of frost."

These things were not said all at once, but at intervals during the day.

Late in the afternoon Edmund was sitting by her side clasping her hand. After a long struggle with himself he was outwardly calm, for he did not wish to grieve Julia ; Frank was on the other side of the bed, and Miss Ray and Kate were near the fire.

Some one remarked that it was Christmas Eve.

" Edmund, dear," whispered Julia, " sing ; I should so much like to hear you sing Gounod's *Nazareth* once more."

With a great effort Edmund controlled himself and kept under command feelings which, but for his strong will, would have broken forth into weeping. In subdued tender tones he sang the exquisite music, and as Julia listened to the refrain an expression of triumph lighted up her face.

> " Lo, the Lord of Heaven hath to mortals given
>   Life for evermore."

When he had finished she drew down his face and kissed him.

As the night wore on it became evident that the rally was only temporary. Julia was sinking fast ; the end was not far off. In the early hours of the morning there was a sharp struggle, she was in much pain, and then the worst was over, and she sank into a dreamy state of semi-consciousness. She was sitting propped up with pillows, her eyes partially closed, her mouth slightly open, every suggestion of terror gone, and in its place a smile that indicated nothing but heavenly peace and joy. Her dearest friends were around her, her brother, her aunt, Edmund, Kate.

Suddenly with the break of earliest dawn the bells of the city rang forth triumphantly. It was Christmas Day and the air was filled with joyous music. Julia awakened, her beautiful eyes filled with light ; her face became radiant, as though it were the face of an angel.

"Hark !" she said, in a whisper. "Do you not hear the angels' song ?"

She sank bank, her face suffused with a supernatural radiance and peace. One by one they kissed her, and bade her farewell, and as her eyes closed, her lips moved in silent prayer, and the last words they could hear were the refrain from Gounod's *Nazareth*, spoken slowly and feebly, with a pause between each word or two. "Lo, the Lord of Heaven . . . hath to mortals given . . . Life for Evermore . . . for Evermore." And so, whilst the Christmas bells were waking the old city with their glad music, she passed away into the Heavenly Home.

BOOK IV.

"Who is among you that feareth the Lord, that obeyeth the voice of His Servant, that walketh in darkness, and hath no light? let him trust in the name of the Lord, and stay upon his God."

CHAPTER I.

"OUR FATHER."

IT was Sunday afternoon, and Edmund, having walked three or four miles along well-wooded roads, and through green lanes, was sitting on a flat tombstone close to the porch of an old grey church, situated on a bit of rising ground not far from Caistor.

The city, bathed in Sabbath calm, slept out of sight behind low hills. On the left the churchyard sloped down to a plantation of venerable beeches, beyond which rose up a whiff of blue smoke from the rectory below. Southwards rolled a picturesque expanse of undulating country, dotted with pleasant homesteads, and watered by a willow-fringed stream winding slowly among meadows and cultivated fields. A railway cutting and viaduct hardly broke the deep peace of this secluded vale by the suggestion of a wider world. The afternoon sun lit up the sullen gloom of a belt of Scotch firs with a bright gleam, smote the river into silvery ripples, imparted a warm touch to the meadows dappled with sheep and cattle, and filled the whole of the sweeping valley with a golden haze.

As Edmund gazed on the scene a gleam of sunshine played on his own haggard features.

Nearly four months had passed away since the death of Julia, and once more the old earth was renewing its youth. The trees were in blossom, bright spring flowers were everywhere, the lambs were bleating in the fields, and every hedgerow and bush was a concert-chamber for feathered songsters.

But for the familiarity that robs life so often of wonder we should never cease to marvel at this annual re-birth of Nature. It is her great yearly parable, her message of eternal hope to mortals, her witness that life and not death is Lord and King.

Edmund was not consciously reflecting on this parable, but as he sat in the spring sunshine that Sunday afternoon, listening to the sweet sounds that arose on every side, he did feel a gentle lifting of the clouds that had darkened his life, and a reviving breath of hope.

It had been a long, sad winter to him, and he had begun to think the sun would never shine again.

For a few days after Julia's death he hardly felt the full bitterness of his loss. The calmness and beauty of her last moments had cast a hallowed spell over him. In her chamber they had seemed quite on the verge of heaven, and he left it like one looking beyond the things of time and sense to some solemn world which had suddenly opened to his gaze.

But when the last sacred rites were over, and Frank and Kate had returned to London, taking Miss Ray with them, and the old house in the Cathedral Close, that had become so familiar and dear, was shut up, and he was thrown back on his own lonely life—more lonely than ever after all that had occurred—he rapidly sank into a deeper melancholy than he had ever known before.

He went regularly to business, and threw himself with feverish activity into all his duties. He was always ready to remain late, or take work home, and those who watched without understanding him thought how easily he was forgetting his sorrow. But there really was no heart in anything he did. For the time being he had lost all interest in life.

An awful shadow had suddenly fallen on him, and the whole world was changed, darkened, charged with sorrow and anguish. The fair vision he had cherished of the future shrunk up and disappeared, and in its place he saw nothing but a dreary and lonely road to be trodden with what dutiful resignation he could command.

His sorrow brought him face to face with the eternal problems, no longer as curious speculations in which he might take a mild intellectual interest, but in all their implacable solemnity and seriousness. The fundamental convictions on which his life had hitherto rested were disturbed. His own personal loss drew to itself the age-long agony of mankind, and he wrestled painfully with the hard, stony, sphinx-like questions that have tormented the world's sufferers in all ages.

"Was man more than a mere speck, an insignificant atom in a boundless universe? Was not Death conqueror and king? Were not all the higher faiths and hopes delusions? Were all human struggle and sorrow anything more than the trouble of a colony of ants in the presence of a million, million worlds?"

Such were the questions he brooded over whenever his mind was otherwise disengaged.

Those who have passed through a similar phase of experience know the hopelessness of all such efforts to solve the enigma of existence. One question is no sooner answered than a score of others start up. The mind wavers in an endless see-saw of argument, now inclining this way, and now that, until heart and brain, tormented and baffled beyond endurance, give up the problem in despair.

There is only one deliverance from such a state, and that is through the awakening of a new mood, a genial change in the climate of the soul, a rising of temperature which will disperse fogs and clouds no blasts of argument can drive away. Thoughtful meditation may certainly help to bring about that change ; but it often occurs, one hardly knows how or why, and generally through listening to other voices than that of the cold, critical understanding.

Such has usually been the inner history of those whose intellectual and spiritual life has involved a movement through negation to reaffirmation, through the "Everlasting No" to the "Everlasting Yea." It is seldom made quite plain by what means they have regained clearness and calm. They have emerged out of darkness by an unknown path. Fresh fields of moral consciousness have unexpectedly opened up. Old truths have reasserted themselves with new power. The air of a warmer clime has softly swept through the soul, and the black storm-clouds having done their work and spent their force, have glided away by a hidden law of their own. And the result is, that those who have experienced these things are often disappointed to find that when they would account for their altered position to others, and so help them in their spiritual difficulties, they can but very imperfectly retrace their own steps, or explain the movement of their own inner life.

It was so with Edmund Stanford. He was naturally of a morbid and brooding temperament, and although he had strenuously laboured to overcome it by throwing himself eagerly into an active career, and cultivating many tastes and interests, events had gone against him. His mother's sudden death had been a shock from which he never wholly recovered. The years that followed were exceedingly lonely. Then came the brief moment of unspeakable happiness with Julia, when the sun shone out gloriously, to be followed so soon by darkness, silence, and inconsolable grief.

It was the last blow, and he broke down utterly. His life was shaken to its foundations. He walked in the very depths of the Valley of the Shadow of Death, and fought Apollyon himself, and heard spirits of evil whispering dark doubts in his ears, until he well-nigh believed them true. All he had leaned on

seemed swept away. Life had lost its meaning, and
shrivelled up to a span. The grave appeared the end
of all ; and everything the sport of blind accident and
chance. The very sky during those dark winter
months looked a dead expanse, black with the void
from which God Himself had disappeared. He
walked lonely, sad, and would have been glad to die.
Only one thing remained sure, certain, clear to him.
He still clung passionately to the belief that it must
be right to do right. Never for one moment did he
hesitate about that. He might find it impossible to
justify the belief to the cold reason, but he knew in
his heart that it was so. Even if there were no God,
and no Providence, and no future life, it was still
better to be true than false, generous than mean, pure
than unchaste, brave than a coward. To that belief
he clung. Never in the darkest moment did he
waver. According to that ideal he lived. And so,
slowly and silently, his mind began to regain its
balance. The spirits of Doubt and Despair were less
often heard, and with the returning spring a sweeter
and brighter spirit slid into his soul.

During the week preceding this particular Sunday
afternoon he had reflected on the inconsistency of
relying so implicitly on the conclusions of what
Thomas Carlyle called the " logic-chopping " faculty
whilst ignoring the witness of heart and conscience.

" Surely," he thought, " the soul must hold a more
direct and certain relation to the ultimate realities of
the universe through its holiest affections and aspira-
tions than through the senses and the understanding.
What is highest and noblest in man must lie nearest
to the truth ; and what is this but saying that Love,

Eternal and Almighty, is the supreme and final fact ? "

This was the thought that occupied his mind as he sat on the tombstone, and took note of all the signs of Nature's rejuvenescence. He was thinking of his own early days, when he knelt by his mother's knee, and was first taught to pray to a Father in Heaven, when he used to walk by the side of father and mother to church, and sat, listening in the pauses of the service, to the rustling of the leaves and the twittering of the birds outside. All those scenes lived again in his memory more lovely, sacred, and full of poetry than ever.

" If there is any truth in life at all," he said to himself, " surely my father and mother found it. If life is not a hopeless riddle, a horrible mockery, their faith and hope, blossoming out, as they did, into such noble living, pointed to the truth of truths. That must be the supreme reality which they felt in their deepest moments to be trustworthy."

And then he thought of the quiet graveyard in dear old Merton Magna, where they were now sleeping, and the words of Christian confidence thrilled through him, " in sure and certain hope of the Resurrection to Eternal Life." St. Paul's argument struck him as it had never done before : " If there be no Resurrection of the Dead, then is Christ not risen." If there be no life beyond the grave " then they also which are fallen asleep in Christ are perished."

It was monstrously absurd. " The Highest, Holiest Manhood the most mistaken ! " he murmured to himself, incredulously. " The ideal Man further from the truth than the Sadducees who put Him to death ! The Foremost Spiritual Leader of men the victim of the most gigantic delusion that ever haunted a troubled brain ! All the sweet, patient, beautiful souls who have gone through this world trusting in God, and who in the last dark hour cried : ' Father, we are coming to Thee ; we trust in Thee to deliver us '—all these forsaken, deceived, suffered to perish ! Surely man was not born to be so cruelly mocked ! "

As he sat musing thus the service in the church was proceeding, and everything was so intensely still that he could hear the indistinct murmur of voices. Then a gentle breeze came sweeping through the budding beeches, and sighing across the graves. He felt it floating about him, touching his uncovered brow with soft fingers, and heard it whispering round the grey old porch. The oaken door shook slightly and stood ajar. The breeze was gone, but in its place came the voice of the minister :

" That it may please Thee to strengthen such as do stand ; and to comfort and help the weak-hearted ; and to raise up them that fall ; and finally to beat down Satan under our feet."

The door closed, and he could hear only a murmur of voices.

" Ah," he said to himself, " that prayer is the inmost voice of my soul. Surely there is somewhere an Eternal and Changeless Love, an ever-abiding Presence which does not come and go like all else in the world, which is before and after and for ever, which can give us adequate support and strength."

Again, after a short pause, the wind came rustling through the trees, and across the grass, and whispering round the church porch, and setting the door ajar ; and now came forth the voice of minister and congregation.

"O Christ, hear us."

"Lord have mercy upon us."

"Our Father, which art in heaven, hallowed be Thy Name. Thy kingdom come. Thy will be done in Earth as it is in Heaven. Give us this day our daily bread. And forgive us our trespasses, as we forgive them that trespass against us. And lead us not into temptation ; but deliver us from evil. Amen."

And as Edmund heard the familiar words, so suddenly instinct with new life, meaning, beauty, he bowed his head, and the prayer which he had first learned from those dear lips now sealed with the silence of death became the divinest expression of his desire and his hope.

He rose from the tombstone and walked back to his lodgings with a new light in his eyes, and conscious of a new confidence and joy. A change had taken place ; the clouds were breaking; the sunlight was on the hills. He felt no longer alone ; Immortal Love watched over him and all the world. Henceforth he would have to bear a chastened sorrow ; but the future was not wholly dark. So he thought, little dreaming how soon his sky would be again overcast, and his new strength tested to its utmost power of endurance.

In the evening he walked round to the Cathedral Close. Miss Ray had been back in Caistor for a week or two, engaged in settling up her affairs, with a view to taking up her abode with Frank in London. She was to leave again the next day.

Edmund had visited her almost daily, and had been struck with the silent change that had passed over the dear old lady since the death of Julia. Her pale face was lighted up with the same sweet smile, and by an even deeper look of resignation and trust; but she seemed visibly fading away, and looked like one who was inwardly saying, "Lord, now lettest Thou Thy servant depart in peace."

They sat talking for a long time, each with the secret feeling that it might be their last conversation together in this world. Miss Ray loved Edmund very tenderly; she believed thoroughly in him, and was sure that in course of time his wounded affections would heal, though he would never lose the scar of past suffering. She wished him to be happy, and was confident that, should his life be spared, he had before him a great future. She knew that whatever joys might be in store for him in the years to come he would never forget the past, nor the one who had been loved and lost. Once or twice she hesitated, as though there was something she was half-inclined to say, yet could not quite make up her mind whether she should say it. At last she drew from her finger a valuable diamond ring, and said,—

"Dear Edmund, I have been thinking that I may never see you again. There are some things of mine I wish you to possess; you will hear all about them when the time comes, but I wish to give you something now. I want you to accept this ring and to wear it for the sake of all that has been; there is now no one whom I should so much like to possess it as you."

"It is too good of you," replied Edmund; "why

give it to me now? I hope we may sometimes meet for a long time to come."

"I should like you to take it now," said Miss Ray, with a pathetic smile. "I may not have another opportunity of giving it to you myself, or of saying what I want to say. Let me see it on."

Edmund could not speak a word, but he bent over her outstretched hand and reverently kissed it, and then placed the ring on his finger.

"There," she said, giving him another affectionate smile, "it fits your finger nicely. I remember when that ring first came into my possession. It was a time of trouble and darkness, just as the present is with you. My life was overshadowed by a great loss. My cherished dreams had vanished, and I was crushed with sorrow. Life seemed to me a tangled thread. It appeared governed by no large purpose; I could discover in it no worthy end. There was such a look of failure and frustration in everything, that I concluded I was merely the sport of some cruel fate, or of blind accident and chance. It was that which made me so rebellious and impatient. I thought I could have borne all the pain and disappointment and heartache if I could have seen any good in them —seen them working for any adequate result. I dare say you have often felt like that during these last dark months?"

"Yes," said Edmund, sadly. "It is the apparent purposelessness of life that has so often filled me with pain."

"Just so. And yet is not that what we should expect? We take up, especially in youth, a little bit of our life, and often enough we can make nothing of it. It is like a few inches cut out of a large picture, a meaningless fragment. But sometimes there come to us hours of insight when the purpose of life is revealed to us. A new light falls upon the spirit, our eyes are opened, we look back on past years, and see that they were not fruitless. A divine plan has been unfolding through all these sorrows and trials that form a part of life's education ; and when we see that what once looked so full of chance and accident has really been under the control of a secret and hidden wisdom, we feel a deep peace. Of course, we shall never understand things perfectly here ; still it is true that ' The secret of the Lord is with them that fear Him ; and He will show them His covenant.' "

" It is a great comfort," said Edmund, " to hear you say these things. I cannot tell you what terrible and gloomy thoughts have been haunting my mind for a long time ; but I hope that I shall be able now to overcome them."

And then he proceeded to tell her of his walk that afternoon, of his thoughts as he sat on the tombstone, and of how the words of the Lord's Prayer had come to him like a fresh revelation.

" Yes," replied Miss Ray ; " I see how you have suffered ; you have had a hard struggle, and others may follow ; but, dear Edmund, you will rise above them all if you will hold on to the belief that there is a Heavenly Father who has sent you into the world for a wise and loving purpose, and that He is never nearer to you than when the way is dark and sad. And it is another great thing to remember that the end of life is never outward happiness. Had it been so our Heavenly Father could have reached it by a

O

simpler method. No, the end of life is our education as spiritual beings, as the children of God ; and pain, disappointment, and trial are necessary in view of that end. And, therefore, we ought to say with Browning :

> ' Then welcome each rebuff
> That turns earth's smoothness rough,
> Each sting that bids nor sit nor stand but go !
> Be our joys three-parts pain !
> Strive, and hold cheap the strain :
> Learn, nor account the pang : dare, never grudge the throe !' "

They continued to talk a little longer about their various plans in the immediate future, and then Edmund rose to depart.

"Well," said Miss Ray, with a smile, "you will forgive my preaching you such a long sermon ; but I know not whether I shall ever see you again. Something tells me that my time is near. I have a great desire to depart to be with Christ, and those dear ones who are now with Him."

And then she embraced him affectionately, and said : "You will remember what I say, and may our Heavenly Father keep you ever in His love."

CHAPTER II.

A TERRIBLE ACCUSATION.

" I HAVE been looking over the work you took home last week," said Mr. Walsingham to Edmund the following Monday morning. " It is most carefully done, and must have occupied you a great many hours ; this statement is quite masterly. How long were you in writing it out ? "

" I don't remember, Sir," he replied, as a bright smile lighted up his pallid countenance. " I must confess, however, that I had to sit up all Friday night to finish it."

Mr. Walsingham's praise was never indiscriminate, and therefore Edmund valued it the more highly.

" I thought as much ; but don't do that again, Stanford, or you will break down. You are not well just now, and must not put such a strain upon your health and strength."

" Oh, I shall suffer no harm," answered Edmund.

" I am not so sure," replied Mr. Walsingham, raising his eyes off the documents he was examining, and giving him a kindly yet searching glance. " I know you have passed through a great sorrow this winter, and sorrow tests a man as nothing else does. You have tried to bear it bravely, but you

O 2

have suffered, and in the meantime you must be careful not to overtax your strength. Take a complete rest during the Easter Holidays. Go away for a change, and if you are enjoying yourself you need not return for a week or ten days. It will be all right. Only don't look at a book whilst you are away. Live in the open air. Your brain is over-worked, and needs to lie fallow for a time."

" I shall be glad to avail myself of your kindness," said Edmund, " for I feel the need of a change. But I am sure the worst is over, and that I shall be better soon."

" I am pleased to hear you say that," replied Mr. Walsingham, " for I have been anxious about you, and had no idea that you had been working so hard during the last few weeks until I began to examine these papers. But I hope, as you say, that the worst is over. By the way," he added, as Edmund was turning to leave the room, " I was with Lord Merton yesterday. I am going with him to his place in Surrey for a week, partly to attend to some business matters there, and partly for a little holiday. He was asking after you, and I told him how you were getting on."

" His lordship has always been immensely kind to me," said Edmund, standing at the half-opened door, " and I hope he will never see reason to regret it."

And having so spoken he went to his own room.

" What was that Stanford was saying about his lordship never seeing reason to regret ? " asked Mr. Gresham, who had just entered the room by another door.

" Oh, nothing important," answered Mr. Walsingham, with a slightly impatient gesture. "I had merely told him that Lord Merton was asking after him yesterday, and he replied that his lordship had always been very kind to him, and that he hoped that he would never see reason to regret it."

"I hope so too," answered Mr. Gresham, coldly. "Lord Merton, like you, has an extraordinarily high opinion of Stanford—too high in my judgment; for I am not so entirely satisfied with him, but time will prove who is right."

"I shall be greatly disappointed if it does not confirm our opinion. You know you have always had an unaccountable prejudice against Stanford."

"Not unaccountable," replied Mr. Gresham, with some asperity. "I have never been able to put aside the fact that he was seen on three separate occasions coming out of that disreputable billiard saloon, and that when I spoke to him about it he answered very curtly, and would give me no proper satisfaction. And then there was the loss of those bank-notes last summer. That business was never satisfactorily explained. I think I have reason for a certain amount of suspicion and watchfulness."

"The billiard-room affair was certainly unfortunate, and made a bad impression on your mind. But, after all, you must not forget that Stanford declared that he had gone there for no other purpose than to try to prevail on a friend to leave the place. The loss of the bank-notes was also very mysterious, but I cannot bring myself to believe that it was anything more than an accident."

"Well," replied Mr. Gresham, "I hope that you are right; but, as I said just now, time will prove."

While this conversation was going on Edmund was sitting in his room revolving in his mind how he should spend the holiday Mr. Walsingham had offered him. After a few minutes' thought he resolved that he would go to Somerthorpe. Should it be fine he would walk over and take them by surprise. Mrs. Heaviside might even half-expect him, but in any case it would be all right. The idea of a walk of thirty miles into the country was distinctly delightful. He had no thought of coming trouble ; there was nothing to indicate it. He had no suspicion that he was on the verge of the most serious crisis of his life. There was no warning to apprise him of approaching danger. The blow fell suddenly, just when he was beginning to feel a reviving breath of joy and hope.

It happened in this way.

A sum of £500 in redemption of a mortgage had been paid in the early part of the previous year to Mr. Gresham, as executor of an old friend, a Mr. Woodrow. The heir was the testator's nephew, a Captain Woodrow, and as he was away in Canada, and was not expected back for two or three years, and did not need the money, it was lodged in the bank on deposit receipt.

But on the Wednesday following the conversations just recorded, Mr. Gresham received a letter from Captain Woodrow stating that he had been ordered home quite suddenly on account of illness, and was then lying at a hotel in London, and would be glad of the £500.

Mr. Gresham had kept the deposit receipt among his own papers in his own room. But although he searched with the utmost care, he could not find it, and at last had to give it up, convinced that it had been secretly abstracted from his private safe. Considerably agitated by this discovery, he walked down to the bank, and after speaking to the managing partner about other business for a few minutes he casually remarked :

" By the way, on February 12th last year I paid £500 into the bank as the late John Woodrow's executor. His heir has returned home unexpectedly from Canada and is ill in London, and wants the money ; but I regret to say that I cannot just now lay my hands on the deposit receipt. No doubt it will be found as soon as we are able to make a more careful search. I suppose you hold the money ? "

" I can soon tell you," replied the banker, touching a bell, and asking a clerk to make the necessary inquiries.

Very soon one of the higher members of the staff entered the room, and with a serious look handed the banker a slip of paper. He glanced at it, started, turned it over, and then said deliberately :

" Why, the money was paid to Edmund Stanford on the 9th of last September. Here is the deposit receipt, backed by yourself, and with his signature below."

As he spoke he handed the paper to Mr. Gresham, who seized it in the blankest amazement, and then after a moment's careful examination, exclaimed,—

" Good heavens ! Mr. Gordon, my signature is forged."

" Are you sure ? " said the banker, rising to his feet.

"Yes, it is cleverly done; I might have passed it myself, had I not known that I had never backed that paper; but if you look at it carefully you will see that it is not my signature."

As he spoke he tossed the receipt across the table. Every circumstance that had awakened dislike and doubt of Edmund flashed back on his mind, and beneath all his astonishment and annoyance there was a certain grim satisfaction that his suspicions, which had appeared to Mr. Walsingham and others so unreasonable, were now justified.

"Yes," said Mr. Gordon as he carefully scrutinized the signature, "this certainly is not your writing."

"The daring young villain," cried Mr. Gresham, with indignation, "to forge my name; and what a fool too! why, a child might have known that discovery was inevitable."

"He must have felt sure that he would get away before it would be found out," remarked the banker. "Did you not say the money has been asked for unexpectedly?"

"Yes; Captain Woodrow was in Canada, and was not expected back for a year or two, and has returned quite suddenly. I knew nothing of his return until I heard from him this morning."

"Then Stanford has been taken by surprise. He must have been waiting for the chance of making a bigger haul before bolting."

"Do you know," observed Mr. Gresham, "I have never liked this young fellow; but Walsingham believes in him thoroughly; and so do Lord Merton and the Rector of Merton Magna, who introduced him to us four years ago. This, however, will open their eyes."

" Well, I must confess that I also am completely deceived," said Mr. Gordon. " I have spoken to him several times, and have always thought him an exceptionally fine fellow. It is most astonishing how one can be taken in. A friend of mine was lately telling me of a case in the North. A young fellow was cashier in an office, and bore an unblemished reputation. Some of the keenest and hardest-headed men in those parts had the utmost confidence in him. And yet he was detected in a regular system of forgery and embezzlement, carried on through several years, by which he robbed the firm of nearly ten thousand pounds. By the way, this may not be the only money Stanford has put his hands on. It probably explains the loss of those bank-notes. You see both happened about the same time. If I were you I would have him apprehended at once."

" I must consider how best to act," replied Mr. Gresham, cooling down, and looking more thoughtful. " The fact is, in some respects I wish he had got away ; for I have no doubt Lord Merton will make good all moneys that he has taken. But, although he will be terribly grieved and disappointed, I am sure he will be quite opposed to prosecuting Stanford."

" Nevertheless, he ought to be made an example of."

" He ought ; but I cannot do it—at least not without first consulting his lordship and my partner. Lord Merton is not merely our most important client, but my life-long friend, and he has such a regard for this young fellow that if I were to prosecute him his lordship would be greatly distressed. He and Walsingham are away together, and will not be back for a week. Things must stand over until they return ; but in the meantime I will charge Stanford with the crime."

" And then you will find he will disappear, if you give him the chance."

" Perhaps that is the best thing that could happen under the circumstances. There is, however, just one other point. I am sure that my name is forged on this paper. Is it possible that Stanford's name is forged also, and that he never took the money, but somebody else ? "

" I don't think that likely ; but I will send for the teller who paid the cash, and we will hear what he has to say about it."

" Thank you ; I should like to see him."

Very soon one of the most experienced men in the bank entered the room.

" Do you know Edmund Stanford ? " asked Mr. Gresham, addressing him.

" Yes."

" Do you happen to have any recollection of his presenting this deposit receipt, and of paying him the money ? "

The clerk glanced at the paper for a few seconds, and then replied :

" I know his signature, and am sure this is his writing, and I remember paying him the money ; if you will excuse me a minute I will give you my reason for being so certain,"

The clerk left the room, and almost immediately after returned with a book in his hand.

" I am," he said, " the treasurer for the 'Aged Clerks' Benevolent Society,' and when I paid Mr. Stanford that money I asked him for a subscription, and there is the entry in my book, 'Sept. the 9th, Mr. Stanford, ten shillings.'"

" Thank you," replied Mr. Gresham, " that will do;" and then, as soon as the clerk had retired, he added, " Stanford is guilty beyond a doubt."

Half an hour after this interview Edmund was hastily summoned to Mr. Gresham's room. As soon as he entered he was greeted with the stern command :

" Shut the door, Sir, I want to speak to you privately."

Edmund quietly obeyed, but, as he did so, he glanced with considerable astonishment at Mr. Gresham, for he could ill brook that manner of address.

" I regret to say," Mr. Gresham began in a hard and bitter tone, " that I have a most unpleasant duty to perform—viz., to charge you, Stanford, with the serious crimes of forgery and embezzlement."

" What? What did you say, Sir ? " asked Edmund, looking infinitely surprised.

" What did I say ! " retorted Mr. Gresham, angrily ; " don't think you can mislead me by putting on such a look of innocence. I am only too certain of my facts."

" Sir," replied Edmund, retaining his look of surprise, " I don't know what you are talking about : you are suffering from some horrible delusion."

And then, immediately recovering himself, the absurdity of the thing struck him, and he broke into a short laugh. "Really, Sir," he said, "this is too ridiculous ; what on earth do you mean ?"

"How dare you answer me in that way ?" said Mr. Gresham, haughtily. "I have proof that would convict you before any jury in the land ; and were it not for the regard I have for those who have befriended you all your life I would send for a policeman and have you apprehended this moment."

"Sir," answered Edmund, turning deathly pale, "am I really to understand that you charge me with forgery and embezzlement? Give me particulars of your infamous charge, so that I may meet it."

"If there was any possibility of doubt I would do so," replied Mr. Gresham, coldly ; "but there is room for none. I have no reason, however, to think that I know all ; and I am hoping that, now you are aware that you are discovered, you will have the good sense to make a full confession. In that lies your only chance of ever redeeming yourself."

"I tell you," cried Edmund, as the blood rushed back to his face, "that I have nothing to confess ; but I demand the particulars of this odious charge." His eyes were flashing fire, and his blood was boiling, almost as much at Mr. Gresham's cold and cruel tones as at the charge itself.

"You shall have them as soon as Lord Merton and Mr. Walsingham return. You know what you have done, and ultimately we shall find everything out. God only knows what your temptations have been ; but if you hold out in this stubborn way you must take the consequences."

It was in this moment of unspeakable bitterness that Edmund felt the sustaining power of the truth that had come to him so forcibly on the previous Sunday. As he stood there listening to the most odious charges that could be hurled at an honest man there came to him the words of poor Job: "Behold, my witness is in heaven, and my record on high;" and, in spite of all the misery of his position, there slid into his heart a secret peace.

Even Mr. Gresham was startled with the light that began to shine in his eyes, and the new calmness of his voice, as he said :

"And how soon may I hope to be confronted with these definite charges?"

"Lord Merton and Mr. Walsingham will be back soon after the Easter holidays," answered Mr. Gresham. "I will communicate with you as soon as I can arrange for an interview."

"And I must go away, and live with this accusation hanging over me, knowing nothing but that I am charged with infamous crimes that I never committed ? It is cruel, it is most unfair ; I never thought you could be so unjust."

"Leave the office immediately, Sir, and do not add to your sin by further falsehood," cried Mr. Gresham ; and, stepping round his desk, he flung open the door, and motioned Edmund to leave.

He bowed silently and retired.

When he was gone Mr. Gresham sat down, looking both angry and perplexed.

"Had it not been that the proof is just as clear as daylight," he said to himself, "he would have made me believe that he is innocent ; but, bah ! it was only clever acting. I am as certain that he took the money as if I had stood by and seen him do it."

An hour later Edmund found himself in one of the suburbs of the city ; how he had got there he hardly knew : what he was to do he could not tell. To go back to his lodgings and remain there all alone until Mr. Gresham sent for him was too dreadful to contemplate. He would go mad before the week was past. Where should he go ? What should he do ? Suddenly a thought struck him—he would walk over to Somerthorpe. It was a long way, and he was very late in starting, and was not on the direct road ; but never mind. He must do something, and the very idea of turning back into the city was horrible ; and so, already weary and sick at heart, and half-dazed with tormenting thoughts, he started on his long journey.

CHAPTER III.

THE evening was well advanced, the light almost gone, and everything betokened the early setting in of a black, stormy night.

The old gipsy, Elizabeth Earne, came to the door of a large covered van, that stood in a sheltered hollow of Somerthorpe Heath, and watched the gathering storm.

Although more worn with age and exposure than when we first saw her, her eyes remain bright and piercing, and the red shawl tied round her head gives a touch of colour to wrinkled and swarthy features which still retain a suggestion of their former beauty.

She looked towards the west, where the sun, shedding down fitful gleams between flying clouds, had slowly disappeared behind the dark woods. Then she turned round and watched the lowering sky that almost touched the range of sand-hills girting the coast. The sea was hidden from her view, but she heard its heavy, sullen roar, growing louder and louder with each fresh blast of the rising tempest.

All around her spread the heath, a wide, wide, sandy flat, covered with coarse grass and ling, and great clumps of furze and bramble bushes, with deep sandholes and circular pits here and there, the latter supposed to be ancient earth-dwellings of prehistoric times, among which, according to local tradition, the wraith of a woman, with wild, dishevelled hair, flitted at night, wringing her hands, and uttering bitter cries of disappointment as she vainly searched each pit for those whom she had lost.

A weird, lonely, barren land ; yet in the morning, when the sun was brightly smiling, a region of strange beauty, the furze bushes flashing into gold, the air filled with sweet scents and the droning hum of bees, the noble beech-wood, on the landward side, bursting into leaf, while along the coast the green waves of the North Sea broke into lines of snow on the yellow sands, and over all spread the wide arching sky tremulous with the songs of innumerable larks.

But about noon the wind had shifted into the north-east, and freshened into a gale, the clouds had rolled up faster and faster, and now, under a leaden sky, the heath was a desolate, melancholy waste.

The old gipsy watched until she saw her son fighting his way across the common with a load of brushes and other goods on his back, and then, with a shiver, withdrew from the bitter wind and closed the door.

"Joe is coming," she said, picking up a short pipe, and sitting down beside the fire. "He'll be here in a minute or two."

"I'm glad," replied a handsome young woman, lifting the lid of a saucepan standing on the hob. "It's a good thing he'll get in afore the rain comes on. I ha' got a nice supper for him."

The latter remark was amply confirmed by the savoury odour pervading the van.

Both women had the pure gipsy type of features, but whereas old Elizabeth Earne's beauty was gone, her daughter-in-law was just ripening into the fulness of hers.

Rachel was about three-and-twenty, above the average height, with dark hair clustering over her forehead, and black piercing eyes. She was strongly, though not clumsily, formed, and although the colour of her gown was rather loud, it was neatly and modestly made. Her sleeves were rolled up above the elbows, showing strong, well-shaped brown arms. Altogether she looked a clever, capable, attractive young woman, the very best of her class, a wife of whom Joseph Earne might very well be proud.

Presently footsteps were heard outside, and she went to the door.

"Well, Joe," she said, "I'm glad you're home. How ha' ye fared to-day?"

"Just middlin', lass; but throw us out a rope or two, and I'll make things a bit faster; there's a terrible storm blowin' up."

"Now, mother," said Joe, as he entered the van, after he had lashed everything up with extra care, "you can't say I never bring you anything. Here's a parcel of tea and a bottle of cream Mrs. Heaviside ha' sent ye with her good wishes, and she says that you and Rachel must go and see her to-morrer, if it's fine; and she said I was to give this to my bonny wife," he added, deftly throwing a bright silk handkerchief round Rachel's neck.

"Oh, that's fine!" she cried, delighted; "Mrs.

P

Heaviside knows how to please a gipsy lass ; " and she took an occasional glance at herself in the glass whilst dishing up the supper.

" Ah," said the old gipsy, " she's one o' the right sort is Mrs. Heaviside, and so is her good man : he was always kind to our people."

A pleasant enough picture did the interior of this big four-wheeled van present, when an hour or two later the horses had been attended to, and the various jobs were all done, and Joe Earne sat before a bright fire telling his wife and mother his day's adventures.

Outside the storm was raging with increasing bitterness ; but its full force was not felt in this sheltered hollow. Yet even here the wind came in gusts that shook the van violently, and caused the glass and metal goods hanging on all sides to keep up a continual jingle, and to flash from their polished surfaces the glow of the fire and the light of the lamp in a myriad dancing reflections.

As Joe's mother listened to the howling of the tempest she glanced round the van with a grim smile of contentment, thinking of the wild nights in bygone years which she had had to face without such comfortable quarters.

For, although belonging to the chief family of her tribe, she had suffered many hardships in her childhood, and even during the first years of her married life had been very poor. Her husband was thriftless, and what money he got through tinkering, and other less reputable ways, went mainly to the public-house.

One Sunday, however, while they were still young, and before Joe was born, he listened to some

Methodists who were preaching on a common, and that was the beginning of better times.

Joe followed, as we have seen, in the new ways of his father. The instincts of his race kept him to a wandering career, but he grew up a keen, sober, industrious lad, attended the Methodist chapels on the Sundays as he followed his business rounds through the Eastern Counties, and then, after his father's death, pushed forward to still greater prosperity in his way of life. Just lately he had married Rachel, a girl of pure gipsy blood, and had exchanged the single horse and cart, which until then had served their purpose, for this large and well-appointed van, and had stocked it with a variety of useful goods which would have done credit to a good-sized shop in a country town.

The old gipsy, his mother, was glad of the added comfort these changes brought, and was thankful to see her son prosperous and happy; but in many respects she still kept to her old ways. Her position among her people gave her great influence among them, and provided her with innumerable links of information; so that it would be hard to say what she could not find out.

Joe had not an implicit faith in his mother's power: but he knew that she had an almost superhuman gift of reading character, and that her ability to find out things was almost unbounded.

" Did Mrs. Heaviside say anything about the young gentleman, Mr. Stanford ? " she asked, laying her hand on her son's knee, and shaking him out of a doze into which the warmth of the fire had thrown him.

"What ? " he asked, with a yawn. " Mr. Stanford, did you say ? "

" Yes, to be sure ; you haven't forgotten him, have ye ? "

" Forgotten him, mother ! No ; I'll never forget the look of his face the night we helped him home, and the parson told him his mother was dead. I think I can see that look now : I believe it will haunt me to my dying day."

" Well, what did the good lady say about him ? How long is it since she heard from him ? "

" I don't know ; but she said that she'd been ex-pectin' to hear from him every day this week. She has a notion that he will come to spend Easter at Hall Farm. It seems that he's had a lot o' trouble. Mrs. Heaviside didn't say much about it ; but she wants to see you. I told her we only got here last night."

" I'll go and see her in the mornin', and tell her all about it."

" What can ye tell her, mother ? "

" A lot o' things ; some that ha' happened already, though she hasn't heard the truth o' them, and others that are still hid in the dark womb o' the future."

" Tell us what has happened, mother ? "

The old gipsy hesitated a moment, and then laid down her pipe and proceeded to relate the scenes on the ice at Brookside Meadows. So long as she spoke of Edmund she talked quietly and gently ; but when she began to speak of Bertram Elles her eyes dilated and grew wild and fierce. She sprang to her feet, her grey hair fell about her shoulders, and her voice became charged with tremendous excitement.

After that there was silence for some minutes, and the three sat and listened to the storm raging outside. They heard the wind screaming and moaning across the heath, the sea breaking with hollow, thunderous roar upon the beach, and the rain sweeping down upon the roof of the van. All the "spirits of the storm" seemed abroad that night, and the very air to writhe and tremble in their clutches.

At last Joe could sit still no longer. Opening the door on the sheltered side of the van, he looked out. His wife and mother came and stood beside him. The night was black, weird, gruesome, overpowering.

As the old gipsy gazed out, the look of exultation and vengeance left her. Her eyes became pitiful, tender, horror-stricken. The whole sad tragedy of human suffering, disaster, and loss appeared reflected in her deeply-marked face.

"Ah!" she cried, wringing her hands, whilst a shudder passed through her whole frame, "it is a wild, soul-summoning night. The Angel o' Death is abroad, spreadin' his wings over the cruel, man-devourin' sea, and the dark, treacherous moor. The gallant ships are driven in distress ; they mount to the heavens, they go down to the depths, they reel to and fro like drunken men. Wanderers miss their way on the dark, lonely heath, and brave men lie dead and dying, their white faces all marred and bruised."

"Hark!" cried Joe, "What is that I heard?—A minute-gun?"

They listened, straining their ears to catch the sound. A pause, and then another boom rose and rolled inland, above the roar of the gale. It could not be very far off, just across the sand-hills. And now they hear it again and again.

Who has ever heard this signal of distress rolling in from the sea on a stormy night and forgotten the sensations it produced? People who have lived all their lives on some dangerous coast, and who are acquainted with all the tragic horror of the sea, never learn to listen to it calmly. They feel as though it would be wicked to continue to sit by their comfortable firesides, or to lie still in bed and go to sleep whilst brave men are perishing. Men and women alike will hurry down to the shore, and watch and wait, even though sadly conscious of their inability to help.

"Ah!" cried Rachel, "it's a ship in distress: pity the poor sailors whose vessel strikes on these treacherous sand-banks. They are worse than rocks."

"There it is again," exclaimed Joe. "I must go. I must try and help those poor fellows."

"Oh, Joe," cried his wife, "don't go. You can do nothing. I know this coast, and with this high wind only a life-boat can reach them, and perhaps not even that. The night is pitch-dark, you will lose your way on the heath, and fall into one of those deep, dangerous pits."

Suddenly the old gipsy roused herself; for a few moments she had been standing like one in a trance; her eyes were fixed as though she saw something far away.

"Let him go," she cried, "let him go!" and Joe hastened to pull on his oil-skins. "Go," she repeated, "you are wanted. I hear someone calling ye ; I see a white face lying on the sand : I see blood. Seek and save the lost ; pluck him out o' the jaws o' death."

"Then I will go too," said Rachel, excited by the old gipsy's words, and firmly convinced that she had seen a vision. "Perhaps it is some one cast up from a wreck."

"Yes, go," exclaimed her mother-in-law. "Be an angel of pity to-night ; hasten before it is too late."

And now the prophetic frenzy was past, and the old gipsy was all practical energy and shrewdness. She lighted the lantern, fetched a flask of brandy, and then followed Joe and Rachel to the door, and raised her hands to Heaven and prayed that their steps might be directed to the place where they were needed.

The hollow in which the van stood was the remains of a disused gravel pit, partially filled up, and overgrown ; with rough, sloping sides, covered with nettles, furze, and bramble bushes. Towards the south it was open to one of the wide, straggling roads that led from the neighbouring fishing village across the heath to the highway.

In this hollow Joe and Rachel were partially protected from the fierce onslaught of the wind ; but as soon as they struck the path leading to the sea they encountered its full strength. The night was, as Rachel said, pitch-dark. The road was badly defined, without hedges or other marks to distinguish it from the heath, and but for the lantern they might have wandered all night without making any progress. But the lantern threw a faint light around them, and keeping in the direction from which could be heard, above the wind, the roaring of the sea, they bravely struggled on.

What a night in which to be out! All the elements of earth and sky and sea appeared to have broken loose, and to have met in wild, unreasoning conflict. Nothing could be distinguished but one awful hubbub of contending forces, a confused welter and shaking of all things. The wind swept like charging cavalry across the heath; it screamed and shouted among the bramble bushes, tossed and tore their long, thorny canes bare, and moaned and wailed among the ancient earth-dwellings like unhappy spirits. The rain came down in one blinding sheet, whilst above all there was the heavy, sullen roar of the breakers on the lonely beach.

What a gruesome, black night! and what useless exposure for Joe and Rachel! What good can they do? If there is a ship in distress there are fishermen and coastguards, brave, heroic men, ready at any moment to risk their lives for others. Joe and Rachel may be quite sure that they have heard the signal of distress, and are already doing all that mortal man can do, and that if any poor fellow has been thrown up on the shore he has been already found and cared for. What a piece of madness for them to expose themselves so uselessly! Far better go back and get to bed, and pray Heaven to have mercy on all poor wanderers and drowning souls.

But what is this against which Rachel has just kicked, and of which she got a momentary glimpse as it went flying into a furze bush?

"Stop, Joe; what was that?"

With one hand Rachel held up the lantern so as to see better.

P. 217.

"Where? What? I saw nothing; come along, lass."

"But I did; I struck my foot against it, and saw it; I'm sure it was a man's hat."

"Where did it go?"

"Just here; hold the light down. Ah, here it is; it looks as though some one had just lost it."

"Listen, Rachel, didn't you hear a moan? I did. There; I hear it again."

"So do I; hold the light up, Joe. See, there's a deep hole; that's where the groan came from."

"Good God! some one has fallen in. You stop here, Rachel, I'll get down."

Joe leaped into the pit. It was only a few feet deep, the bottom covered with coarse grass and bushes, with here and there a big stone lying half-buried in sand.

Suddenly he gave an exclamation.

"What is it, Joe?" asked Rachel, excitedly. "Have you found some one?"

"Yes! Here is a young man; he has fallen and struck his head against a great stone; he's bleeding, but I believe he's alive."

"Oh dear; who can it be?" cried Rachel, scrambling down beside her husband.

Joe knelt down and gently raised the prostrate form in his arms.

"You've got the flask, Rachel; pour a drop of brandy into his mouth."

With one hand Rachel held up the lantern so as to see better, and with the other she held the flask to the pale lips. The light fell upon a haggard, white face; but the eyes were closed, and there were no signs of life.

"Poor fellow!" cried Rachel; "I'm afraid he's gone; whatever could he be doing here this wild night?"

Joe had been too much occupied to carefully notice the face of the stranger whom he had so unexpectedly found. Now he gave it a keen, searching glance, and started.

"Hold the lantern, Rachel, so that I may see his face better."

Again he looked at the pallid, handsome face.

"My God! it is he, and no mistake."

"Who is it? Do you know him?"

"Why, it's young Mr. Stanford, and, thank God! he's alive; I feel his heart beating. Give him another sup of brandy."

Edmund slowly opened his eyes, and gazed into the faces of Joe and Rachel.

CHAPTER IV.

IN THE GIPSY'S VAN.

IN a few minutes Edmund was able to sit up. Rachel examined the wound on his head, which bled profusely, and hastily tied her handkerchief round it, and then noticing that he had no overcoat on she drew a shawl from her own shoulders, and wrapped it round him.

"I hope you are not much hurt, sir," said Joe, anxiously; "but you are wet to the skin, and will get your death o' cold if you stop long here. We must help you to my van, and to-morrer mornin' I'll drive ye to the Hall Farm."

Edmund, though still confused, looked up in surprise.

"Oh yes, sir," observed Joe, understanding the glance, "I know you; you're Mr. Stanford. Mrs. Heaviside told me this mornin' that she was expectin' ye. Now let Rachel and me help ye up."

They raised him gently to his feet; but he was so weak and dazed that he would have fallen again had they not supported him. Rachel again held the flask to his lips, and the brandy revived him; so that he was able with their help to clamber out of the sand-pit. And then, with Joe on one side helping him and Rachel on the other, he was almost carried across the heath.

The storm was behind them, and they were soon over.

A light streamed upon them as they turned into the hollow where the van stood, and the old gipsy was waiting at the open door.

After Joe and Rachel had left on their apparently blind errand she had wandered up and down the van in a sort of prophetic frenzy, muttering strange incoherent words to herself, a medley of charms, prayers and odd bits of Scripture; but all through her passion there ran the belief that Joe and Rachel had not gone out into the storm in vain; there was someone in trouble, someone whom it was Joe's fate to help, and the very darkness and tempest that seemed to hinder, would really further, their search, and force them to the spot where they were needed.

After a time she grew calm, and, as though she saw them bringing Edmund home, she went to the inner compartment of the van, and opened out the bed, put the blankets before the fire, and placed a kettle of water on the hob. And before it would have been thought possible for her to hear footsteps or voices she hastened and threw open the door.

" Here they come," she cried, " they have saved him ! they have brought him out o' darkness and the shadow o' death."

" Mother," said Joe, " it's Mr. Stanford; we found him on the heath ; he'd fallen into a pit."

"Wonderful ! Wonderful ! " exclaimed the old gipsy ; " but did I not tell ye that ye were wanted ? "

Joe and Rachel lifted Edmund into the van, and placed him in a chair by the fire, and when old Elizabeth Earne gazed into his white face, and saw that it really was Edmund Stanford, ill, bleeding, and suffering from exposure and pain, she raised her clasped hands and prayed that his life might be spared.

Edmund opened his eyes, and gazed with astonishment at the gipsy, who seemed so strangely mixed up with his life, and then he turned to his deliverers, and said feebly,—

"You have saved my life ; I should have perished had you not found me."

"Your good father saved Joe's life," replied the old gipsy, "and as long as we live, if we can serve you we will."

"Mother," said Rachel, "Mr. Stanford is wet through; he's shivering with cold. Do you and Joe help him to remove his wet clothes, and get to bed, and I'll make the kettle boil."

Edmund attempted to rise, but sank back into the chair again and fainted away. When he came round he found himself lying in a little bed in an inner room of the van, wrapped up in warm, dry blankets, and the old gipsy bending over him, putting a fresh bandage round his head.

"Ah !" she was muttering to herself, "he's had a lot o' trouble, but it'll all come right in the end. Winter will change to spring, and sorrow will turn to joy."

She left him for a moment, and then returned, stirring up a smoking cup, over which she seemed to be repeating a charm.

"Drink this," she said, holding the cup to his lips with one hand, and with the other gently raising his head. "It'll do ye a lot o' good, comfort ye, and send ye to sleep."

Edmund drank it, and almost immediately sank into deep slumber.

When he again opened his eyes the light had begun to steal through the little window of the compartment where he lay. For some minutes he felt confused, and tried in vain to collect his thoughts, and recall where he was. In the dim twilight he could distinguish nothing, and all was silent save the twittering of a bird outside. He felt very ill. A dull, weary pain caused him to put his hand to his head and touch the bandage, and then the events of the previous day and night flashed back on his memory, and filled him with a sinking sense of misery.

He had left Mr. Gresham's room almost mad with shame, vexation, and perplexity. He had been suspected : nay, deliberately and vehemently charged with dishonesty. The very thought brought a burning flush of shame to his face, and he hurried away anxious only to avoid everyone, and reach a solitary spot where he could grapple with the hateful and tormenting thoughts that surged within him.

Instinctively he turned into the nearest exit from the old city, and had got beyond the long line of villas, and was passing into the open country, before it occurred to him to ask himself where he was going, or what he proposed to do.

Then came the sudden resolve to walk over to Somerthorpe, and he struck into a cross lane, by which he knew that he would be able to reach the high road, at a point some distance from the city.

As he walked swiftly forward the horror and ignominy of his position were more than he knew how to bear. Yet there was the hateful fact ; he could not get away from it.   Mr. Gresham, though hasty, haughty, overbearing, was a high-minded man, with an essentially legal habit of looking at things, and he must have reasons for believing him guilty, so strong and convincing as to leave no doubt upon his mind, or he would not have made these horrible charges.

What could it all mean? What could be the explanation of the mystery ? Oh, had Mr. Gresham only told him what was wrong, and given him the opportunity of meeting his indictment.

But then came a more paralysing thought. What if he should be unable to clear himself ? He had never been able to explain the loss of the £20. No doubt Mr. Gresham believed that he had stolen the money, and the misery of it was that he could not prove that he had not. What if he were again involved in some strange set of circumstances which would, at least, leave his integrity in doubt, if anyone was willing to question it ? Such things had happened before. Innocent men had been suspected of crimes they never committed ; bad men had escaped justice by throwing suspicion on others, and the truth had only been discovered when it was too late. What if it should be so with him ?

The thought tortured him almost beyond endurance, and in his extreme mental excitement he hastened on so rapidly that before long he was compelled to pause.

He had come to a bridge, beneath which flowed a broad, deep stream, and being too exhausted to go further without resting he descended

to a grassy bank, and sat down by the river-
side.

It was the darkest hour he had ever passed through ;
the most bitter cup he had ever been called to drink.
Again and again he recalled Mr. Gresham's cruel
words ; again and again the burning flush of shame
rose to his face. His spirit sank into deeper and
deeper gloom ; God seemed to hide His face ; and all
his old doubts of the moral order of the world returned
with new force.

" Where are the signs of Immortal Love?" he sadly
asked himself. " What proof is there of reasonable
purpose, of presiding wisdom in the universe ? "

He smiled bitterly as he thought of Browning's
words :—

> " God's in His heaven ;
> All's right with the world."

"Instead of Reason and Love governing the world,"
he said, mournfully to himself, " is it not rather the
scene of inextricable moral confusion, the playground
of blind accident and chance, or the sport of a mocking fate, which throws some to the top and others to
the bottom, utterly regardless of their deserts, which
pets and feasts the villain and curses and starves the
saint, which crowns the tyrant and crucifies the
Christ ? "

As he sat by the side of the deep, calm-flow-
ing river, tortured by such questions, he was fast
sinking into a state of morbid depression that borders
on insanity. His brain had been overwrought for
months, and his body reduced and weakened with
neglect and sorrow. He had been ill for weeks,
although he had paid no attention to it.

And now this terrible charge, coming so unexpectedly, had thrown him down into a depth of darkness and bewildered thought, so profound, that the one security against his committing some desperate deed was the hope, that the doing of right and resisting of evil had become with him a principle and a habit so strong and commanding, that the temptation to do a rash and sinful act would be immediately repelled by an instinctive and unreasoning impulse.

The sky had become overcast, but he did not notice it. A cold, chilly wind moaned among the willows that fringed the river's bank, but he was too much absorbed with his own misery to heed it.

" What is life worth to you now ? " a voice seemed to say in his ear. " How will you face the world with this infamous charge resting on you ? Would it not be better to die ? to lie in the quiet grave, where the wicked cease from troubling and the weary are at rest ? "

The river flowed at his feet, calm and deep, the very emblem of rest and peace.

And then there appeared to come a whisper, soft, subtle, alluring, from the little wavelets glancing against the bank.

" Rest is here, peace is here," they seemed to gently murmur ; and for one brief moment he bent over, and looked and listened, just for a single second, to realize what it meant, and then, with a groan, he sprang to his feet, and hurried away, crying, " No, no ; not that way ; not so."

He regained the road and pressed towards Somerthorpe. The whispering voice was gone, and in its place he heard his mother's voice, singing, as he

Q

had so often heard her sing, the hymn she loved best :

> " Lead, kindly Light, amid the encircling gloom,
> Lead Thou me on."

He walked on wearily and painfully, while the black clouds gathered overhead. The wind rose, and, at last, the storm broke on him in all its fury. Before he had reached Somerthorpe Heath it was pitch-dark, the rain was coming down in torrents, and the wind was blowing a hurricane. There was no house or shelter that he could see anywhere. He had left the office without an overcoat, and was soon wet to the skin. He grew dizzy, missed his way, stumbled on blindly, recklessly, completely worn out in body and mind. Then came a sudden fall, a sharp blow, and he lost consciousness, and knew nothing until Joe and Rachel found him and brought him round.

And now all his misery returned upon him again as he opened his eyes and recalled where he was.

" Ah ! " he murmured, " would it not have been better if they had not found me ? A few hours in that pit would have finished me, and there would, before now, have been an end to this weary struggle, and in course of time, no doubt, the truth would have been discovered."

He had not been awake long before the door was quietly opened, and the old gipsy glanced in. Seeing that he was not sleeping, she came forward.

" How have you slept ? " she asked, pushing back the window curtain, and letting down a panel in the side of the van. She bent over him, and scanned his face with keen searching eyes.

" I have had bad dreams ; I seem to have been in trouble all night, and my head is full of pain."

" Ah, I can see ; you have got a bad shaking."

" Yes."

" Rachel is making ye a cup o' tea ; here she comes with it."

Edmund looked up, gratefully, as she entered.

" You are very kind," he said, feebly. " I hope you did not take any harm by last night's exposure. You drew off your shawl and put it on me ; I was too weak to resist, but you should not have done that."

" Oh no," she replied ; " I am used to being out in all weathers."

Her voice was pitiful, for she saw the look of pain and trouble in his face.

" Let me help you to sit up," she said gently. " The tea will do you good, and I have made you a nice bit of toast, which you must try and eat."

" I was thinking, when you came in," remarked Edmund, wearily, to the old gipsy, as she took the empty cup from him, " that it would have been as well if I had remained where I fell last night, and never got up again alive. I see nothing before me but a world of trouble and sorrow."

" The darkest hour is just before the dawn," she replied eagerly. " See, look out o' the window. The black night is gone, the sun is touching the hills with gold, the heath is gay with flowers, the birds are singing in every bush. Don't be discouraged, Master Stanford ; darkness will not last for ever. Be patient and wait."

" That is what you said long ago," he answered,

slowly. "What made you deliver that strange prophecy?"

"Because I knew it was true, and you will see it by-and-by. I am only an old gipsy, but years and years ago I learned that gain comes through loss, and joy through pain.

"When I was only a little lass, wanderin' about with my people, more than seventy years ago, I often used to sit on the heath all day alone watchin' the sky, and the birds, and the sea; and I used to lie awake all night listenin' to the wind, and peepin' out o' the tent at the stars.

"And when I grew older I watched men and women, and after a lot o' pain and sorrow I learned to read the Bible, and so I came to be sure of a good many things.

"I saw that sorrow and pain and death are only tools in the hands o' the Almighty, and that when He has done His work there will be no more need o' them. Isn't that what the good Book means when it says that He holds the keys o' Hell and Death? When it says that He must reign till He hath put all enemies under His feet? It means that He has taken hold o' the worst things and conquered them all, and holds the mastery over them, and compels them to do His work, and serve His purpose, and when His work is finished they will be cast aside like worn-out tools, and they will be thrown into the lake o' fire, and be destroyed for ever."

Weak and ill as Edmund was he listened with intense interest to the old gipsy's words. While she was speaking her face was full of power, her eyes grew larger and brighter, and her whole countenance suggested remarkable intellectual force. When she had finished he said,—

" Then you believe that anguish and loss are working for good ? "

" To be sure. Not good in themselves, not part o' God's order, but working good in us. That is what I ha' learned. I ha' watched the lives o' men and women for threescore years and ten, and I ha' seen that those who ha' suffered nothin' ha' learned nothin', and that the serenest faces bear also the traces o' sorrow. There is no other path to the secret o' life."

" Well," said Edmund, "you declare a wonderful gospel."

She watched him with keen eyes, and then said, gently,—

" Ha' patience, and things will come all right before long. Joe has gone to Hall Farm to let them know how he and Rachel found you last night. I expect Mr. Heaviside will be here for you very soon. And here," she added, taking a bit of crumpled paper out of a little black book, " is a letter you had better keep ; it may be useful some day. That bad man Bertram Elles dropped it in my tent on Brookside Meadows, the night of the carnival. I ha' been keeping it for you. And now I will go and brush your clothes and get them ready for you to put on. They are quite dry now."

And so saying she handed him the letter, and went into the other apartment of the van.

Edmund read the letter with surprise and indignation. In a moment it flashed upon him that here was a clue to the mysteries that overhung his life.

He lay back and tried to think the matter out. He felt sure that in some way Bertram Elles was connected with these infamous charges of forgery and embezzlement. He had robbed the firm, but contrived to implicate him. How had it been done? The more, however, he tried to think clearly the more confused he became. The sudden shock of discovery had sent the blood rushing to his brain, and had caused a fresh outbreak of pain. He moaned aloud in agony.

Just then the old gipsy returned with his clothes. He lay back in great distress. With one hand he clasped his head, with the other the letter.

"You are not so well," she said, hastening to his side.

"My head is worse," he answered. "Everything is going round and round."

"Oh!" she cried, "I am sorry I gave you that letter to read. It has upset you."

"It is a very important letter," he replied, with an effort. "Put it in my pocket-book." And then he moaned again, "Oh, my head, my head!"

"You must not try to get up," she replied. "Lie still, and I will give you something that will send you to sleep again ; and Joe shall put the horses into the van, and drive you to Hall Farm, and when we get there we will carry you to your bed in the blankets."

When Mr. Heaviside arrived he found Edmund in a dull, heavy sleep or stupor.

CHAPTER V.

IN PROFUNDIS.

"STRANGE! strange!" muttered Mr. Heaviside to himself as, some three hours later, he walked up and down his dining-room in great perplexity. "Whatever set the lad to come off like that? I could ha' driven in for him, or he might ha' come by the coach to St. Peter's. And what a mad thing to try to cross the heath in such a storm, and the night as black as pitch! I wouldn't ha' done it myself; no, not for a hundred pounds. It's a wonder he wasn't killed, and he would ha' bin but for those gipsies. How strange things do happen! If that ship, whose crew the coastguards saved last night, hadn't been in distress, the gipsies wouldn't ha' been out, and he would ha' died o' cold and exposure. And he was without an overcoat or anything. He must ha' come off quite unexpectedly. I can't understand it. I wonder whether the loss of that girl has so upset him that he's not altogether right in his head just now? Maybe that is it; I know how near I came to losing my reason when poor Mary died. Evidently he has suffered a lot; his whole system is down. It will be all he will be able to do to pull through; and it's an awful pity, he was such a

splendid young feller, and would ha' been certain
to ha' made his mark in the world."

Further reflections were cut short by a movement
on the stairs. Mr. Heaviside hastened to the door.

"Well, doctor, how ha' you left him?" he asked,
eagerly.

"He's dozing now; he was a long time coming
round, and then he was only half-conscious. But he
knew where he was, and recognized Mrs. Heaviside,
and looked round the room as though he was glad to
be here."

"Did he say anything? Did he explain why he
came off in such a queer way?"

"All he said was: 'There's trouble at the office.
I'll tell you all about it by-and-by; I shall go back
in a week.' And then he became delirious, and
talked wildly and incoherently about a great storm
in his head. He's in a kind of dull stupor just
now."

"Do you think his head is hurt much? Is the
brain injured?"

"I can't say anything definite yet. The external
wound is slight, and should soon heal; but the brain
may have suffered. So far, he reminds me of a case
I had many years ago. A son of Squire Waring fell
down a clay pit and broke his collar-bone. His head
was also bruised a little, but to all appearances it was
nothing serious. Things went on all right for several
days; then he suddenly became quite delirious, and
passed from that into a comatose state, and lay for
three months at death's door, utterly unconscious. I
never thought he would rally; but he did, and completely recovered. I don't like your young friend's

look. He's a strong, well-built fellow, and has youth on his side ; but he seems as though he has suffered a good deal lately, and has been working too hard. I am going to send off at once for a trained nurse ; for he is certainly seriously ill. I shall be back again soon, and in the meantime he must be kept absolutely quiet. Much will depend on how he gets through the next few days."

Having said this the doctor left.

After a short time Edmund awakened, but was more confused than before. He did not clearly understand where he was, and still complained that a fearful storm was raging in his head. The doctor did what he could to relieve the pain, but with little success. Through that day, and the following, which was Good Friday, he grew worse, slept less and less, and when awake became more and more restless and incoherent in his talk. On the Saturday he seemed to rally slightly, and there was a glimmer of hope that the more serious symptoms were disappearing ; but he became worse during the night, and the next day there was a complete collapse.

It was a lovely day, an ideal Easter Sunday, and all nature seemed joining with man in celebrating the great victory over woe and death. The warm April sun shed a glory over land and sea, and sent even a soft glow through the window-blinds into the silent and deeply-shaded chamber where Edmund lay.

Mrs. Heaviside was keeping watch by his side. She noticed that a more deathly pallor had over-spread his face. His eyes were closed, and but for a slight and scarcely perceptible twitching about the lips and nostrils there was hardly a sign of life.

For a time she sat silently watching him. In the great stillness every sound without reached her ears. A blackbird was pouring forth his mellow notes in the garden ; from the more distant fields came the happy songs of larks ; whilst from across still wider spaces there gently floated into the room the rich, liquid notes of church bells, soft, ethereal, like the soul of all music, telling of the past, the distant, the dead.

Unconsciously her mind went back through the bygone years to the time when Edmund was a little child, and his father and mother were living, and no dark shadow had fallen on his path. She recalled how he used to look and talk then, and many of his childish sayings and questions came back to her.

One scene especially, which she had not thought of for many years, now flashed on her memory, and seemed strangely suggestive. He had gone with her into a cottage at Merton Magna, and stood silently gazing on a picture of Grace Darling saving some shipwrecked sailors. Then he turned and, with a look of trouble in his face, asked : "Does God send the storms ? " and when she replied that He did, the troubled look deepened, and he said : "But my mamma says that everything God sends is good."

As Mrs. Heaviside thought of these things her eyes filled with tears. She loved Edmund very tenderly, and it was with something approaching a mother's anguish she now bent over his wasted features, and saw that the shadow of death had begun to fall upon them.

"Ah," she mused, "he was always so good and thoughtful, always trying to understand these things ;

but they seem beyond our fathoming. At the bottom of half our sorrow lies the mystery of God's ways. Now we see through a glass darkly; but he's drawing near to where the veil is removed, and they see face to face, and know even as they are known."

The tears chased each other freely down her cheeks, and a choking sob rose to her throat. "I see it all now," she cried to herself. "The old gipsy said that loss would bring gain, and she was right, for 'to die is gain.' She said his joy would come through pain, and through much tribulation he is entering into the Kingdom of Heaven."

In her distress she fell on her knees and prayed: "O Father, spare his young life, and make his future noble and happy; but not my will, Thine be done."

Hardly had these words escaped from her lips when Edmund gave a sudden movement, which caused her to rise quickly. He tossed up his arms and moaned, as if in great anguish. Then the pain seemed gone; for he smiled and lay still.

Mrs. Heaviside seated herself near him, and took up her Bible. Her eyes lighted on the magnificent words beginning with: "The Spirit itself beareth witness with our spirit, that we are the children of God." She had read the words: "If so be that we suffer with Him, that we may be also glorified together," when another movement caused her to glance up. But it passed off, and again Edmund became quiet. She read on: "For I reckon that the sufferings of this present time are not worthy to be compared with the glory which shall be revealed in us." She lingered over the words, trying to take in their grand meaning, and had reached the end of the verse : " For we know that all things work together for good to them that love God," when Edmund gave a violent start, and in a moment she was standing by his side. He was wide awake, and staring wildly into a dark corner of the room.

" Away!" he cried, in a voice of fierce and proud disdain ; and springing up demanded : "how dare you come here ? "

" Dear Edmund," said Mrs. Heaviside, laying her hand gently, but firmly, on his uplifted arm, " there is no one here except me. You will do yourself harm ; let me help you to lie down again."

" Do you not see him ? " he asked, excitedly. " Away ! Get you hence, you liar, slanderer, deceiver. There," he whispered, as he fell back exhausted, " he's gone now."

" No one shall come near you that does not love you," said Mr. Heaviside, advancing to the bedside. He had heard Edmund's loud and angry tones, and had hastened to the room. " You have had a bad dream," he added, as he clasped his hand.

" No, no, it was not a dream," cried Edmund, with a wild look in his eyes. " It was that deceiver ; and now he's gone to slander me. I must go after him ; I must face him." As he spoke he tried to get out of bed, and it required all the strength of his friends to hold him back.

" Let me go," he cried, piteously, "do let me go ! I must face my accuser."

" Not just now, dear Edmund," answered Mrs.

Heaviside, soothingly. "As soon as you are better you shall go; but no one accuses you of anything."

"Yes, they do," answered Edmund. "They charge me with horrible things, infamous things." And then the wild look of delirium returned, and he said proudly: "But I will face them; I will meet my accusers before the great white throne, and Jesus will plead my cause. He knows that I am not guilty. You believe me, don't you?"

"Oh yes," replied Mrs. Heaviside, "everybody believes in you."

"No, no, not now," he said, in a tone of infinite sadness. "You don't know; you don't understand; but it will all come right some day, I know it will."

For a few moments he lay still, and seemed satisfied with this last thought. "The Lord is on my side," he murmured, "I will not fear. What can man do unto me?"

But the next minute the madness returned,—

"There," he cried, in wild excitement, "there he is again! Put him out; he shall not come here."

With one sudden and vehement effort he flung both Mr. and Mrs. Heaviside from him, and, before they could recover themselves, sprang out of bed.

He was able to make two or three steps forward, and raise his hand as if about to strike, then he gave a deep groan, swayed on one side, and fell apparently dead into the farmer's arms.

.   .   .   .   .   .

On the morning of the day on which Mr. Walsingham had arranged to return to business he descended as usual to breakfast, but was surprised to see Lord

Merton already down, and walking about the room in great excitement.

" I am glad you have come," he exclaimed ; " here is strange news from Gresham ; but I can't believe it. Read this letter and tell me, for goodness' sake, what you think of it."

He thrust the letter into Mr. Walsingham's hand, and turned to the window.

An expression of blankest amazement slowly overspread the lawyer's face, as he proceeded to read his partner's account of what had occurred in relation to Edmund and the deposit receipt.

" Had I followed my own sense of what was the strictly right course to take," Mr. Gresham wrote in conclusion, " I should have given Stanford in charge there and then. But considering the great interest you have always taken in him I hesitated to do that. Although I was exceedingly grieved and angry at the violent and determined way in which he protested his innocence, I urged him to consider his position. I said that he must leave the office immediately, but that I would send for him as soon as you and Mr. Walsingham returned. I told him that if he made a full confession of his guilt, and showed himself truly penitent, and gave satisfactory assurances for the future, he would not be so severely dealt with as he deserved. But, I regret to say, that he only took advantage of my leniency to disappear altogether, and has not been heard of since."

" Well," said Lord Merton, as Mr. Walsingham laid down the letter, " of course it's all a wretched blunder ? "

" It's a most extraordinary story. I would no more

think of suspecting Stanford of forgery and embezzlement than my own son. I wonder whether Gresham
has thrown any further light on it in his communication to me?"

Mr. Walsingham picked up his letters, and tore
open the one from his partner and glanced hastily
through it.

"No! he only adds that he thought it would
be a pity to spoil my Easter holiday by sending such
unpleasant news, and so delayed writing until it was
practically over."

"I am confident," said Lord Merton, "that
Stanford is innocent. There's some ugly secret in
this affair that has yet to be discovered. The very
idea is absurd. I should laugh at it, had it not already
assumed such a serious aspect. I know the lad, and
I knew his father, and the thing is impossible. His
disappearance is the strange thing. Good heavens!
I hope that he has come to no harm."

"I am not so surprised at his disappearance," remarked Mr. Walsingham. "He was not well, and I
told him that he might go away for a week or ten days.
He will have repudiated the charge vehemently, and
then, when he found that he could make no impression
on Gresham, will have gone away, intending to return
as soon as he could meet us. And yet, if that theory
is correct, I am amazed that he has not written."

"It's no use speculating," said Lord Merton. "I will
return with you to-day, and I have no doubt he will
be there to meet us, and the affair will be cleared
up."

They arrived at Caistor too late that night to do
anything, but the next morning they repaired to Friars'

Court, and at once began to investigate the matter with Mr. Gresham.

That gentleman went into every detail with lawyer-like clearness and precision: he produced the deposit receipt, and it was examined. They drove to the bank and interviewed Mr. Gordon and the clerk who paid the money. A special messenger was despatched to Edmund's lodgings, but he returned to say that nothing had been heard of him.

Lord Merton and Mr. Walsingham were completely baffled; they refused to believe that Edmund was guilty, and yet they saw that the case against him was quite unassailable. They could urge nothing on the other side but an instinctive faith in him. They were beginning to discuss what should be done to trace him, when a clerk entered, and, addressing Mr. Walsingham, said:

"You are wanted, sir: a gentleman has driven up, and says he wants to see you very particularly."

"Ask him his business."

"He says that he has important news of Mr. Stanford."

"Bring him in at once," said Lord Merton.

The next minute Mr. Heaviside entered the room, with an unusually grave look on his great, honest face.

"Mr. Heaviside of Somerthorpe!" cried Lord Merton, recognising him as a well-known countyman. "Is it really you that brings us news of young Stanford?"

"Ay," said the farmer, "and I'm glad to meet your lordship, although I bring news that I know will grieve ye."

"Why? What is the matter with Stanford? Where is he?"

"He's at Somerthorpe, my lord, and he's dyin'."

"Dying? No, surely not."

"I fear it is only too true," replied Mr. Heaviside. And then he proceeded to relate the whole story of Edmund being found on the heath by the gipsies, and brought the next day to Hall Farm, and of his subsequent illness.

"And he is now quite unconscious?" asked Mr. Walsingham.

"Yes," answered Mr. Heaviside; "he is lyin' just as if he were already dead; but the saddest thing about it is that a brave and honest young feller like that should die under the delusion that he is accused of doin' something wrong. It was heart-breakin' to see his look when he said: 'God knows that I'm not guilty; you believe in me, don't you?' And, when my good wife told him that everybody believed in him, he shook his head and said: 'No, not now, but some day they will.' I would give anything for him to know that it is all a delusion."

"This is a very sad affair indeed," said Mr. Gresham; "but Mr. Stanford was not the victim of a strange delusion when he spoke as he did. You are not alone in believing in his honesty; nevertheless there are serious charges against him, which I fear are only too true."

"I don't believe they are true," said Mr. Heaviside, indignantly; "and I never will believe it unless I hear Edmund Stanford confess it with his own lips, and he'll never do that."

"Does the doctor hold out no hope?" asked Lord Merton.

"Very little, my lord."

R

"Will you drive over to Somerthorpe with me to-morrow and see the poor lad?" he asked, addressing Mr. Walsingham.

"Certainly."

Mr. Walsingham spent the afternoon in searching through all letters and papers in Edmund's desk ; in the evening he drove round to Mrs. Muriel's, and told her what news they had received of him, and then asked to be shown into his room in order to look for some papers that were required.   In Edmund's interest he considered himself justified in examining his books and letters, but could find nothing that compromised him in the slightest degree. Everything indicated that his private life was all that it ought to be—one of strict purity and integrity.   Mr. Walsingham went home more convinced than ever that Edmund was innocent.

The next day he and Lord Merton drove over to Somerthorpe. They saw Edmund, and the sight deeply touched them. He lay absolutely still, his hands clasped across his breast. His eyes were closed and sunken, with dark rings beneath them, and his features, thin and wasted beyond what would have been thought possible in so short a time, were white as alabaster. There was on them a look of perplexity and sorrow, as though he had passed into unconsciousness under the burden of life's mystery. The slightest movement of the pulse, and heaving of the chest, were the only indications of life.

They looked long and earnestly at him, and then with a sad and silent farewell turned to leave the room.

Mrs. Heaviside, who was now outwardly calm went with them to the door.

" I suppose," said Mr. Walsingham, " that you found no papers about Mr. Stanford's person, nothing that would throw light on this painful mystery ? "

"Nothing, except his pocket-book. You can examine it if you wish. It has never been opened since he came here."

" As I would not leave a stone unturned, I will glance through it, and then leave it with your husband."

Mrs. Heaviside brought the pocket-book, and they descended to the dining-room.

" I am going to look through this book belonging to young Stanford," said Mr. Walsingham to the farmer. " One never knows where a clue may turn up."

As he opened the book a crumpled letter slipped out and fell on the floor. Lord Merton observed it, and stooped and picked it up. He opened it, and read :—

" I have called to see you about business. I need go into no details, but I warn you that I will not any longer trust your assurance of a speedy marriage with a rich young lady. Unless you pay up I will apply to those who will give me my money ; but the disclosures I shall make will ruin you."

Twice Lord Merton read it through before he could believe his own eyes. Then he dropped the letter and said,—

" Alas ! alas ! after all it is true : Stanford took the money."

BOOK V.

"And we know that all things work together for good to them that love God."

> "The year's at the spring,
> And day's at the morn;
> Morning's at seven;
> The hill-side's dew-pearled;
> The lark's on the wing;
> The snail's on the thorn;
> God's in His heaven—
> All's right with the world!"

CHAPTER I.

HOME AGAIN.

"WHAT a glorious morning for the first of May!" said Mr. Sedgewick to himself, as he stepped outside the door, and gazed on the Rectory garden. His eyes filled with gladness as he surveyed the scene. "Home, sweet Home," he murmured, "and I don't think I ever saw it more beautiful."

It was the spot on earth he loved best, and this was his first view of it for nearly four years. They had arrived the night before in the rain and growing dusk, and so had seen nothing then. But this morning Nature was in her happiest mood.

The sky was high, cloudless and intensely blue ; a gentle breeze stirred among the bursting foliage of the trees ; the air was full of song, and the gardens, in the brilliant sunshine, looked lovely.

At the Rector's feet some beds of tulips and hyacinths displayed a perfect blaze of colour ; beyond them the lawn spread out a fresh, bright carpet of green ; and further still stood the stately elms, breaking into leaf, between which could be caught glimpses of the brimming river sweeping by, a myriad dancing wavelets sparkling on its broad bosom. On his right a chestnut reared its vast dome, the pink and white blossoms swaying bravely among the rustling foliage, like toy ships on a tossing sea of green ; whilst the shrubbery on his left was fringed with long lines of spring flowers that nodded and waved their white and gold heads gaily in the morning breeze.

Everywhere there was the throb and excitement of early summer, an indefinable suggestion of abounding life, joy, rapture, which seemed to find, at last, its most perfect expression in a voice which suddenly broke into song in a corner of the garden hidden from the Rector's view.

" Oh ! merry goes the time when the heart is young,
  There's nought too high to climb when the heart is young ;
      A spirit of delight
      Scatters roses in her flight,
  And there's magic in the night when the heart is young."

It was a sweet mezzo-soprano voice, and the Rector walked across the lawn, and found his daughter seated upon a swing that used to be one of the delights of her childhood.

"Good-morning, papa; you are just in time to give me a swing," cried Evelyn, stopping her song, and holding up a face, glowing with life and happiness, for a kiss.

"Indeed," said the Rector, as, with a grim smile, he started her off; "don't you think a substantial young lady of your age should put away childish things?"

"Not while she has such a delightful dad to teach her the secret of perpetual youth," laughed Evelyn, at the same time throwing herself back, and doing her utmost to swing higher. "But higher, papa, I want to touch the branch of that elm with my toe."

"Then I must call one of the gardeners to help me."

"But you used to send me as high as that."

"Yes, but I'm getting older, and you are a great deal heavier."

"Just once more and I shall manage it," cried Evelyn, urging the swing upwards herself. "There, I have done it, and knocked off a leaf. That will do. Let me die, and then I'll give you a swing."

"Thank you," answered the Rector, wiping his forehead, "I prefer to go to breakfast; there's the bell ringing."

"How is the dear little mater?" asked Evelyn, as she skipped along gaily by his side.

"Nearly as happy as her madcap daughter, I believe, only in a quieter way. She has stood the journey home better than I expected, and has slept well, and to all appearances so have you."

"Oh yes, as sound as the 'Sleeping Beauty,' till Phœbus Apollo roused me. Then I lay in a dreamy half-awake state of bliss for a long time listening to the birds, and unspeakably happy to think that we were really back again at dear old Merton Magna."

And again she broke into song:

"Oh! sparkling are the skies when the heart is young,
There's bliss in beauty's eyes when the heart is young;
  The golden break of day
  Brings gladness in its ray,
And ev'ry month is May when the heart is young."

"It is delightful to be home again, is it not?"

"Delightful! There's no word strong enough to express it. It is like a rich perfume distilled from a million rare flowers: it suggests everything that is sweet and beautiful."

"Would it not be better to compare it to a rich wine, apt to get into a girl's head, and make her a little extravagant in her speech?" asked the Rector, humorously, as he seated himself at the breakfast table. "However, it's a weakness that leans to virtue's side. May the thought of home, my dear, always make you equally happy. By the way, speaking of your mother, she will not be able to go out this afternoon; so, as soon as she is up, I am going to take her for a drive. Will you go with us?"

"If you don't mind, dad, I would rather make some calls in the village. I want to see Mary Bell —I mean Mrs. Hallam now—I hear that she has got a dear little baby boy, just a fortnight old. And then I should like to run into the school and speak to Miss Woodburn, the new mistress, who, I am told, has captivated everybody by her pleasant, lady-like ways. After that I would return home by the common, and visit poor old John Rickwood. He is quite confined to bed now, and it is a marvel to everyone how he survived last winter."

" Bless me, Evelyn, you know all the gossip of the parish already ; but you can go into the village after lunch."

" Not very well ; I want to put my books and papers in order to-day. I feel, however, too excited for that this morning, and then Edmund may ride over this afternoon."

" I hardly think so," replied the Rector, somewhat gravely. " There's no letter from him this morning, and I was surprised that he was not at the railway station at Caistor last night. I sent him a telegram before leaving London to say when we should arrive."

" Oh, I was not aware of that," said Evelyn, turning rather pale.

" No ; I hoped he would be there to give both you and your mother a pleasant surprise."

" Where did you send the telegram to, papa ? "

" To Mrs. Muriel's ; I thought he would be certain to get it there. He may have been out, of course ; but in that case I wonder he did not write."

" I am afraid he is ill," replied Evelyn, anxiously.

" I know no reason for thinking that," said the Rector, seriously ; " but I have had a fear for some months—which I never expressed before, even to your mother—that Edmund Stanford is, for some un-accountable reason, drifting from us. We have heard very little from him since he sent word of his engage-

ment to Julia. Doubtless while she was living he
was engrossed with her ; but afterwards I was hoping
the old familiar correspondence would be renewed.
However, we have been away a long time, and must
not be surprised to find changes on our return."

"I feel sure that you are wrong, papa, and that he
is ill."

"What can make you think that, my pet?" asked
the Rector, kindly, for he saw that his daughter was
unusually disturbed.

"I will tell you ; I should have done so before,
only I had no opportunity without mamma hearing,
and I was anxious not to alarm her. You know that
while you were resting at the St. Pancras Station
Hotel, waiting for our train, I went out to Kensington
to see Kate?"

"Yes."

"As I told you, neither she nor Frank was at
home ; but I saw that dear old lady, Miss Ray, and
although she spoke with reserve I learned enough
about Edmund and Julia to make his conduct quite
intelligible. Miss Ray saw him about three weeks
ago, and says that he looked dreadfully ill. Since
then she had heard nothing, and was sure something
was wrong. I then thought her fears were very likely
groundless ; but now you confirm them."

"Dear me ; did she say what was the matter with
him?"

"Oh, there has been such a lot of trouble ; not
merely the shock of poor Julia's sudden death, but
before that. Miss Ray says that they never had
more than one week of real happiness together."

"Indeed! how was that?"

"Bertram Elles caused great mischief. While Julia was in London he met her frequently, and insinuated all sorts of wrong things about Edmund, and unfortunately she believed them. And then he went down to Caistor and tried to win her from Edmund, and Miss Ray says that it was all for her money. She hints at some very ugly things in his life."

" Ah, I have sometimes condemned myself that I did not make more inquiries into his character before I urged Edmund to be friendly with him. I never think of that long walk he had with you without a shudder."

" Miss Ray blames him entirely for poor Julia's death ; for Edmund she has unbounded admiration. She spoke of the goodness and nobility of his character, and of how much he had suffered, and of his beautiful affection for Julia. She says that he has passed through great darkness and perplexity, and so that, no doubt, accounts for his comparative silence. And now I am very much afraid that she is correct in thinking him seriously ill."

The Rector ate his breakfast in silence for a minute or two, and then he said :

"What you have told me is quite consistent with Edmund's character. These troubles will have thrown him into a state of melancholy, and he will have been too unhappy to write. But I don't think it likely that he has broken down. He has a splendid constitution, and is too brave to allow grief to utterly prostrate him."

" That was my feeling when Miss Ray was telling me of her fears. Hence I did not think so much of it until you mentioned about the telegram."

"But, after all," said the Rector, brightly, "we have at present no serious grounds for anxiety. Edmund may have been out when my telegram arrived, and got home too late to write. In that case, you may depend upon it, he will be over this afternoon. If he cannot come before, he will ride over as soon as the office closes, and be here in time for dinner. If he does not do that we shall have reason to fear there is something wrong, and I will send a messenger into Caistor to-night, to make inquiries; but you may be pretty confident that we shall see him in a few hours."

"I do hope so," replied Evelyn; but, for all these assurances, the glad excitement with which she had begun the day faded from her eyes, and she finished her breakfast with an anxious look upon her face.

"Now," said the Rector, "I cannot allow you to make yourself unhappy over suppositions. It is too early for you to begin your visits. Put away these gloomy thoughts, and come with me into the garden for an hour; there never was a lovelier morning."

Evelyn roused herself at once, and, with something of her former brightness, replied:

"You are quite right, dad. I will run up and speak to mamma for a few minutes, and then join you in the garden;" and, so saying, she tripped away.

Mr. Sedgewick sauntered out among the flower-beds, thinking about his daughter. Four years previously he had taken her away a child, and now he had brought her back a woman. In heart and intellect, as well as in personal charm and beauty, he could not be otherwise than proud of her. She had gone from home a well-educated girl, but during those years had grown immensely. She had seen much, read much, and had been brought into personal inter-course with many highly-trained minds. And thus she had become familiar with the most powerful ideals and thoughts of the age. Nevertheless, she remained without affectation—a lovely, true-hearted English girl.

Still the Rector was not without a certain amount of anxiety as to her immediate future. He knew that the ordinary ideals of a woman's life would prove inadequate for her. She was filled with the charac-teristic spirit of the age—the new enthusiasm for humanity—and eager to carry out Thomas Carlyle's advice : " Find your work and do it."

So far as she had given any indication of her wishes and schemes, he had been glad to see that she expected to find her vocation at home—in his own parish—and that she distrusted all plans for setting the world right by a re-arrangement of outward circumstances that left untouched the springs of inner life and character.

He had resolved that if possible he would gratify her wishes, and was now curious to know what she would propose.

He was not long alone : in a few minutes Evelyn joined him.

" Here is a seat sheltered both from the wind and sun," he said ; "let us sit down."

"I was expecting you would suggest a ramble over the whole place, to see how things have grown."

" Not just now ; you will have sufficient walking in

making your visits. You are quite resolved to begin your work in the parish to-day ? "

" Yes ; I dread a life of elegant idleness : I want to begin right."

" Well, now, give me exactly your ideal of your life."

" That's rather a large order, dad ; I must consider. Briefly, I think I could express it in this way : Most of the ideals of woman's life and work are good, only inadequate ; I would like to blend and harmonize them in something higher. I crave for a life that is many-sided. The ideal life is like a diamond, with innumerable facets receiving and reflecting the light in all directions. Does not Thomas Carlyle say of Luther that he could both play the flute and fight the devil ? That is one way of expressing it : a saint engaged in spiritual conflict, and yet delighting in all the beautiful things of this world. Let me see ; you have taken me by surprise ; but I will quote to you some familiar lines from Wordsworth. They exactly express my ideal of the perfect woman."

And, so saying, she quoted the lines :

> " A creature not too bright or good
> For human nature's daily food :
>
> .   .   .   .   .   .
>
> And yet a spirit still, and bright
> With something of an angel light."

" Ah," said the Rector, " that is a beautiful ideal ; but what I should have asked you for is your idea of what you would like to do in the parish. You wish to help me ; what would you like to do ? "

" Oh, I have nothing very revolutionary to suggest. I would wish to be your curate, as far as a woman can. I will visit, teach the children, organize the various societies, and all that sort of thing."

"Then you would like me not to keep a curate?"

"Yes."

"And give you his salary?"

"Yes."

"And what would you do with it?"

"Spend it on the one change I should like to make."

"What is that?"

"Well, first I should like to see a substantial and handsome building erected in the parish, and surrounded by its own beautiful grounds. I should like to have in it one large good room, in which concerts, lectures, and all sorts of meetings could be held, and which could occasionally be cleared for a dance. Then I should like a number of smaller rooms—reading, smoking, recreation rooms, etc. I should like the care-taker to provide simple refreshments at cost price; and the place should be open with its grounds summer and winter, week-days and Sundays, to all the parish."

"And you would encourage the people to go there instead of to church?" said the Rector, with a twinkle in his eye.

"There is no fear of their wishing to do that while you are their Rector."

"The curate's salary then would go to the up-keep of your scheme?"

"Just so."

"And you wish me to erect the building?

"You would give a handsome subscription, and I would beg the rest of the money if the scheme were

approved. Of course it would have to be considered
carefully. Lord Merton would have to be consulted ;
we could not do it without his approval."

"Well," said the Rector, rising, "you can soon
have a chance of submitting your scheme to him.
There he is, just entering the gate."

CHAPTER II.

"I DON'T BELIEVE IT."

LORD MERTON walked towards the Rectory too much occupied with his own thoughts to notice that Mr. Sedgewick was coming across the lawn to meet him.

"Good morning, Lord Merton," he cried, as soon as he was within easy speaking distance; "have I been away so long that you don't know me?"

The nobleman started, glanced round, gave an exclamation of pleasure, and went towards him with extended hand.

"My dear Sedgewick," he said, "I should know you a mile off if I saw you; for you don't look a day older, and I can't tell how glad I am to see you back again."

They were life-long friends, and were eagerly asking and answering the usual questions put under such circumstances, when Evelyn came towards them.

Lord Merton saw her approaching, but before he had recognized her she was by his side, smiling and saying:

"I expect you don't remember me at all."

He gave a look of astonishment and admiration.

"Evelyn! Miss Sedgewick! is it indeed you?" he

exclaimed, clasping her hand, and looking as though he wished she would hold up her face to be kissed, as she always used to do. " I will never again say that time spoils all things."

When they last met Nature had already given many broad hints of her intention of making Evelyn Sedgewick an exceptionally beautiful woman. These promises were now generously fulfilled. She was tall, lithesome, well-proportioned, with features as lovely as they were refined and intellectual. A simple morning-gown of perfect fit set off her graceful figure, while a wide-brimmed garden hat, beneath which peeped her hair, threw a soft shadow into the depths of her large violet eyes. Her face, animated by the conversation that had just taken place, seemed a living mirror for the reflection of a soul of ideal sweetness and beauty.

" It is rather odd," said Mr. Sedgewick, " but your name was upon Evelyn's lips when you turned into the drive."

" Ah," he replied, still clasping her hand, " and what were you saying about me ? Not threatening, I hope, to exclude me from your friendship because I did not visit you abroad."

" Oh dear no," answered Evelyn ; " we knew of your dislike to crossing the Channel."

" I expect," said the Rector, with a merry twinkle in his eyes, " that Evelyn will be courting your favour and friendship more than ever ; for she has been occupied during the last half-hour in explaining to me some of her plans for revolutionizing the parish, and if they are carried out we may expect a serious attack upon our purses. But we must not keep you

standing here. Shall we go into the house? I am
sorry my wife is not down yet."

"This sheltered corner looks most inviting," said
Lord Merton, pointing to a cosy garden seat hard
by; "and it is delightful outside. Come and sit
down, Evelyn, and tell me all about these revolutionary plans of yours which are to cost such a lot of
money. You will have some little pity on my conservative prejudices, will you not? You have not
become a disciple of those French and German
Socialists, have you?"

He had hardly withdrawn his eyes from her fresh
young face since he caught sight of it, and he wanted
to hear her talk.

"The fact is," he added, without waiting for her to
answer his questions, "after your long journey
yesterday I scarcely thought anyone would be moving
about so early except your father; meeting with you
is quite an unexpected pleasure, and I'm not going
to let you run off at once."

As he spoke he led her to the sheltered corner, and
he and the Rector seated themselves by her side.

The subject of Evelyn's plans, however, seemed
quite forgotten, for they chatted about what had
gone on at Merton Magna, and of their experiences
abroad; and the clouded and anxious look that had
rested on the worthy baron's face, when he entered
the Rectory grounds, cleared, and it regained its
usual expression of kindness and good-humour.

At last Evelyn, judging that he had come to see
her father more especially, rose.

"Oh, don't leave us, unless you really must go," he
said. "I have not yet heard anything about these

schemes of yours." He clasped her hand, and drew her down again by his side. "Now," he said, as the merry wrinkles gathered round his eyes, "I am all attention."

"I think," replied Evelyn, laughing, "that I ought not to trouble you with my plans to-day, which, how-ever, are not nearly so revolutionary as my father would suggest. By-and-by, when I have thought them out more fully, I shall be glad to hear what you think of them."

"You can't do better than explain them to Lord Merton at once," suggested the Rector.

"Exactly so," said his lordship, looking half amused, and half in earnest.

And so Evelyn gladly seized her opportunity. The knowledge that she was speaking to one who had it in his power to do so much, could she only win him to her views, stirred her to the utmost. A sweet maiden modesty set her cheeks in a flame, and gave a pretty hesitation to her first words, but these soon disappeared, and she spoke with a charm and per-suasiveness that captivated her listener.

She began with a reference to one or two early experiences that had led her to think of the absence of all brightness and joy in the lives of the poor.

In a few graphic sentences she drew a picture of their sordid homes, their dwarfed and impoverished childhood, their lack of all interest in anything beyond the gratification of a few animal instincts as they grew older, their bitterness, discontent and hope-lessness as they looked onward to old age.

Then she referred to the new sense of brotherhood that had awakened in the foremost minds, and which

S 2

was doing so much to strengthen the bonds that held the different classes together, and with delicate tact spoke of what Lord Merton himself had done upon his own estate.

"Still," she said, eagerly, " I ask myself: Cannot something more be done ? Healthy cottages and better wages are not everything. Are they to be for ever excluded from all those higher things that give interest and joy to us, and really make life worth living—knowledge, books, pictures, music, healthy and innocent amusements ? I want to awaken their souls, to widen their sympathies, to offer them a larger share of our spiritual heritage."

"Well," said Lord Merton, "we have not been altogether forgetful of this work in the past ; what more do you think we should attempt ? "

" Your question," replied Evelyn, " brings me to my one revolutionary proposal—as my fathe1 calls it ; " and then she proceeded to explain her scheme for the erection of a sort of " People's Palace " in the centre of the parish, which, though a novel idea then, was so soon to be realized.

" There ! " she exclaimed at last, the colour rising again, " I have said ever so much more than I intended ; and yet I hope that I have not wearied you, and that you do not consider my plan wholly visionary and impracticable."

" Not at all, not at all, my dear Evelyn ; far wilder dreams than yours have been realized," replied the aged baron, somewhat pensively. " Most of what you say is only too true, and it was very good of you to speak of what I have already tried to do on my estates. If I thought I could effect any good by taking up your scheme I should seriously consider it. Unfortunately my feeling is one of bitter disappointment at the results of what I have attempted. I feel just now as though I could say : 'I have laboured in vain, and I have spent my strength and my money for nought.' I have been much grieved lately by some for whom I have done most. I might as well have left them to themselves."

"Why, you have become quite pessimistic in my absence," said the Rector.

"It seems to me that the older you get the more you feel how little you can do to help your fellow-creatures," replied Lord Merton. "You pity them, you try to assist them, and end by discovering that you have done nothing but harm. Still, I don't want to throw cold water on Evelyn's ardent enthusiasm. She will find it all out soon enough. There is, however, another objection that one might raise to this scheme of yours. It is one I have often heard stated against some of the things I have done already. Is there no danger of doing too much for these people? May you not relax the springs of their self-reliance, until they look to you for everything?"

"It would be so if we undertook what they could and ought to do for themselves. But that is not the case with my scheme. And consider how many beautiful things even the upper classes enjoy which they do not provide for themselves. How much we inherit from the past! If we were stripped of everything which we have not obtained by our own individual skill and effort we should be poor indeed."

"There is another question that occurs to me," said

Lord Merton, smiling. " Supposing that you got your building erected, and your grounds laid out, and all that sort of thing : how would you propose to keep the whole scheme working ? All this machinery for elevating the masses would require a great deal of superintendence. Your meetings, and concerts, and lectures, and various classes would require a small army of curates to organize them."

" And yet she asks me to give up the one curate I do engage," said the Rector, with affected astonishment.

" What for ? "

" In order to be my curate herself, and take his salary ; but to use it to buy books, newspapers, and so on for this Institution."

" But, my dear Evelyn," cried Lord Merton, inwardly gratified at the girl's enthusiasm, " you could not undertake a half nor a quarter of the work which would be required to keep your scheme going."

" Of course not," she replied, brightly; " but I should hope to enlist the sympathies and co-operation of all who could render assistance in the neighbourhood."

" Who would help you ? "

" I am sure my father would, for one. Then there are Mr. and Mrs. Hallam. You will remember what a splendid girl Mrs. Hallam used to be before she married ; and I am sure she would help in all good things still. The school master and mistress would give us their assistance, and I have a host of friends in Caistor. And, besides these, there is Edmund Stanford," she added, slightly colouring.

" Edmund Stanford ! " cried Lord Merton, raising

his eyebrows, and looking grieved and surprised. "Alas! I'm afraid not. Have you not heard?"

"Heard what?" asked Mr. Sedgewick and Evelyn in one voice, the latter growing very pale.

"Why, that he is charged with forgery and embezzlement! Walsingham wrote all about it to you; have you not received his letter?"

"No," said the Rector, with a look of utter incredulity. "I have not heard from Walsingham; but we have been moving rapidly from place to place on our way home; so there is nothing surprising in that. But you don't really mean that *our* Edmund Stanford is charged with the crimes you have mentioned?"

"Indeed he is," replied Lord Merton, sadly.

"Oh, dreadful! Poor Edmund!" exclaimed Evelyn, with a half-stifled sob. "I am grieved."

"Forgery and embezzlement!" repeated Mr. Sedgewick, hoarsely. "Impossible! How can such an absurd charge have arisen?"

"I fear it is true," said Lord Merton, with a deep sigh. "I was thinking of him when I spoke of my disappointment, but did not like to refer to him then more definitely. I could not believe this charge at first, neither could Walsingham. He still hopes that some explanation will be discovered that will clear Stanford, for he had the utmost faith in him."

"Well he might have!" cried Mr. Sedgewick, emphatically. "Really, Lord Merton, this must be either a horrible blunder or else a wicked plot to ruin Stanford."

"I am grieved to say, my dear Sedgewick, that I fear it is true. It would seem that we have all been mistaken as to the character of this young man, except Gresham. He never perfectly trusted him, and he found him out."

"I don't believe it," cried Evelyn, vehemently. "I never will believe it unless Edmund confesses it himself."

"I sympathize with your feeling," said Lord Merton. "It is how I felt myself when I first heard of the charge; but look at this." He drew from his pocket the deposit receipt. "Is that his signature?" he asked, handing it to the Rector.

Mr. Sedgewick scrutinized it carefully.

"It certainly looks like his. Yes, I believe it is. What do you say, Evelyn?" He handed the paper to his daughter.

She looked at it carefully.

"Yes, it is his," she replied, handing it back to Lord Merton.

"Well," he said, "that is a deposit receipt for £500. It was abstracted from Mr. Gresham's private safe, and his name forged on the back of it, to all appearances by Stanford. What is certain is that on September the 9th of last year Stanford presented it at the bank, and drew the money, and that is his signature. What can you say to that?"

Evelyn had recovered from the first shock; she stood absolutely white, but outwardly calm, and her mind was working swiftly. The idea that Edmund had committed forgery and embezzlement she set aside as absurd. The question she was trying to solve was, how the guilty person had not only contrived to escape, but to involve Edmund in suspicion.

"Why may not someone else in the office have abstracted this paper from Mr. Gresham's safe, and forged his name, and then asked Edmund to go to the bank and draw the money ? " she asked.

" A very pertinent question," replied Lord Merton, " and one that had occurred to me ; but unfortunately there are other proofs that it was Stanford. I fear there is not a jury in the land but would convict him."

" What is the other evidence ? " asked the Rector.

Lord Merton took out the crumpled letter, and handed it to him.

" That letter Walsingham and I found in Stanford's pocket-book."

Mr. Sedgewick read it, turned it over, and looked perplexed beyond measure.

" There is something exceedingly strange about this paper. A guilty man would not have been such a fool as to keep it in his pocket-book. There is no date on it, no signature, and no evidence that it was sent to Stanford."

He handed it to Evelyn.

" I feel reluctant to press the points of evidence," said Lord Merton. " For I would give anything to discover that he is innocent. Evelyn should have her Institution, and whatever she liked to ask for if that could be proved. But really we must face the facts. In July Stanford professes to lose £20, yet gives a very rambling account of how he lost them. On the 9th of September he presents a deposit receipt, that was not expected to be inquired after for two or three years, at the bank, with a forged signature, and draws £500, which he certainly never paid over to the firm. When the forgery and embezzlement are discovered this paper is found in his pocket-book, on his very person, which shows that the receiver of it was being pressed by somebody for money, who had the power and intention of ruining him unless he got what he wanted. You must acknowledge that the case against Stanford is strong. To all human appearances he took this £500 to prevent the exposure threatened in this letter."

"I admit that your theory seems plausible, and yet I don't believe that he is guilty—I can't believe it. You might as well tell me that my own daughter has done these things. What does Stanford say himself?"

"Oh, he repudiated the charge, I understand, with the utmost vehemence and indignation."

"Did you not say that the deposit receipt was presented on September 9th?" asked Evelyn, who had been busy considering every word of the letter.

"Yes."

"Well, then, assuming that this letter was sent to Edmund, which, of course, I don't for a moment believe—but accepting your theory for argument's sake—it is at least certain that it could have no connection with his presenting this deposit receipt at the bank. There is the utter improbability that he would keep such a paper in his pocket-book all these long months; but there is much stronger evidence than that."

"What is it?" asked Lord Merton.

"This letter says: ' I warn you that I will not *any longer* trust your assurances of a speedy marriage with a rich young lady.' Now, on September 9th of last year Edmund had not been engaged to Julia

Ray twenty-four hours, and at the time of his engagement he did not know that she had any money. She wrote and told me so. I am convinced that Edmund is the victim of a foul plot, and oh! I cannot help having suspicions that I know who is at the bottom of it."

" Bertram Elles ! " said the Rector.

" Strange ! " exclaimed Lord Merton. " Walsingham also spoke of someone of that name, whom he had no faith in. It seems that he left the office only a few days after this money was taken."

" But cannot Stanford himself throw any light on this terrible business ? " asked the Rector, suddenly.

" Alas ! " replied Lord Merton, more sorrowfully than Mr. Sedgewick had ever heard him speak before, " I keep forgetting that you don't know the worst of this affair. The poor fellow is beyond giving explanations. Gresham charged him in a general way with forgery and embezzlement, but refused all details, hoping that he would confess everything. Walsingham was away with me in Surrey. And when Stanford vehemently asserted his innocence Gresham was so convinced of his guilt that he ordered him out of the office. The same night he was found on Somerthorpe Heath by some gipsies. In the midst of a terrific storm he had fallen down a pit, and injured his head, and has been unconscious ever since. He is now lying, apparently dying, at Hall Farm."

Evelyn sprang to her feet with a cry.

" Oh, papa, papa, how cruel! how dreadful! Go and see him. He must not die like that," and with a great sob she turned towards the Rectory.

CHAPTER III.

HOW THE CURSE WROUGHT.

ABOUT the time Lord Merton called on the Sedgewicks Mr. Walsingham seated himself in his chair at Friars' Court, and began reading his letters.

The first he opened was one from Mr. Heaviside. It stated that Edmund was still living, though unconscious, and had given one or two indications of an approaching change. He had that day opened his eyes for a moment, uttered a moan, and then relapsed into his former state. Mr. Heaviside went on to say that a London physician had been down, and held a long consultation with their own doctor, but that it was not necessary to repeat his opinion, as he had said that he was intending to write to Mr. Walsingham himself.

The physician was a Dr. Berkley, an eminent specialist on the brain, whom Mr. Walsingham had asked to visit Edmund. There was a letter from him, in which he stated how he had found the patient, and expressed a slight hope of his recovery. "It is a singular case," he said, "but I have had one or two like it before under my charge that have come round. Should he regain consciousness there will be danger of a relapse. He is suffering not merely from exhaustion and the injury caused by his fall, but from the effects of extreme mental distress, and the likelihood is that, as soon as consciousness returns, his mind will hark back on whatever has caused that distress, and he is too weak to endure any more. He must be watched closely, and when he awakens his thoughts must, if possible, be drawn to something else. If that is done he may be saved."

"That is as favourable as anything I could expect," Mr. Walsingham considered. He opened his book and wrote a cheque for fifty guineas, and addressed it to the physician, and then turned to the rest of his correspondence.

Whilst he was so doing Mr. Gresham entered the room.

"Have you any news? Is he still living?" he asked.

Mr. Walsingham pushed the two letters towards him, and went on with his reading.

As Mr. Gresham laid them down he said : "I do hope that he will live ; I would give anything to have this wretched business cleared up. I suppose the detective you have engaged has brought nothing to light?"

"All that he has discovered tends to confirm my opinion rather than yours," replied Mr. Walsingham, dryly. "He has learned that Elles had frequent dealings with old Abraham Jacobs, and he has cleared up that billiard saloon incident which so much influenced your mind against Stanford. He was only there twice, and in each case it was to get Elles away from the gambling-table."

"Indeed," answered Mr. Gresham. "Of course that only awakens the suspicion that we have been harbouring two rogues in the office instead of one."

Mr. Walsingham made no remark for a minute or two, and then said somewhat sharply :

"As soon as I have finished with my letters I shall drive over to Merton Magna. I wish to see the Rector ; he returned home last night ; and I also want to see Lord Merton."

"Well," said Mr. Gresham, as he turned to leave the room, "you have a pleasant day for your drive."

Just then a clerk came up, and said that two people were downstairs, one of them a woman, an old gipsy, and they wanted to see both the partners about Mr. Stanford.

"Bring them up," said Mr. Walsingham, and then turning to his partner he remarked : "You know that Stanford was found on Somerthorpe Heath by gipsies ? I have been wishing to see some of them."

The next minute old Elizabeth Earne was shown in, followed by a sullen, dark-visaged, and dissipated-looking man, who seemed to enter, not through any choice of his own, but under some kind of compulsion.

"The seal o' the day to ye, Mr. Walsingham," she cried, dropping a short curtsey, and adopting the broad dialect of the country people ; "and the same to you, Mr. Gresham," she added, repeating the movement, which suggested more of contempt than respect for the two lawyers. As she spoke she turned her eagle eyes on the one and then the other, and read them with a glance.

Neither of them had ever before seen in their office such a strange-looking woman. She was dressed in her wildest and most extravagant attire ; her grey hair was disordered, and coiled about her neck and shoulders in a sinister manner, while her eyes seemed in a flame.

"And ye are two lawyers?" she asked, with a perceptible sneer.

"Yes," answered Mr. Walsingham, adjusting his glasses, behind which shone a pair of dark eyes almost as keen and searching as her own.

"Oh yes, ye be lawyers, great lawyers, clever lawyers ; and ye ha' got a fine office," she said, glancing round, and speaking with withering sarcasm ; "and ye kaap a lot o' clerks a-writin' all day long. And lawyers are 'mazin' wise, and can tell rogues from honest folk, and black from white, and truth from lies."

"Not always," replied Mr. Walsingham, thinking it better to humour this wild creature. "Some people say we often try to call black white, and lies truth, and rogues honest men."

"Then they say the truth, for that's what you two ha' been doin'," she cried, with a hoarse laugh.

"How dare you come here and say those things?" asked Mr. Gresham, haughtily. "I will send for a policeman. Who are you? What have you come here for?"

"Listen to me, and I'll tell ye. Ye had in yer office two young men, Bertram Elles and Edmund Stanford. The first was a thief, a liar, and a slanderer, but ye sent him away with a gude character. The other ye charged wi' shameful things, none o' which

wor true, and then ye put him to the door. The
rogue ye took for a honest man, and the honest man
ye nearly murdered—his blood, if he die, be on yer grey
head," she hissed, raising her long hand threateningly.

Mr. Gresham grew pale with rage, and Mr.
Walsingham rose to his feet.

"Now," he said, sternly, "we cannot allow this any
longer. If you can tell us anything about either of
these young men we shall be glad to hear it, and if
you help to clear up things which we don't understand you shall be amply rewarded ; but, if not, you
must go away at once."

"Reward ! I want no reward ; I ha' come to clear
the innocent."

"Make haste, then, and tell us all you know,"
replied Mr. Walsingham, resuming his seat.

"You found a letter in Mr. Stanford's pocket-book,
did ye not ? I know ye did, for I wor at Somerthorpe
last night, asking after the young gentleman, and I
heard all about it. And I ha' come to tell ye, and to
prove to ye, that I got that letter from Bertram Elles
last Christmas, and I put it in Master Stanford's
pocket-book wi' my own hands, just afore we carried
him to Hall Farm, and if ye'll listen to me I'll tell ye
all about it." And then she proceeded to tell her
story with a dramatic power and force that riveted
the attention of the two lawyers.

"But you said that you could prove that that letter
belonged to Bertram Elles."

"And so I can. If you'll go with me to that
scoundrel Abraham Jacobs, the money-lender, he'll
not deny it. It is in his handwriting. I know him,
and I can make him speak the truth."

Mr. Walsingham's glasses could not hide the gleam of satisfaction that shone in his eyes as he listened to the old gipsy. Even Mr. Gresham heard her with a nervous twitching about the mouth and eyebrows that showed his excitement.

" Is there anything more that you can tell us ? " the former gentleman asked. " What have you brought this man with you for ? "

" He's Daniel Wright, the locksmith, and I s'pose lawyers know that false keys and duplicate keys are nice handy things for thieves ? "

" Well ? " said Mr. Walsingham, gazing at her intently, as he placed his elbow on his desk and his hand under his chin.

" Daniel Wright will tell ye that this Bertram Elles went to him with a key."

" I don't know no names," interrupted the old man, sullenly. " I told ye he didn't tell me his name."

" Hold yer tongue, ye owd fule ; it's all the same."

" It wor a tall young gentleman, wi' small grey eyes, and he spoke wery nice, and paid me all I asked him, that's all I know."

" Very well ; he took a key last summer to Daniel Wright, and asked him to make one 'xactly like it. Don't ye think, gentlemen, that that ha' somethin' to du wi' the £20 Maaster Stanford lost ? "

" It's impossible to say, my good woman," replied Mr. Walsingham.

" Can't ye find out ? "

" How ? "

" Show Daniel the key o' Maaster Stanford's desk, and he'll tell ye whether it's the one that the young

T

gentleman brought to him. He oan't lie; he daren't."

Mr. Walsingham left the room, and returned in a few minutes, and laid down about a dozen keys before the locksmith.

" Is the key among those?" he asked.

" I oan't say anything," said the smith, doggedly. " I don't want to get nobody into trouble."

" You'll answer the gentleman's question, or I'll curse ye, I will," said the old gipsy, raising her hand.

He turned the keys over, looked at them carefully, and then picked one out.

" That is it," he said, flinging it down on the desk. " Now let me go; I don't like this sort o' work," and so saying he slouched away.

" Well?" asked Mr. Gresham.

" It is the key of Stanford's desk," answered Mr. Walsingham.

" I thought so," said the old gipsy, chuckling; as without another word she disappeared from the office.

.   .   .   .

A few days after this interview Mr. Gresham was engaged in his room, when the door opened and Captain Woodrow was announced.

" Oh," said Mr. Gresham, " I heard that you were better, and had come down to Caistor, and I was hoping that you would soon call, as there are several things I would like settled while you are here."

" I have been wanting to see you," he replied; " but I had no sooner arrived than I left again to spend a few days with a friend in the country. You would be surprised that I sent for that £500 so hurriedly?"

"I was rather. I hope you haven't been speculating or gambling."

"No, indeed, that's not in my line; but I was glad the money was safe."

"Why?" asked Mr. Gresham, raising his eyebrows.

"Because of something that happened just before I came away from Canada—about the most blood-curdling thing I ever experienced. It might have cost me my life."

"Oh!" exclaimed Mr. Gresham, wondering what he was going to hear. "Tell me all about it."

"I will; in fact that is what I have come for."

Mr. Gresham pushed back his chair and listened.

"It was in this way. Towards the end of February I left Ottawa to spend a couple of days at a country house. There were a good many of us, some nice girls, and we had a glorious time sleighing and tobogganing. The second day there was a big dinner party, and several other guests arrived from neighbouring houses, who intended returning home the same night. But before dinner was over the wind changed, and such a tremendous storm came on that hardly any of the guests could leave. The ladies, especially, had all to stay, and arrangements were made for their sleeping. I was asked to give up my room, and to share a double-bedded room with a fellow who seemed to be courting one of the young ladies of the house. The storm was terrific, and some of us sat late in the smoking-room, though my

bed-room companion retired early. Being a bad
sleeper, at any time, I knew the storm would keep
me awake ; so I was one of the last to go upstairs.

" The room that had been hastily prepared for
us was at the top of a tower, connected with the
main building by a stone staircase, and some distance from the other sleeping apartments. It was
exposed to the full force of the gale. The other
fellow was asleep when I entered the room. I put
out my candle and lay awake listening to the
tempest. The wind howled and shrieked round the
house, and crashed and moaned through the trees.
The room was pitch-dark. By-and-by, however, I
began to feel drowsy, and was dropping off, when a
low, inarticulate murmur commenced in the other
bed. I paid no attention to it until the fellow grew
excited, and shouted out in his sleep :

" ' What did you send Captain Woodrow here for,
you old hag ?   How dare you say I took his money ?
What do you know about it ?   Go to the devil with
you ! '

" The fellow is dreaming, I thought.

" He lay still for a few moments, murmuring some
thing I could not make out, and then he cried, like
one in mortal terror :

" ' Keep off ! Keep off ! Don't touch me with
your crooked fingers.   Murder ! She's choking me !
Murder ! ' and in his excitement he wakened himself
up.

" I thought I would lie still and appear to be
asleep, and then I heard him mutter : ' By Jove !
that was a bad dream.'

" After a long time I fell asleep, and must have slept soundly for some hours ; for when I awakened again the storm was over, and I saw the full moon sailing among drifting clouds. I must have been awakened by my companion, for he was sitting up, and waving his hands.

" ' Drive quicker ! ' he shouted. ' How the old hag can run ! She's gone now,' he whispered, after a pause. ' Gone to hell, I hope, and will never come back again to torment me. No ! ' he screamed, ' there she is again, and a thousand wolves at her heels. Here they come ! here they come ! Drive faster, you old fool ! My God ! What eyes ! What teeth ! They are gaining on us ! They will be at our throats in a second.'

" The fellow was so excited that I thought he would do himself harm, and I jumped out of bed and went to him.

" ' Wake up,' I cried, ' you are dreaming ; ' but in a moment he flung his arms round my neck, and dragged me on the bed, and had his fingers at my throat. ' You limb of Satan,' he cried, with a fiendish laugh, ' I'll stop your cursed capers now ! ' Fortunately I was the stronger man, and flung him off, and before he was properly awake I got back to bed, and lay quite still.

" ' This horrid place is full of devils,' I heard him mutter to himself. ' I can't stay in it another hour.'

" He got up and dressed himself, and went out. When I went down I found that he had left. As he seemed to be looking after one of my host's daughters I thought it better not to say anything of what had taken place, and merely referred to the wild storm that had alarmed us all during the night.

"Almost immediately after that I was invalided home. One of my fellow-passengers was a young merchant from Ottawa, and, as I was ill, he often used to come and sit with me in my cabin, and to beguile the time one night I told him this story.

"'What was the fellow's name?' he asked. 'I don't know,' I replied; 'though, no doubt, I heard it at the time.'

"'It is very singular,' he said; 'but there is a fellow in Ottawa who is subject to strange hallucinations. I can't remember his name; but I know he has only lately come out to Canada. Before that he was in some law-office, in your old city of Caistor. I don't know him, but I have heard nasty rumours about him.'

"I was somewhat startled with this news, and wondered whether the fellow's dream could have any basis in fact, and hence I determined to write to you for my money as soon as I got to London."

"Was his name Bertram Elles, do you think?"

"I believe it was."

"Then, I think," said Mr. Gresham, "that it was something more than a dream!"

CHAPTER IV.

" IN THE KISS OF ONE GIRL."

" Truth, that's brighter than gem,
Trust, that's purer than pearl,
Brightest truth, purest trust in the universe—all were for me
In the kiss of one girl."—BROWNING.

MR. SEDGEWICK left Edmund's bedside with his head bowed very low. Only once or twice before in his whole life had he felt so utterly sad. He had expected to find him much changed, but was not prepared for so great a shock.

When he entered the room Mrs. Heaviside was endeavouring to give her patient a little food. She had to watch her opportunity, and do so whenever his mouth slightly opened, as it did occasionally. Whilst she was so engaged the Rector waited near the window, gratified to see that not even in his own rectory could Edmund have had more loving attention or greater comfort. The room was large, airy, and filled with the sweet scent of lilies of the valley ; everything about the bed was exquisitely white, and a thick carpet on the floor rendered all movement noiseless.

Presently Edmund's mouth closed firmly, and Mrs. Heaviside turned to the Rector, and extending her hand, said, with a faltering voice :

"Oh, Mr. Sedgewick, I'm thankful you've got home; this dreadful disaster would not have happened had you been at Merton Magna."

"Ah," he replied, "I'm grieved beyond measure; but it's a great mercy he reached you. No stranger could have brought him through the first crisis as you have done. Lord Merton and Mr. Walsingham told me all about it yesterday." And then he added: "You would hear the news last night that the whole mystery is practically cleared up? Everybody now believes that Edmund is innocent."

"I am more than surprised that any one who knew him should have ever believed otherwise," she replied, with an impatient movement, as she placed a chair by the bedside.

The Rector walked forward deeply moved. During the years of separation Edmund had grown more and more like his father. There was the same noble forehead, and firm mouth and chin; the same look of refinement and courage. As Mr. Sedgewick gazed mournfully on the statuesque and silent figure the past came crowding back on his memory. Above all, there flashed on his inner eye with great vividness the white face of Edmund's father as he lay in the calm majesty of death. The likeness was painfully striking; only that on the father's face there was an expression of perfect peace, almost of triumph; whereas here it was one of wistfulness and trouble, a questioning look of sorrow and wonder.

While he sat by the bedside, unable to tear himself away, Mrs. Heaviside's words echoed again in his mind. "It would not have happened had you been at home." They expressed an idea that had haunted him from the moment of his interview with Lord Merton. But now, also, another thought, still more distressing, came to him. He could not blame himself for any lack of interest in Edmund during his childhood and youth at Merton Magna. Never forgetting that he was the son of the brave man who had sacrificed his life in saving Evelyn, he had endeavoured to take the dead father's place, and had watched over him with solicitude and affection. But still, during the later years, and especially since his engagement to Julia Ray, had he not allowed his interest in him unconsciously to decline? He had thought that engagement a hasty and ill-considered step, and when Edmund had ceased to write as frequently as he formerly did, had he not too readily allowed the old friendly correspondence to lapse? Above all, during the last few months, should he not have shown more of a father's anxiety for Edmund's welfare? The least inquiry would have elicited the reason for his silence. How differently things might have gone with the poor fellow had he not been allowed to walk in the darkness alone, and struggle with his doubts and sorrows unaided! Surely he ought to have thought of all this before, and then insisted upon a change of scene. Then these extraordinary charges would either not have been made at all, or they would have been made under circumstances that would have rendered them harmless. The plot would have been disentangled without such a disaster.

From these painful reflections he was roused by Mrs. Heaviside.

" What do you think of him?" she asked.

" I only once before saw anything so sad," he
replied, mournfully.

" The face of his dead father ? "

" Yes."

" It comes to my mind almost every time I look at
him," said Mrs. Heaviside ; " but I feel sure a change
will come soon.   He will be better or worse."

" Do you think he will recover ? "

" I hope so—I pray so, though he is very weak ;
but it will be something if he only comes round
sufficiently to be told that it was all a horrible
mistake.   I can't reconcile myself to his dying under
such a cloud."

She could say no more, and bent over the silent
form and smoothed the pillow.

" He has a good constitution, and I pray God that
he may recover," said the Rector, fervently.   " Should
he do so he will be dearer to us all than he has ever
been."

" He will, indeed," remarked Mrs. Heaviside; and
then, looking intently at Edmund, she asked, " Don't
you think there is just the slightest flush of colour on
his cheeks ? "

" I don't notice any change," replied the Rector,
taking a long, earnest glance at him ; " but I do trust
that he will come round soon.   I must go now and
send Evelyn up.   She would come with me.   I must
have tried her patience by remaining so long.   She
was terribly upset yesterday when she heard the
news of his illness.   I will not say good-bye, as I
shall come up again before we leave."

And then, with another sad look at the white face
of Edmund, and a gentle pressure of the hand, from

which there came no response, Mr. Sedgewick withdrew.

As Evelyn touched the door it was quietly opened by Mrs. Heaviside, who, having greeted her with great tenderness, led her to the bedside. For one startled moment she gazed at the silent figure, and then broke completely down. The sight of her old playfellow lying pale and motionless, like breathing marble, with closed eyes, and hands clasped across his breast, was too great a shock for her already overstrung nerves, and flinging her arms round Mrs. Heaviside, she fell upon her neck and sobbed out :

" Oh, cruel, cruel men ! They have killed him ! They have killed him ! How could they believe such things to be true ? "

After a time she became calmer, and stood leaning over him, her right hand gently clasping his, her left resting on the pillow. There she stood thinking of all that had been in the past, the happy days when they played together in the Rectory garden, and fished in the river, and galloped on their ponies across the common. Then, as she thought of the anguish through which he had passed since then, the tears silently flowed down her cheeks, and fell unheeded on his pillow. Mrs. Heaviside was greatly touched as she watched her, and thought that she looked like an angel bending over him, and fervently wished that he could open his eyes and see her.

" It is very, very hard," cried Evelyn, " after these long years of separation, to return home and find him like this."

" And all through a wicked fellow who did the wrong, yet contrived to throw the suspicion on him."

" I don't know how I can ever forgive those who
have so wronged him, should he not recover."

" I do hope and pray that he may," answered Mrs.
Heaviside, bending down and regarding him with
fixed attention. " I believe there is a greater flush of
colour on his cheeks than when you entered. Oh,
how I wish he would come round just now ! "

" Do you think he would know me ? Every one
says that I am so changed."

" Ah, but you were so much together, and he was
so fond of you. If he knows anyone, it will be you."

As Mrs. Heaviside spoke the sound of an approaching carriage was heard.

" Here comes the doctor," she said.

Evelyn heard the outer door open and the doctor
speaking with Mr. Heaviside in the hall.

" I will go now," she said, " but I will come back
when the doctor is gone."

She gave another lingering glance at the noble
face, and then moved to retire. But as she did so a
sudden, terrible thought struck her. What if the
next change should be—the end ?

" I may never see him again," she said, with a low
sob, and, stooping down, pressed her lips to his, and
then turned to leave.

But an exclamation from Mrs. Heaviside arrested
her footsteps. "Look ! " she cried, " he's coming
round."

Evelyn's heart gave a tumultuous leap of joy, as
she bent over him again. A perceptible agitation
passed over his features, a faint colour rose, his lips
moved, and slowly his eyes unclosed. For a moment
or two they appeared vacant, as though no soul was

there, and Evelyn turned pale. Then there was another quiver of his whole frame, a tremulous flutter as of incoming life ; the soul had regained possession of its earthly tenement, and shone out of his eyes in conscious intelligence, and sent a smile over his wasted face ; while the name " Evelyn " faintly trembled on his lips. The next moment he gave a deep sigh of relief, and fell into a natural sleep.

Late that night Evelyn was still watching by his bedside. The doctor had strongly urged that it would be for his patient's good for her to remain. The London physician had especially pointed out the danger of a relapse. When consciousness returned they were to do their utmost to keep his mind from the late unhappy events. What, urged the doctor, could do this so effectually as the presence of Miss Sedgewick? It was impossible to say how much good she had done already. These cases were very mysterious, and the patient's life often seemed to hang upon a thread. Why had he come round at the moment she was there? Who could tell but that the sound of her voice by his bedside had reached down to the more secret depths of his being, and touched some tender chords of association with the past, and re-awakened the slumbering soul? And why did he fall off into a calm, natural sleep, as of a weary child, as soon as he recognized her? The doctor did not profess to know ; but he was a man of thought and imagination as well as of science, and he suggested that his patient had slipped back into the days of his childhood, and that for a time the immediate past would remain a blank, and only slowly come back. It was most desirable that it should be so, and if Miss

Sedgewick remained, and he found her there again
when he awakened, she would help to keep up the
illusion. If they got through the next two or three
days all danger would be over.

So the Rector left her and drove home alone, unspeakably thankful that he had allowed her to go with
him. He had not consented very willingly to her
taking the long journey; for there had been a great
strain upon her all through the previous day, and she
had passed a sleepless night. She had left the interview with Lord Merton in much distress; but had
fought with herself and mastered her feelings, and
then gone out and paid her visits. She returned to
the Rectory to find Mr. Walsingham and Lord Merton
there again, and heard of the visit which the gipsy
had made to the office, and the report of the London
physician. Everyone was excited, and a special messenger was despatched to Somerthorpe; and Evelyn
had begged her father to allow her to accompany him
the next morning, to which, at last, he had consented.
Now he was glad he had done so.

Evelyn, on her part, remained watching Edmund.
On no account would she leave him for more than a
few minutes. But he slept on calmly, peacefully,
healthfully, during the whole afternoon and evening,
and on into the night. The doctor called two or
three times, and was greatly pleased with the turn
things had taken; and left full directions how
they were to act when the patient came out of his
sleep.

About ten o'clock he began to show signs of
waking. He made several movements, and then
opened his eyes. Evidently he had recalled none of

his dark experiences of trouble ; he was only in a state of semi-consciousness ; for, though he recognized Evelyn, he evinced no surprise at seeing her there. She clasped his hand, and said,—

"You've had a delightful sleep, and will be better soon."

"Yes," he answered, "I'm better."

Mrs. Heaviside began to give him some food.

"You must not trouble about anything," she said. "We will soon get you well again."

Almost immediately after he fell asleep again, and Evelyn retired. He slept through the whole night ; and the next morning, when he awakened, he was so clearly conscious, that Evelyn, who was already up and by his side, managed, with great skill, to inform him, without any sudden shock, that his late troubles had arisen through plots and mistakes that had been since nearly all cleared up, and that no one was more glad than Mr. Gresham.

A smile gathered when he heard the news ; but when he began to ask further questions Evelyn said that she only knew that all was sufficiently explained for the time being, and persuaded him to let the whole matter go by, until he was stronger and more able to enter into it.

CHAPTER V.

GOD'S TOOLS.

EDMUND was sitting in the Rectory garden at Merton Magna reading the book of Job. It was the beginning of July, and he had left Somerthorpe nearly a week. Two months had passed since he had recovered consciousness, and he was now in an advanced stage of convalescence. As soon as he was a little stronger he was going north with Lord Merton for a yachting cruise on the west coast of Scotland, from which it was expected that he would return completely recovered.

The last week or two had slipped away like a dream. He was free from pain, and most of the time had passed in one of those delicious moods of restful contentment that looks neither before nor after, and is often experienced by those recovering from a serious illness.

During the few days that Evelyn had remained with him he was too weak for conversation, but her presence had made him happy. It was such a wonderful thing to see her again. Whenever he was awake, and she was in his room, he lay silently watching her. She was still her old self, the dear companion of his childhood and youth, unspoiled by travel and study, and more beautiful than he had ever imagined she would be, or than her portraits had given any idea of. For in her countenance there were life and grace, especially when she was speaking to him, that the camera could never reproduce. Her presence took him back to his childhood, to the happy days at Merton Magna, and kept his mind from dwelling on the trouble and sorrow through which he had so lately passed, and from brooding over the hard problems of life which he was only too ready to face.

Thus he grew stronger rapidly, and when the Rector returned for his daughter he was delighted with the progress he had made.

Their meeting was touching—a moment both of happiness and pathos. So much had happened since they shook hands at the railway station at Caistor, and the Rector had said, little thinking how much his words involved : " Whatever befalls you, trust me." A world of varied sensations now rushed into their hearts as they clasped hands again, and thought of all the darkness and suffering that were past.

Mr. Sedgewick brought the kindest of messages from all Edmund's friends. They were coming to see him as soon as he was stronger. Not the shadow of suspicion rested any longer on him. Even Mr. Gresham was perfectly satisfied. He wrote and assured Edmund that he deeply regretted his mistake, and that henceforth he would make it his pleasure and duty to further his interests. He would be sure to keep his word ; for although devoid of imagination and sympathy he was a good man, with a certain nobility of character which would impel him to do his utmost to atone for any injury he had done.

The old gipsy had gone to Abraham Jacobs and

compelled him to disclose facts that placed the guilt
of Bertram Elles beyond doubt. The only question
that remained was how Edmund had become involved
in the transaction. How had it come to pass that he
had taken the deposit receipt to the bank, and drawn
the money? That question, however, he was able to
answer at once; for he remembered the incident perfectly. Bertram had professed to be suffering from
a sprained ankle, and had asked him to go to the
bank for him. He had gone without question, for
the request seemed reasonable, and when he returned
Bertram was standing at Mr. Gresham's door. The
door was open, and Edmund saw Mr. Gresham sitting at his desk.

"Oh, here he is, sir," exclaimed Bertram, advancing a step or two. He took the notes, and Edmund
could have sworn that he saw him hand them over to
Mr. Gresham.

When that gentleman heard Edmund's explanation
he, also, was able to recall the incident. He had
asked Elles to go to the Stamp Office to get some
agreements stamped; but he had made the excuse
that he had a sprained foot, and had said that he
would ask Stanford to go. It was now evident that
while Edmund was at the bank Bertram had gone to
the Stamp Office, and then had adroitly substituted
the agreements for the notes, keeping the latter, and
handing the former to Mr. Gresham.

Edmund was tremendously indignant when he
heard of the plots by which Bertram had successfully
committed forgery and embezzlement, and yet contrived to throw all the suspicion on him. When Mr.
Sedgewick and Evelyn had left him alone he lay

thinking about it until it began to do him harm. Bertram Elles had been the evil genius of his life. Gradually, however, his indignation cooled down. It was not likely that they would ever meet again. What action the firm might take in the matter he could not tell; but there was no probability that Bertram would ever return to England of his own accord, unless he came back a changed man, ready to undo the wrongs of the past, as far as that was in his power—which was saying little.

And so, slowly, Edmund's anger and bitterness somewhat abated, and feelings of pity swayed his mind. Bertram Elles had been most unfortunate in his early surroundings and education: his character had received a wrong bias from the beginning. And yet, in spite of that, there was something pleasant and good in him. No man is altogether hideous when he is truly known. Edmund had caught glimpses of a real man beneath the mask of falsehood; he had seen a wistful look occasionally in his cunning eyes, as though he were still haunted by some nobler ideal. Perhaps the time would come when the better nature would recover from the blight that had fallen upon it; when the alien element that had grafted itself upon his true life would be expelled by those avenging powers that vex and plague the erring soul, not in mockery, but to save it from the death that cannot die. So Edmund tried to think of him as kindly as possible, and then let him pass out of his thoughts like an evil dream.

But much in that tragic past, he knew, would for ever abide with him. The memory of those loved and lost would never fade. The world could not again be quite the same for him which it was before he underwent that discipline. What might be hidden in the future he could not tell ; but one great period of temptation was over. He had suffered where he was most keenly sensitive, and the scars would remain. He had been led down into the lowest depths of darkness and humiliation, where he had heard fiends whispering horrid blasphemies in his ears, which in his bewilderment he had almost mistaken for the voice of his own spirit. He had fought a hard battle with Apollyon, and, though not vanquished, had been sorely wounded. In the hour of black darkness he had not surrendered his faith, but he trembled to think how near he had come to yielding.

And thus one effect of what he had gone through was to make him conscious of the need of some more adequate solution of the deeper problems of life— some reconciling principle which would enable him confidently to assert Eternal Providence in the presence of all wrong and misery, and to justify the ways of God through all contradiction and evil.

He knew that many of the best and noblest men and women had found it enough to believe simply in the wisdom and love of God. In the strength of that faith they had gone through sorrow, desertion, and martyrdom without angry questioning. To them it was natural that God's ways should be beyond our mortal fathoming. It was so with his revered mother. But he was conscious that he could never be one of those. He felt a burning passion to solve the Sphinx-riddle, to penetrate the inmost shrine of the sanctuary of sorrow, and learn its secret meaning.

Such were the thoughts working in his mind as he sat in the Rectory garden reading the book of Job. It was a beautiful morning ; high summer had come, and, as far as the immediate outlook was concerned, the world was untouched by woe. But he knew that such appearances were delusive. It would not do to look merely at the sunny side of life. An optimism of that sort would last just so long as things went well, and no great shock of sorrow or disappointment was experienced.

That was not enough. It was no good glossing over difficulties. No reconciling theory was of any use that did not embrace all the evils that flesh is heir to. He could never accept an optimistic faith unless it fathomed the utmost depths of the world's evils. But was such a faith possible?

"Well," he said to himself, " surely reason cannot ask questions which it is beyond the power of reason to answer ; surely there must be some solution of a problem that has always confronted man. To-day the child asks, If God is good, why does He send pain and death? and here is the book of Job, one of the oldest and noblest poems in the world, occupied with the same theme.

He was musing in this way when Mr. Sedgewick came and sat down beside him.

" So you have been reading the book of Job," he observed. " Well, what do you think of it ? "

" A noble poem ; but I like the ending least of all," Edmund answered. " Is this really the solution of the mystery : ' The Lord gave Job twice as much as he had before ? ' A somewhat impotent conclusion of such a splendid poem."

"True ; but you must remember that the poet had to submit to the limitations of his age."

"The ending, then, was a mere concession to his readers ; they demanded then, as now, a pleasant finish ? "

"Not that merely ; for it suggests, in a crude way, a truth for all time. Unless the universe is a moral chaos goodness and happiness must finally coalesce."

"It was just a popular way, then, of setting forth the moral order of the world ? "

"Exactly so ; but has it ever struck you that there is another and much deeper solution to the problem of evil in the book of Job ?   This ancient poet represents Satan, like Goethe's Mephistopheles, as a sneering, contemptuous spirit of depreciation. He has no faith in human virtue. 'Doth Job fear God for nought ? ' he asks. It is all a bargain. Job knows that honesty is the best policy. Men serve God for what they can get. Now this magnificent poem was written to prove that Satan's taunt is a lie—that disinterested goodness is a reality. In other words, it shows that through suffering and disappointment man's dignity and greatness are developed and revealed, and God is seen to be One who can inspire man with a genuine love for Himself. It is a splendid truth. The troubles of good men are not unmixed evils when they accomplish that."

"No," answered Edmund, musingly, and speaking almost to himself, "they became what my old friend the gipsy called them, 'God's tools.' "

"Just so ; there are not many of us who have

looked deeper into life than that old gipsy. But leaving that," he added, " of course the deepest solution of the problem of evil is found where good and evil come into sharpest collision—in the life and death of our Lord. Jesus was the greatest optimist that ever lived, and His cross throws a light on the mystery of evil we find nowhere else."

" Ah," said Edmund, " state that thought, please, a little more fully."

" Well, it is clear to me," answered the Rector, " that a universe without a cross would have meant a God the deepest principle of whose life was hidden. The presence of suffering and sin in the world has become the grand occasion for making known to us that God is Love, and that Love means self-sacrifice. Had things never gone wrong, pity, sympathy, heroism, self-sacrifice, and all that is sweetest and divinest in life would have been unknown."

" And that is the secret of the optimism of Jesus ? "

" Yes ; He did not gloss over the difficulties of life, but sounded them to their depths. He did not hide away from evil, but directly encountered its utmost malignancy. And yet He saw that in the end it must further the highest good. His was a victorious optimism that transfigured the very phenomena that have given rise to doubt and despair ; an optimism that showed calamity, suffering, conflict as a necessary means of spiritual growth ; in other words, to use the gipsy's phrase, showed them to be ' God's tools.' "

The Rector had hardly spoken these words when Evelyn came up, looking very happy.

"You are not too deep in philosophy or theology, I hope," she exclaimed, "to hear a bit of good news?"

"No, come along," replied the Rector, "come and sit down under the shadow of these trees."

"You look warm," said Edmund, making room for her, "and also immensely happy. What is your good news?"

"I've two items—one specially for you, and the other for us all."

"Indeed!"

"Yes;" said Evelyn, taking off her hat and throwing it on the grass. "Guess what they are."

"Tell us," replied the Rector. "I'm all attention."

"Then you must wait, dad. You must cultivate patience. Here comes mother; she also must hear my news."

"Come along," cried the Rector, looking towards his wife. "Come and sit down. Evelyn says that she has got some delightful news; but she won't tell us until you come."

"Oh, indeed," replied Mrs. Sedgewick, smiling, "I have just come to tell you something pleasant."

"Bless me!" ejaculated the Rector, "Dame Fortune is propitious this morning."

"Well," said Evelyn, turning to Edmund, "I shall gratify your curiosity first. I have seen Lord Merton; he will be here in the afternoon; but he asked me to tell you that he has received a letter from Mr. Walsingham, and that he is going to join you on your yachting cruise."

"That is pleasant news," said Edmund; "now let us have item number two, which is for us all."

"Yes, but specially for me. Lord Merton is going to carry out my scheme. He is most generous. He wants to do everything himself, and he is coming here this afternoon with an architect to talk over the plans with us. I did not know how to thank him enough."

"That is wonderfully good of him," said the Rector ; "but we must do something."

"So I told him, and he said that he would think it over. And now what is your news, mamma ?"

"I have seen Mrs. Hallam, and told her of Edmund's idea. I said that when he returned to business again he thought of residing at Merton Magna, and riding to and from the office each day. And she replied that she was confident that Mr. Hallam would be glad for him to board with them, as she would be herself ; so you will be able to have your old rooms, just as in the old times."

"I am glad," answered Edmund. "It's very kind of Mrs. Hallam. I seem to be just slipping back again into my old life."

"You have had a long talk together," said Mrs. Sedgewick. "I hope that you have not been thinking too much and too deeply for your strength Edmund."

"I found him working at a pretty stiff problem," replied the Rector. "He has been reading the book of Job, and trying to fathom the mystery of evil. And I have been preaching Christian optimism, by pointing out how often suffering and disaster are made to subserve a purpose of goodness. Tell us what you think about it."

" I can say nothing fresh : but I have often thought lately of those lines of Wordsworth in 'Despondency Corrected,' beginning with the words,—

> "One adequate support
> For the calamities of mortal life exists."

" Yes! those fine lines express the idea we have been working out," remarked the Rector. "Of course faith grows more and more assured as we discover a divine love working through the deepest sorrows."

" That is a note in all our best modern literature," said Evelyn. "I was reading Mrs. Browning's 'Vision of Poets' yesterday, and was struck by it. Several beautiful sentences still linger in my mind : 'Pain is not the fruit of pain. Not to suffer is to want the conscience of the jubilant.'"

> "Knowledge by suffering entereth,
> And Life is perfected by Death."

" Let us be careful not to think too much about the mystery of evil," said Mrs. Sedgewick gently. "Our thoughts may grow too sad and strenuous. We have all drunk of the bitter cup ; let us hope that it is our Heavenly Father's will for us to taste the cup of joy. We must not live constantly under the shadow of these solemn thoughts, but let our hearts sometimes be young and glad."

" That is what I feel," exclaimed Evelyn, jumping up. "Just now I feel mad with delight. Come, Edmund, let us go and have a swing, as we did when we were children."

" I do feel more of a boy," he said, rising, " than I

have done for a long time." And with a merry laugh they went off together.

The Rector and his wife followed slowly, and found them swinging side by side, as when they were children, and singing,

" Oh ! merry goes the time when the heart is young,
  There's nought too high to climb when the heart is young."

EPILOGUE.

"LIFE," says Schopenhauer, "may be represented as a constant deceiver in all things, great and small." Everything, in his opinion, reaches the wrong conclusion, and the world is merely a scene of frustrated purpose and disappointed hope.

Is that true? Most people, no doubt, have experienced moments when they have been tempted to think that the pessimistic philosopher was right; times of darkness and suffering when they did not see life clearly. But those moments have passed away, and happier and saner thoughts have returned.

It was so, as we have seen, with Edmund Stanford. All that, however, has gone by; he has no such thoughts now.

This is a bright morning in spring, two years after his accident on Somerthorpe Heath. He and Evelyn Sedgewick are by the river's side, at the very spot where we first saw them together six years ago. And this is the happiest moment of their lives. They are standing on one of the topmost points of earthly bliss, and there we propose to bid them farewell for the present, after a brief account of how they found their way thither.

Since we last saw them their lives have been full of activity and enterprise.

Edmund went back to the office, although he need

not have done so, had he chosen otherwise. For while he was in Scotland with Lord Merton his venerable friend Miss Ray passed away peacefully, leaving the bulk of her property to him. Frank was amply provided for, seeing that he had his own and his sister's fortune, and " there is no one else," so ran Miss Ray's will, "for whom I have such sincere respect and affection as for Edmund Stanford." The property was considerable, though not equal to what Edmund's forefathers had enjoyed prior to the family misfortunes during the political troubles of the seventeenth century. Still it would have supplied him with ample means for a life of leisure had he chosen to follow it.

But that was not his ideal. He went back to the career he had deliberately adopted, and threw himself with his customary ardour into his work, and as soon as he was fully qualified he was offered a junior partnership in the firm.

As time passed he not merely regained his physical strength, but his early melancholy disappeared. He stood in the sunlight of a larger and stronger faith. In the fires of anguish the discordant elements of his character were fused into harmony, and his life now rested immovably in the Divine Fatherhood. The storm and stress period was over, and he was like a sailor who, after a black and dangerous night, spreads his sails to a favourable breeze, and sweeps onward into the golden dawn.

Evelyn also found great joy in her career. She endeavoured to carry out her ideal of a rich, full life. Her enthusiasm and tact in the work she had taken up were conspicuous. Without condescending airs or haughty reserve, she would, on entering a cottage, drop quietly into a chair and begin to play with the baby, and draw the hard-worked mother into talk about her children and her troubles, and so gain an insight into the wants and struggles of the poor that was of the greatest service to her, while her sympathy and friendly help did them good. "Come again soon," they would say, as she rose to leave, "for ye allus bring a bit o' sunshine wi' ye."

As soon as Lord Merton returned from Scotland the foundation-stone of the new Institute was laid ; but she did not wait until it was built before putting many of her schemes into operation. In most of them she had the enthusiastic co-operation of Edmund as well as others.

Among the more important of these was an adult school. The Education Act of 1870 had only just been passed, and there was great need for such a movement. They taught the men on the Sunday mornings before the service, and the bigger boys and girls on the week evenings.

In another matter Edmund was able to render her the most efficient help. She had discovered that the hot-bed of disease and vice in the whole parish was a cluster of wretched hovels belonging to an old miser, who had permitted them to fall into the utmost dilapidation. They were mere sties, and the families huddled in them grew up sickly, and accustomed to sights and habits that made decency and morality well-nigh impossible. Edmund set the law in motion against the proprietor, and so thoroughly frightened him that he was willing to part with the property for a fair price. Then Edmund bought it, and had it put in good repair, and so removed a great evil.

They could not engage in these practical measures without coming face to face with the political and social questions that were appearing on the horizon of the national life. Thus, during those two years the Rectory became the scene of many an eager debate. Mr. Sedgewick took almost as much delight in them as Edmund and Evelyn, whilst Mrs. Sedgewick was content to sit and listen. Evelyn generally showed herself the most advanced in opinion, and the Rector the most conservative, while Edmund was always seeking for some reconciling principle.

But these discussions, and the careful reading they provoked, did them all good, and especially Edmund. His mind was definitely turned to the great practical problems of the day, and during the second winter he frequently lectured on them in the school-house, and by so doing showed a gift for public speaking which not only surprised the Rector and delighted Evelyn, but caused him to be much talked about in political circles as a coming man, from whom great things might be expected.

In this way, then, the months swiftly passed, and Edmund and Evelyn were thrown more and more together. For a long time the former was conscious of nothing beyond a deep brotherly regard. It was only the early intercourse renewed, and he found it inexpressibly sweet. Love, in the ordinary sense of the word, had passed below the horizon of his life. He had had his day, and it had closed with a tragedy that left him with a bruised and lacerated heart.

But Evelyn's projects and enthusiasm drew him out of himself. With her he passed his happiest hours. His countenance brightened when she appeared. The thought of her often haunted his quiet hours. And so slowly his wounds healed, and the friendship that had its roots in the inmost depths of his being, and was entwined with every recollection of childhood, began to assume a new character. The movement was silent, like the secret growth of a seed, and he only became clearly conscious of it as it burst into bloom.

With Evelyn it was different. In her thoughts Edmund had always stood apart from all others. As a boy, he held a unique place in her life. She returned from her long stay on the Continent with her feelings unchanged, and became clearly conscious of what they signified when she bent over him as he lay apparently dying at Somerthorpe. In that bitter moment, when she was taking, as it seemed only too sadly probable, a final farewell of him, she realized that she loved him with something more than sisterly affection.

But that was a secret she divulged to no one. Her father and mother might have their suspicions, and Mrs. Heaviside, who had witnessed the touching scene in the sick-room, had drawn her own conclusions ; but nothing was ever said, and Evelyn, with beautiful modesty, and wonderful self-control, never let Edmund suppose that her regard for him was other than what it was when they were children together.

The moment, however, of full awakening dawned on Edmund just when it seemed too late for his happiness.

Evelyn had been working hard, preparing for the opening of the new Institute, and greatly needed a change. So the final arrangements were left with Edmund, and the Rector, taking Evelyn and her mother with him, went up to London for a few weeks in the early spring.

The Institute was to be opened in June, and Edmund worked with his usual energy and thoroughness, but found that the absence of Evelyn made a great blank in his life. His thoughts were continually going out after her. He had slowly recovered from the blow that had crushed and stunned him more than two years previously, and one day, as he stood gazing at her portrait, he awakened to the fact that his love for her was something which neither friendship nor a sister's affection could satisfy.

It came to him like a sudden revelation, and yet he was so certain and clear about it that he marvelled that he had not recognized the truth before. For in becoming conscious of it he knew that it had command of his whole being. It was not a stormy and unregulated passion, but the rising up of all the tides and currents of his nature, in response to an attraction that drew him with an irresistible charm. It was the reverential homage of his whole mind and heart for a woman worthy of all that he could offer her.

But it was not enough for him to be conscious of his affection for Evelyn. Could he offer her a love which was not his first passion? Why should he suppose that she would accept him? And dare he risk being rejected? For so long as he kept his secret he could continue to enjoy her society; but if

X

he were to confess it, and be refused, he would be compelled to leave Merton Magna.

These questions disturbed him, and he was still considering how he ought to act,—whether he should go up to London and see Evelyn, or write, or wait— when Mr. Walsingham handed him a letter with the remark that it contained news that would interest him.

It was from Lord Merton, who was in London, and among other things stated briefly that Evelyn had made quite a sensation in society, and that several young men were paying her great attention. Among these was Sir Harry Seymour, who was unmistakably in love with her. She had inspired him with her enthusiasm, and he was quite willing to sit by her side the whole evening and talk about the elevation of the masses. "However, jesting aside," wrote Lord Merton, " he's a fine young fellow, to whom any father might be willing to entrust his daughter's happiness. The estate is one of the finest in Surrey, and if we are not to keep Miss Sedgewick at Merton Magna— which I once thought might happen—I am glad there is a prospect of her settling so near my place in Surrey."

Edmund read and re-read the letter in the greatest dismay. How was he to act now? One thing was clear, he must neither go to London nor write. If Evelyn loved Sir Harry Seymour her happiness should never be marred by the knowledge of his disappointment. She should never know that he had ever thought of her in any other light than as a dear friend. On the other hand, he knew that if she did not love this young baronet neither title, position, nor wealth would induce her to accept him. So there was nothing for it but to wait, and he did so with an anguish of spirit that only too visibly recalled the sad and terrible past.

Fortunately he had not to wait long. Several days before the time fixed for the return of the Sedgewicks he received a letter from the Rector, saying that they would be home that evening, and that he would like very much to see him, as he had some most interesting and important news to communicate.

To Edmund it seemed like a sentence of doom, and he was thankful that he had an engagement some two miles away, which would make it impossible for him to reach the Rectory before Evelyn and her mother had retired.

" I should not know how to congratulate her to-night without betraying my secret," he said, sadly, to himself ; " but I should have to do it if I saw her. It may come easier after I have had a little time to reconcile myself to my fate."

So he sent a message to say that he would call late in the evening ; and then, after delaying the hour until he was sure of meeting no one but the Rector, he summoned up his courage, and walked down pale and agitated.

" Halloo ! " exclaimed Mr. Sedgewick, as he entered the study, " you are very late. I began to think you were not coming. And, bless me ! you are not looking well. What's the matter ? "

" Oh," said Edmund, with a forced smile, " I've had a long, busy day, and I've not slept well for several nights."

" Had I known that I would have come round to

you. I wanted to see you to-night. I suppose you have not heard the news?"

"Oh, yes," replied Edmund, somewhat surprised to see the Rector so delighted. "I saw Lord Merton's letter to Mr. Walsingham."

"That's strange; I understood him to say this morning that he had not breathed a word to any-one."

"He just mentioned it in a postscript to a business letter, and had very likely forgotten that he had done so."

"Still it is odd. However, never mind that. We are all delighted. But, boy, what is the matter? You don't look particularly well pleased about it."

"Don't I?" answered Edmund. "Well, you see, it has come very suddenly. It's hard to realize what Merton Magna will be like without Evelyn."

The Rector looked searchingly at him, and then he replied, thoughtfully:

"I see you have heard about Sir Harry Seymour. I was not aware of that; but that's not what I alluded to in my note. It is something that concerns you."

"Indeed!" said Edmund, thinking that nothing in the world just then concerned him so much as Evelyn.

"Yes; our present member of Parliament has re-signed, and several of the leading men in the county are resolved to bring you forward. It is almost certain that you will be unanimously proposed by the Committee."

"Oh!" said Edmund, with a momentary expression of surprise and pleasure, which immediately gave place to one of perplexity and pain.

"Yes," answered the Rector ; " but what's troubling you ? What's the matter? You don't seem a bit interested."

Edmund hesitated, and then asked with an effort :

"What sort of man is Sir Harry Seymour ? Will he make her happy ?"

"He's a fine fellow, a splendid fellow," answered Mr. Sedgewick, thoughtfully and kindly ; for he began to understand Edmund now, "and if Evelyn could have returned his affection he would have made her happy."

Edmund sprang to his feet.

"Then she refused him ?" he asked, with an intensity of feeling which he vainly tried to conceal.

"Yes," answered the Rector, quietly.

Edmund walked backwards and forwards for a few seconds in silence. Mr. Sedgewick saw that he was deeply moved. His face quivered and worked under the influence of emotions that he could not wholly hide. At last he controlled himself, and walking up to the Rector, said :

"Sir, I love her ; will you trust her to me if I can win her ?"

And then, without waiting for a reply, he proceeded to tell briefly how his love for Evelyn had unconsciously grown up and dawned upon him.

When he had finished Mr. Sedgewick rose. For a moment he grasped Edmund's hand in silence, and Edmund knew that what he had asked for was granted.

"And now," said the Rector, "you must go home

and get some sleep, or your pale looks will frighten
Evelyn. You have my consent to tell her what you
have told me."

.   .   .   .   .   .

It was a beautiful morning, and Edmund was
early astir. He had been too much excited to get
more than a few hours' sleep, and had risen soon
after the dawn, and gone for a long walk. He was
now slowly returning home. From the old grey
tower of the church came the soft chiming of bells
and then the deep note of the clock, striking the
hour of seven. He turned into the path by the
river's side, and loitered along till he reached the
spot where his father had saved Evelyn's life, and
there he sat down on the gnarled root of a tree.

His mind was unusually stirred. He had been
suddenly raised from the deepest despondency to the
utmost verge of hope. That day he proposed to
speak to Evelyn. Should she respond to his love
he saw before him a life full of promise and joy.

From these thoughts of the future the scene called
him back to the past. This morning he was
peculiarly open to its impressions. It was holy
ground. It seemed to draw him into mystic communion with the unseen, the Eternal, the departed.
All the deeper chords of his nature were touched.
His whole life rose up before him, and there came to
him a fresh intuition of an Immortal Love that had
ordered all his steps, and turned his sorrow into joy
and made the bitter waters sweet.

While he was thus musing he heard a light step
along the path, and glanced round the tree to observe
who was approaching. Evelyn, looking somewhat

paler than usual, but beautiful as ever, was within a few yards of him.

He sprang to his feet with a beating heart, and stepped towards her. At the same moment she saw him, and gave a start of surprise and gladness.

"Dear Evelyn," he exclaimed, clasping and retaining her hand, and speaking with a voice that thrilled her, "this is an unexpected pleasure. I was coming after breakfast to see you." And then he added, significantly: "Your father gave me permission last night."

She glanced at him inquiringly; but only for a moment could she meet his ardent gaze. Instinctively she read his love, her eyelids dropped, and the rich blood mounted to her cheeks.

"We have been life-long friends, dearest Evelyn," he said, still clasping her hand, and leading her to the seat from which he had just arisen. He sat down by her side, and for a moment there was golden silence. His heart was very full.

"Life-long friends," he went on, slowly; "but in your absence I have become conscious that my friendship has blossomed into love. What am I to do? May I, dare I, hope that you will accept me as a lover in place of a friend?"

He paused, and fixed his eyes upon her. She gave him a glance so beautiful and tender that he read half her answer in it. Then she said, softly:

"You have made me very happy. . . . . I cannot tell when mine first blossomed, but it was a long time ago."

.   .   .   .   .   .

Half an hour later they rose hand in hand,

supremely, radiantly happy. As they did so a tall figure appeared coming from they hardly knew where. It was Elizabeth Earne, the old gipsy. For a second or two she fixed a keen glance on them ; then a soft light shone in her eyes, and, advancing towards them, she said :

"Did I not tell ye, Edmund Stanford, that the black night would pass, and the time for the singin' o' birds would come ?"

Then she raised her hands and blessed them.

Woodfall & Kinder, Printers, 70 to 76, Long Acre, London, W.C.